## Cheryl Robson FRSA

Cheryl was born in Australia and studied Drama & French at University of Bristol then worked at the BBC in London for several years before setting up a theatre company producing and developing feminist plays. She gained a PGCE in Drama (Middlesex University) and an MA in Playwriting Studies (University of Birmingham) and went on to create the award-winning publishing company Aurora Metro Books, well-known for its diverse and inclusive range of titles, with translations from over 20 languages, and over a dozen unique world drama collections.

As an editor/publisher, Cheryl's work has won the Pandora Prize, the Raymond Williams/Arts Council Publishing Prize, a Special Jury Prize for Peace, Best Innovative & Best Seasonal Foodbook from Gourmand World Cookbooks, and was shortlisted for the People's Book Prize and for the IPG National Diversity awards in 2019 and 2020. www.aurorametro.com

As a playwright, she has won the Croydon Warehouse International Playwriting Competition, been shortlisted for the Roger Leach Memorial Prize and longlisted for the Bruntwood Prize. Several of her plays have been produced to acclaim in London. She has edited or contributed to over 150 books with work also published in *The Guardian,* the *Chicago Tribune, Culture Trip, Riviera News* and more.

Her documentary film *Rock 'n' Roll Island,* won several awards at film festivals and was broadcast on BBC4 in 2020, garnering a *Sunday Times* Critics' Choice and *Radio Times* Pick of the Week.

Cheryl is perhaps best-known for her successful 5-year campaign with sister charity (aurorametro.org) to erect a full-size bronze statue of Virginia Woolf which was unveiled in November 2022 on Richmond riverside and has proven a popular attraction.

She co-owns the independent bookshop Books on the Rise in Richmond, which offers weekly literary and arts events and hosts Feminist Book Fortnight. booksontherise.com

For more see cherylrobson.net

First published in the UK in 2024 by Aurora Metro Publications Ltd under their Supernova Books imprint. 80 Hill Rise, Richmond, TW10 6UB
www.aurorametro.com    info@aurorametro.com
x: @aurorametro Instagram: @aurora_metro
*Feminist Theatre Then & Now: celebrating 50 years* copyright © 2024
Aurora Metro Publications Ltd.
Introduction copyright © 2024 Elaine Aston
Cover design copyright © 2024 Aurora Metro Publications Ltd.
Interviewer and editor: Cheryl Robson
Individual contributors retain the copyright to their own essays.
We'd like to thank the following photographers: Barnaby Aldrick, Almeida Theatre, Grant Archer, Simon Annand, Lauren Baxter, Ruby Belassie, Bayrem BenMrad, Brett Boardman, Patrick Bouillaud, Christine Bradshaw, Graeme Braidwood, Sheila Burnett, Phyllis Christopher, Dee Conway, Donald Cooper, Suzy Corker, Richard Davenport, Suki Dhanda, Graham Fudger, Hugo Glendinning, Steve Gregson, Willoughby Gullachsen, Julian Kronfli, Pat Langford, Hector Manchego, Hannah McEachern, Topher McGrillis, William Murphy, Keith Pattison, Carol Rosegg, Mark Rusher, Mark Savage Photography, Lee Searle, Chris Webb, Meier Williams, Robert Workman, Ali Wright, Josie Morrison Young. All the photographs in this volume are reprinted with permission or presumed to be in the public domain. Every effort has been made to ascertain and acknowledge copyright status, but should there have been any oversight on our part, we will endeavour to rectify the error in subsequent printings.
Contact: editor@aurorametro.com
Printed on paper which has been sustainably resourced by 4edge Ltd., Essex.
ISBNs:
978-1-913641-38-2 (print)
978-1-913641-39-9 (ebook)

# FEMINIST THEATRE
## THEN & NOW

celebrating 50 years

Introduced by
Elaine Aston

Edited By
Cheryl Robson

SUPERNOVA BOOKS

Paislie Reid in *Sugar* by Open Clasp Theatre Company
Photo: Topher McGrillis

# CONTENTS

Monstrous Regiment Theatre Company 1976. *L to R*: Josefina Cupido, Gillian Hanna, Susan Todd, Chris Bowler, Mary McCusker, Sue Beardon (behind her) Ian Blower, Linda Broughton, Helen Glavin, Roger Allam, Meri Jenkins

F-Bomb Theatre Company 2023 International Women's Day Showcase. *L to R:* Chelsea Grace, Michelah Desnai, Valerie Andrews, Marion Geoffray, Sally Cairns, Linzi Devers, Louisa Chang, Kirsten Hutchison, Rachel O'Regan, Kira Mason, Jess Ferrier, Rebecca Wilkie, Niloo-Far Khan, Lintong Zhang

# INTRODUCTION
## ELAINE ASTON

Autumn 2023 finds me reaching for the boxes that house my feminism and theatre papers: a personal archive of documents collected over the past 35 years or more of feminist-theatre research – articles, programmes, reviews, publicity, unpublished scripts, correspondence. My recollections of feminist theatre also reside in embodied memories of shows and of encounters with practitioners – workshops, interviews, informal conversations. Such archival traces inform this introduction, the aim of which is to provide a framework that will resonate with the past-present histories of feminism and theatre brought together in this anthology. These histories need to be preserved – told and re-told – otherwise the danger is that they risk being erased by patriarchal interests and narratives. As playwright **April de Angelis**[1] astutely observes: 'Women's history, it seems, gets disappeared on a regular basis' (see also **Lucy Stevens**).

Spanning 50 years of women's theatre, the history that unfolds in *Feminist Theatre Then & Now* is one that recounts the rich and valuable contributions women have made to UK theatre in their roles as playwrights, performers, directors, or producers; as solo artists or as members of women's theatre companies, past and present. It also records the persistent inequalities and discriminatory practices of the profession, from the maldistribution of state funding to the systemic malestream culture that moulded the industry into a toxic workplace, as outed by the #MeToo Movement. Moreover, from the outset, it is important to note that this is not a solo-authored monograph but a collection of first-hand accounts by a cross-generational mix of women theatre makers who variously detail their work processes and productions; offer insights into the form and content of their theatre; explain how feminism influences their work and why feminist theatre is still necessary; and reflect on strategies to implement change including the idea of a dedicated women's theatre. Not only does this afford an opportunity to create an experientially voiced, multifaceted account of feminism and theatre, but it also reflects the collective ethos foundational to the rise of women's theatre in the climate of second-wave feminism.

## Second-Wave Feminism and the Rise of Women's Theatre Groups

Opening up the box labelled 'second-wave feminism and theatre', on top of a disorderly pile of papers I find a letter from Pam Gems in which the playwright reminisces about Ed Berman, founder of Inter-Action, asking her for '"two sexy pieces" for his Fun-Art Bus'. She notes her 'indignation (!)', but goes on to explain how, despite this inauspicious beginning, she successfully pestered him for 'a season of plays by women':

> We did a season of plays by women, directed by women, designed by women. We even (a small number of us) painted out the theatre, dried out the basement for a creche and I – newly up from the country, cooked food every day and took it in to be sold (alas, our profit from this little bourgeois venture was stolen). (12 January 1999)

The women's season that Gems describes took place in 1973 and was instrumental in founding the Women's Company and The Women's Theatre Group (WTG). The former was short-lived; the latter, with its roots in street theatre and activism in support of the Women's Liberation Movement, evolved into what would become the longest running of the 70s groups, subsequently renamed as Sphinx Theatre Company (**Sue Parrish & Susan McGoun**).

As a women's company organised through non-hierarchical, collaborative structures, the WTG typified the burgeoning number of groups founded by the close of the decade – groups that were not building-based, but small-scale touring companies reaching out to audiences not only in theatre spaces, but community spaces, church halls, or schools. These groups included: Monstrous Regiment (1975; **Mary McCusker**), Clapperclaw (1977), Cunning Stunts (1977), Beryl and the Perils (1978), Mrs Worthington's Daughters (1979), Siren (1979), Spare Tyre (1979;

Pam Gems, playwright

**Clair Chapwell**) and Clean Break (1979; **Anna Herrmann**).

Although these groups 'then' may seem distant to us 'now', a feeling of just how vibrant this flourishing women's theatre culture was to the feminist landscape at large emerges from

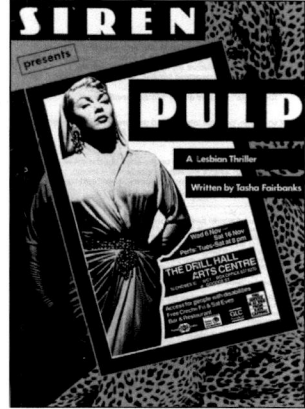

Poster for *Pulp* by Siren Theatre

the reviews in *Spare Rib*. As I sat leafing through the theatre columns I collected from the magazine, moving from review to review, immersed in the descriptions of shows seen from the feminist perspectives of reviewers, I came away with a sense of the anarchy and clowning of Cunning Stunts; the musical, feminist satires of Clapperclaw; the agit-prop influences of WTG's early shows; or the preoccupation of Mrs Worthington's Daughters with women and history. Overall, this re-awakened a feeling of how exceptional it was for women's theatre to be reviewed and embedded in the issues and concerns of a *feminist* magazine.

Feminism was the backdrop against which the groups were formed. These were the exciting years of the Women's Liberation Movement, forged in the four demands: for equal pay, equal education and opportunity, 24-hour nurseries, and free contraception and abortion on demand.[2] Where these demands evinced something of a consensus, the question of *how* to advance women's rights was hotly debated among feminists – differing significantly according to whether women espoused bourgeois-, radical-, or socialist-feminist politics. Similarly, women's theatre groups varied both in their relationship to the women's movement and their feminist politics. Some, like WTG, were closely aligned with the Women's Liberation Movement, others, like Cunning Stunts, did not identify as a feminist company. In my archival box, I recover correspondence with Rose Sharp, former administrator of Monstrous Regiment, in which she explains how, 'Monstrous Regiment has always been and is now a socialist, feminist company. This is reflected most importantly in our "work process" – we have always encouraged women in all areas of the production' (23 October 1989). Contrastingly, as a lesbian collective, Siren found inspiration in radical feminism and the ideas of Mary Daly and Andrea Dworkin. There were also groups whose identity and purpose were forged through a particular issue: Clean Break's fight for women affected by the criminal justice system, detailed by **Anna Herrmann**; Spare Tyre's Susie Orbach-inspired work on women's weight, body image and well-being, outlined by **Clair Chapwell**. But whatever their feminist

-political differences and affiliations, the rise of the groups consolidated the "demand" to move women's stories centre stage.

In turn, this raised the issue of how women's lives and experiences were to be represented or told. In these formative, counter-cultural years, groups developed their signature styles; they often drew on popular-political traditions of agit-prop, music, comedy, or cabaret. Whatever the form, the dominant drive was towards the presentational rather than representational: the breaking of the fourth-wall theatre tradition that confined and subordinated women to the patriarchal "drama" of male-dominated subjects and interests. Retrieving my well-thumbed, now barely legible copy of Gillian Hanna's (Monstrous Regiment) influential 1978 interview, I revisit her explanation of needing to explore dramatic forms that capture women's 'broken backed' lives and experiences; of working on the production of Caryl Churchill's *Vinegar Tom* (1976), using 'music to smash' the 'regular and acceptable theatrical form' of a 'traditional play'.[3] She speculates that in future years 'women theatre practitioners will increasingly come up against the discovery, or the need to discover, new forms'.[4] The fortunes of feminism and women's theatre will prove decidedly mixed in the ensuing decades, but the quest for 'new forms' will endure.

## Gains and Losses in the 80s

Into the 80s, these companies remained important to the evolution of feminism and theatre. Many of the women playwrights during the decade were indebted to opportunities created by them. Bryony Lavery, Deborah Levy, Winsome Pinnock, and Timberlake Wertenbaker all had plays performed by WTG. Lavery's work also featured in Monstrous

The Drill Hall now RADA Studios

Regiment's 80s repertoire, alongside a raft of European writers. Additionally, gay and women-friendly venues such as London's Drill Hall or the Oval House Theatre provided alternative, counter-cultural stages for playwrights and companies. Elsewhere, at the Royal Court Theatre, England's premiere venue for new play-writing, there were indications of women's playwriting progress: in contrast to how only 8% of plays produced between 1959

Mel Taylor & Dulice Liecier in *Spell #7* by Ntozake Shange

and 1980 at the Court were by women – chiefly two women, Ann Jellicoe and Caryl Churchill – from 1980 to 1989 it rose to 29%.[5] That said, the percentage was consistently higher in the studio, upstairs space than the downstairs, main auditorium. In other words, plays by women dramatists increased, but did not frequently cross over into larger spaces. This was an inequality that The Women's Playhouse Trust, inaugurated in the 80s, sought to redress by 'demand[ing] a place for women in the mainstream'– a 'demand' that encompassed the idea of obtaining a West End theatre (**Parrish**). Although the West End theatre did not materialise, what the WPT exemplified was the strategy of a dedicated women's theatre working within the mainstream to close the gender gap.

Meanwhile, the ongoing need for women to carve out their own counter-cultural spaces saw more groups forming in the early to mid-80s. These included **Peta Lily's** Three Women Mime company (1980), **Julia Pascal's** company devoted to new writing (1983), and regional groups like Birmingham's issue-based Women and Theatre (1983) and the working-class trio of older women who formed The Chuffinelles in Sheffield (1986). Highly significant were the theatre collectives set up by Black women artists to address the lack of plays and roles by and for Black women: Theatre of Black Women (1982); Imani-Faith (1983), and Munirah Theatre Company (1983). A *Spare Rib* review of Theatre of Black Women's production of *Silhouette*, a performance that invoked the history of slavery, draws attention to a common purpose of these groups and to Black women's relationship to feminism:

> The stated objective of the Theatre of Black Women is to give artistic expression to the experiences of Black women past and present. By reliving our history and current struggles in front of our eyes, these aims, I believe, will be instrumental in helping Black women to define and name our own brand of 'feminism', a noun which so far means little to me, appropriated as it has been to describe white women's experiences.[6]

What these comments reflect is the need for Black women artists to have a space of their own and for a feminism that is not exclusively defined and circumscribed by 'white women's experiences'. As **SuAndi,** performance poet and champion of the Black arts sector, movingly attests, 'differences matter'.

The difference that the publication of a playscript makes to the possibility of sustaining a playwriting career is significant: vital to ensuring plays have a wider circulation, audience/readership, and to securing future productions. Women playwrights found it significantly harder to get published given the risk-averse trend of publishing male dramatists and canonical texts. Pioneering, feminist playwright and critic Michelene Wandor sought to address that imbalance by establishing Methuen's *Plays by Women* series. Volume One published in 1982 included plays by a cross-generational mix of writers – Caryl Churchill, Pam Gems, Louise Page, and Wandor.[7] These anthologies were hugely important to those of us seeking to make a feminist difference to the male-centric texts and practices of university theatre departments. Moreover, as collections of plays by different dramatists, the volumes highlighted the diversity of women's drama in terms of content *and* form. As Volume One exemplifies, subjects are wide-ranging: the witchcraft of Churchill's *Vinegar Tom*; sisterhood and politics in Gems' *Dusa, Fish, Stas and Vi*; breast cancer in Page's *Tissue*; and Wandor's depiction of the poet Elizabeth Barrett Browning in *Aurora Leigh*. And in terms of form, to encounter the plays side by side is to register the Brechtian-feminist terrain of *Vinegar Tom*; the scenic fragmentations of *Dusa, Fish, Stas & Vi*; the reporting style of *Tissue*; and the poetry of *Aurora Leigh*.

Poster for *Vinegar Tom*

To come out from under the canonical past proved a significant feminist, theatre-making strategy in the 80s, exemplified by Monstrous Regiment's visual-theatre production of *Shakespeare's Sister* (1980, 1982), inspired by Virginia Woolf's image of the bard's fictional sister as a woman deprived of an artistic life; Timberlake Wertenbaker's *The Love of the Nightingale* (1988), a feminist re-telling of the ancient Greek myth depicting the rape of Philomela, and Elaine Feinstein and WTG's

*Lear's Daughters* featuring three daughters, a fool, a nanny, but no King Lear. *Lear's Daughters* lingers in my memory because of its finely crafted feminist resistance to the Shakespearean canon that even now continues to occupy the British stage at the expense of new writing, and Hazel Maycock's larger-than-life, money-grabbing, androgynously depicted fool that captured the greed and socio-economic divide of the Thatcherite 80s – as well as my involvement in getting the script published.

Correspondence in April 1989 with the actress Adjoa Andoh (Regan in *Lear's Daughters*) reminds me of the interview we arranged with the company in London – an interview that was instrumental in seeding the idea for publishing WTG scripts. An approach to Sheffield Academic Press on the part of my then colleague Gabriele Griffin, secured contracts for two collections of plays: *Herstory Volume 1 & 2.* (A buried memory of typing up Bryony Lavery's *Witchcraze* for Volume 1 surfaces as a I write this – a somewhat painful exercise in the era of floppy discs and basic Amstrad computers!) All of the plays published in the volumes (six in total) were from the 80s and all deployed what we termed 're-visioning' strategies, whether this was the re-visioning of mythological and literary heritages (Vol. 1) or of "real" women's lives in the early 20th century (Vol. 2). Overall, these two volumes were an attempt to redress the way that, like women's erasure from patriarchally written history, 'women's theatre groups' work disappears as it appears'.[8]

However, the phenomenon of appearing and disappearing is what ultimately characterises the state of women's theatre by the end of the decade. Despite the gains I have outlined, there were significant losses for feminism and women's theatre-making. Firstly, while the 80s saw more women playwrights emerging on the British stage, they were still statistically small in number. Introducing *Plays by Women 3,* Wandor estimates 'that women in this country constitute somewhere between 10% – 15% of produced playwrights'.[9] As previously indicated, they were also mainly confined to studio spaces and to the small-scale touring circuit of the women's companies, thus reducing public profiles and income. In terms of the reception and reviewing of their work, they also had to contend with the negative perceptions attached to the label 'woman' or 'feminist' playwright. Hence, the reluctance of some women writers to be published in a 'volume with the label "by women"'.[10]

Gender bias in theatre reviewing was a constant source of complaint.

Of all the volumes in the Methuen *Plays by Women* series, my most worn copy is Volume 6. This is because time and again over my years of teaching, I drew students' attention to Mary Remnant's introduction[11] and her case study of the misogyny heaped on the radical-feminist playwright, Sarah Daniels, notably in the wake of *Masterpieces* (1983), a play that powerfully opened up a debate on pornography at the same time as igniting a huge anti-feminist rant voiced by a majority of male theatre critics. In short, this served as a feminist consciousness-raising exercise, fostering awareness of gender bias in theatre reviewing 'then' (and 'now').

Moreover, the feminist movement was in difficulty. Identity politics that were crucial to recognising differences of class, sexuality, or race (as evinced in the formation of the Black women's theatre groups), made it harder to find common, feminist-political ground. Compounding that struggle was mainstream culture's disarticulation of feminism as a socially progressive movement: its promotion and positing of feminism as an individualistic mode of bourgeois, self-empowerment, a phenomenon powerfully and memorably critiqued in Churchill's state-of-the-nation play, *Top Girls* (1982). Hence, the collective ethos and work processes foundational to women's theatre groups were now antithetical to the 'top-girl' syndrome. More concretely, the increasing shift to a 'post-feminist' climate saw the loss of synergies that had existed between the Women's Liberation Movement and women's theatre in the 70s – synergies that had proven advantageous to building networks and audiences, securing venues and bookings.

Above all, it was the increasing Thatcherite drive towards private sponsorship and the drastic reduction of state subsidy for theatre that made it so very difficult for the women's theatre groups to survive.[12] Although the Arts Council always publicly denied operating any political agenda, many of the alternative, political theatre groups found their funding withdrawn, as reflected in **Mary McCusker's** account of the Council's rejection of Monstrous Regiment's 'new plans for the company's future'.[13] To stand any chance of survival, groups were forced to forego their collectives: to streamline into small, core management teams who were left to cope with increased administrative labour and the time-consuming task of securing funding – this at the expense of a company's creative output. It is not therefore surprising to find most groups unable to manage. Under these conditions and with a loss of funding, none of

Cover of new edition

the Black women's companies formed in the early 80s were able to continue. Of the groups cited in this introduction only WTG/Sphinx and Clean Break have kept going, with Clean Break the only company to secure a building. Overall, this constitutes a highly detrimental setback to the evolution of women's theatre in the UK: the loss of opportunities for women playwrights to have their work staged; the loss of training grounds for women practitioners in all fields of work (directors, performers, designers, lighting and sound technicians); and the loss of supportive, feminist networking that helped to nurture and/or sustain women's careers in the theatre industry. In short, without the opportunities, training grounds and networks that the groups provided, it was difficult to build on past successes and achieve a sustainable feminist-theatre legacy.

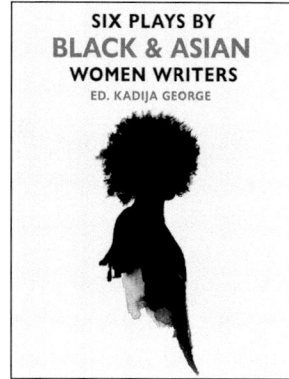

## 'Bad Girls' in the 90s

Although the early 90s saw the disappearance of many women's theatre collectives, thus marking a break in the counter-cultural, collectively-orientated women's theatre tradition, there are nonetheless continuities to be found in the case of women playwrights. Playwriting voices from the 70s and/or 80s such as Gems, Churchill, Lavery, Wertenbaker, Daniels, Pinnock, and de Angelis continued to make a feminist difference to the British stage. Furthermore, although Methuen's *Plays by Women* series was ending, Aurora Metro Press came forward with the collection *Black and Asian Women Writers* (1993). This heralded Aurora Metro's enduring commitment to publishing women's plays: 150 plays by women since published, many in translation from other languages.[14]

From my file on Lavery, I retrieve the programme for *Goliath* (1997). This was Lavery's adaptation of Beatrix Campbell's *Goliath: Britain's Dangerous Places* (1993), a feminist analysis of the nationwide riots sparked in 1991 by the social and economic disenfranchisement of those dwelling in the UK's rundown council estates, rioting rendered and distilled into a solo, one-woman performance by Nicola McAuliffe. *Goliath* was commissioned by **Sue Parrish** for Sphinx (WTG) and directed by Annie Castledine. I pause on this production as testimony not only to the enduring, collaborative, feminist energies that fuelled the production, but also to its exemplification of feminist theatre tackling epic questions of social inequality and economic deprivation. There's publicity too for Lavery's *Kitchen Matters* with Gay Sweatshop and *Her Aching Heart* for WTG (Sphinx) – both in 1990-91, both comedic, defiant rejoinders to funding cuts and the notorious, anti-gay legislation Section 28 (popularly known as 'Clause 28').[15]

Significant among new women's writing voices of the 90s was the attention given to the dead-end lives and deprivations of young women: the girl-gang plays *Ashes and Sand* (1994) by Judy Upton and *Yard Gal* (1998) by Rebecca Prichard. Both premiered at the Royal Court that subsequently also staged Irish playwright, Stella Feehily's working-class, Dublin-girls-in-trouble play, *Duck* (2003). And elsewhere, despite the hardship entailed in forming a women's group, the northern company Open Clasp (**Catrina McHugh**) set up in 1998 with a commitment to girls and women on the socio-cultural margins and to "acting" in the interests of social change.

These playwriting examples of what I termed 'bad girl' theatre[16] along with Open Clasp's founding concern with young women on the margins – the girls, who like working-class Angie in Churchill's *Top Girls*, are not going to make it – stood in stark contrast to the vaunting of 'ladette' behaviour and girl power in the British media. Like its 'top-girl' predecessor in the 80s, the individualistic, sexually aggressive mode of 90s girl power (think Spice Girls), disarticulated feminism from a socially progressive agenda. Now there were proclamations of a 'new feminism' antagonistic to the second-wave and promoting the idea of women's self-empowerment.[17] But this ideological shift from the notion of women helping each other to the idea of women helping themselves, merely served to perpetuate rather than ameliorate persistent inequalities. As to bringing about change in

British theatre, as Gems observed: 'the only way is for women in the theatre – actors, designers, directors, administrators – to get together' – to be supportive of each other.[18]

In her 1999 study of women's directing based on interviews with 13 directors, Helen Manfull notes that irrespective of whether the directors identified with feminism or not, all were 'adamant about their desire to help and

Stella Feehily, playwright

Cover of Methuen edition

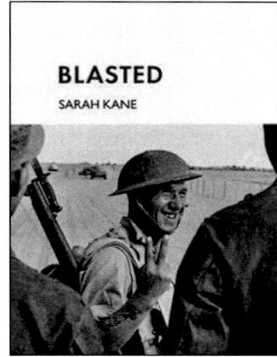

support one another'. She adds: 'To a person they are hopeful about their roles as women directors and encouraged about their abilities to nurture the work of women writers or emphasise plays with female protagonists'.[19] Although there were constraints on just how supportive women directors could be given the persistent male-dominated "direction" of British theatre, as directors and/or artistic directors of venues and companies, women were in a position to nurture and assist the development of women's playwriting. Some notable examples from the 90s include: **Parrish's** enduring and sustained commitment to women playwrights in her role as Artistic Director of Sphinx/WTG, Lisa Goldman's founding of The Red Room, a London fringe venue and company that supported early plays by Judy Upton and Kay Adshead, and Castledine's feisty, feminist championing of women's work. Equally, to cite an example from Irish Theatre (see **Jaki McCarrick**), during her tenure as Artistic Director at Dublin's Abbey Theatre (1991-93), Garry Hynes 'committed to doing at least one play by a woman in the Abbey's season of new plays',[20] an initiative that proved instrumental in the launching of Marina Carr's career. Carr is now recognised as one of, if not the, leading contemporary playwright in Ireland. And yet, as the 21st century approached, a level playing field in British theatre (and on the Irish theatre scene) remained elusive – an aspiration rather than a reality.

Despite the rich, diverse qualities of women's playwriting exemplified here and the supportive efforts of those women in the industry seeking to bring about change, the struggle to close the gender gap was fraught with difficulty. The 90s wave of 'in-yer-face' plays by predominantly 'angry young men' had a silencing impact on women's theatre voices.[21] Antipathy to feminism (on and off the stage) also marginalised women's work as did the prevailing negative preconceptions of theatre critics – a largely unchanged cadre of male, white, Oxbridge-educated reviewers. The latter often (albeit not always) evinced little enthusiasm for women-centred subjects and were notably unreceptive to the experimental forms women explored and developed. How different the reception of her controversial debut play *Blasted* (1994) would have been, Sarah Kane surmised, if she had crafted and confined her war-torn landscape of masculine violence to a mode of familiar realism. Kane's disavowal of the 'woman' writer label saw her categorised as a member of the angry boys' brigade.[22] But her iconoclastic, experientially formed theatre expressive of damaging and violent masculinities resonated with a feminist sensibility – a renewed structure of feminist feeling in British theatre.

## 21st-Century Feminist Directions

Feeling the structures of inequality in the 21st century, many women playwrights reinvigorated their resistance to the status quo. Over the next two decades, the "cast" of women playwrights continued to expand. It now includes: Bola Agbaje, debbie tucker green, Ella Hickson, Lucy Kirkwood, Rebecca Lenkiewicz, Lucy Prebble, Penelope Skinner, Nina Raine, Anya Reiss, Katherine Soper, Polly Stenham, Laura Wade, and Joy Wilkinson. Whether they identify with feminism or not, like their predecessors, these 21st-century women dramatists crafted plays tackling a range of subjects in diverse forms and styles – tucker green's poetically voiced, angry black-feminist critiques of white Western privilege; Prebble's epic treatment of capitalism in *Enron* (2009); or Wade's riotous, darkly comedic dramatization of posh-boy antics (*Posh*, 2010). While eclectic in form and subject matter, this theatre reflects widely shared concerns with the toxicity of patriarchalism, socio-economic privilege and power.

In 2010, explorations of 'Women Power and Politics' came to the fore in a season of nine short plays by women, curated by the director Indhu Rubasingham for London's Tricycle Theatre. It was presented in two parts, 'Now' and 'Then'; I recall how exhilarating it was to see both parts back-to-back. A cross-generational mix of writers included award-winning dramatists Marie Jones (an original member of the Belfast-based, women's theatre company, Charabanc, founded in the early 80s) and **Moira Buffini**, whose one-act comedic rendition of Thatcher and Queen Elizabeth II in *Handbagged* was subsequently expanded into a version that played the West End. In one way, this season testified to the diversity and power of women's writing; in another, it was a salutary reminder of women's under-representation in politics and theatre, 'then and now'.

On the political "stage", 2010 was also the year that saw a transition from New Labour to a Conservative-led coalition. Austerity, fuelled by the global banking crisis (2007-08), deepened; 2011 was a year of strikes and

# INTRODUCTION

Fenella Woolgar in Moira Buffini's *Handbagged*

riots – a groundswell of opposition to the deficits of a bankrupt neo-capitalist system, reduction in state welfare, and escalating hardship for millions of people. It was against this backdrop that the feminist movement renewed and gained traction. A young, intersectionally aware generation of women embraced rather than rejected feminism – initiating a number of campaigns and protests on a range of issues including sexual harassment, domestic abuse, racial equality, and equal pay. In parallel, there was a rise of feminist work tackling the abject state of the British nation: plays that critiqued a competitive, masculine world order endorsing the high-achieving career woman (Lucy Kirkwood's *NSFW*, 2012; Penelope Skinner's *Linda* 2015); dramatized the state's welfare system at the point of collapse (Clean Break's *Joanne*, 2015); demonstrated conditions for young low-paid and unemployed workers (Katherine Soper's *Wish List*, 2016); or, as in Churchill's *Escaped Alone* (2016), protested the ecological damage caused by neoliberal capitalism (see **April de Angelis, Alison Child,** and **Bibi Lucille**).

Also mirroring the feminist movement at large were the escalating demands and campaigns to address the inequalities of the British theatre industry: the calls for the introduction of quota systems, exemplified by 'ERA 50:50', the Equal Representation for Actresses campaign founded in 2015 by actresses Lizzie Berrington and **Polly Kemp**; 'The Act for Change Project' launched in 2014 to campaign and lobby for an end to discrimination and the promotion of equality and diversity in the arts; and Lucy Kerbel's Tonic Theatre, founded in 2011 to support the industry in taking incremental steps towards equality. Collecting and compiling information on gender-parity initiatives for a 'restaging feminisms' book project,[23] I experienced as energising and frustrating – frustrating because of the *déjà vu* feeling. Moreover, while equality strategies are essential to change and potentially impactful, as evinced in Ireland's #WakingTheFeminists Movement,[24] a more seismic shift to the toxic culture of the male-dominated industry is also needed to address the depth of discrimination and harassment occurring front *and* backstage that, **Imy**

**Wyatt Corner; Rebekah Smith** & **Abbie Lowe** (Scylla's Bite) all describe.

With the advent of the #MeToo Movement in 2017 came the outing of sexual harassment. The abuse of power by directors who made use of 'the casting couch' was called out and the ability of women to take to social media to publicise such working practices allowed those who had been fearful of reprisals to come together and share their experiences online. On 28 October 2017, the Royal Court's Artistic Director, Vicky Featherstone, organised a day of action and the drawing up of a Code of Behaviour that encouraged other theatres to take remedial action. There was also a renewed awareness of the "age old" problem of paucity of roles for older women, and of continuing sizeism and colourism whereby darker-skinned women and larger women were unlikely to be cast. As **Rebecca Mordan** (Scary Little Girls) comments, 'The unofficial standard is that no woman who is a size 10 or over is cast in a leading role'. Equally, based on her 40 years in the industry, lesbian comedienne **Clare Summerskill** reflects that 'the road is a rough one' for 'lesbian actresses – especially those who do not conform to stereotypical images of female beauty'. Attention was also drawn to class and intersectional inequalities "acting" as significant barriers to participation in the industry. As producer **Maeve O'Neill** highlights, 'Racism exists in the UK and Ireland, and it exists in our theatres. While the arts industry has begun to address these issues, we still don't see enough representation on stage, backstage or in leadership roles'. Hence the importance of Stella Kanu's #Connect: Black Women in Theatre at the Oval House (2018-19) that created meeting grounds for Black women practitioners to come together, to share experiences and advice in a non-hierarchical, supportive environment.

With so many women working as freelance artists, finding a 'community of like-minded artists' is critical, as playwright **Hannah Khalil** observes, not only for developing creatively, but also for coping with isolation and employment precarity – a precarity that deepens for those

Shazz Andrew in *The Tempest* by Scary Little Girls and The Minack, Cornwall.

women who have children (see **Suzie Miller; Cheryl Robson**). If women are to have 'the chance to succeed and thrive', in director **Sarah Brigham's** widely shared view, what they require is 'a working environment which respects things like caring responsibilities, which offers strong female role models, and asks "what can we do to help"' (see also **Suzanne Gorman; Amy Ng**).

An enduring need to be in the like-minded "company" of women has seen no shortage of women's theatre groups emerging in the 21st century, creating supportive environments for practitioners and writers; reviving and reinvigorating the second-wave, collaborative, group tradition. Intersectional feminism is widely embraced by new and established theatre companies, as reflected in debut works by companies F-Bomb (**Rachel O'Regan**) and Scylla's Bite (**Rebekah Smith** & **Abbie Lowe**), and Scotland's long-running, Stellar Quines company (**Gerda Stevenson**). Intersectional-feminist approaches are those that ensure that women's stories are not confined to white, straight, able-bodied, class and gender-binary privilege (see **Kelly Burke**). Think of the popular-political, inclusive, feminist theatre of Artistic Director Emma Rice and her company Wise Children (2018); the diverse and inclusive casting of Morgan Lloyd Malcolm's *Emilia* (Shakespeare's Globe 2018; Vaudeville Theatre 2019) that joyously and irreverently reclaimed women's writing from the margins of Shakesperean history and culture; or the diverse and non-binary casting that Suba Das, Artistic Director of Liverpool's Everyman Theatre, initiated in the revival of Churchill's *Top Girls* (2023). Equality *and* diversity *and* inclusivity. This is where the future history of feminism and theatre resides.

## Forward and Back

From the vantage point of 'now' the journey of feminism and theatre over the last five decades can be seen as a 'broken-backed' narrative of gains and losses, of cyclical endeavours to challenge the malestream – in the words of actress **Ann Mitchell**, of needing 'to fight the same fights over and over again'. History repeats because of the perpetual cycles of underfunding and discrimination that militate against the expansion of feminist-theatre horizons from one generation to the next, as reflected in the case of women's theatre companies that more often than not struggle to survive, grow, maintain training opportunities, or secure a building base as a means to a more sustainable future. Hence, it comes as no surprise to find that the cross-generational voices brought together in this volume attest to equality as far from achieved.

Contributions highlight the need for affirmative actions that include: a policy change in Arts Council funding to close the gender gap, provide support for childcare and increase numbers of women in leadership roles; theatres to "act" for change by commissioning more women playwrights, employing more women both front and backstage, and creating opportunities for supportive networks; and drama schools as well as theatres to have reporting lines and policies to address discriminatory and harmful behaviour.[25] Equally, contributors draw attention to the enduring need for feminism in society at large and in the theatre. As writer and performer **Roberta Livingston** comments: 'If feminism isn't implemented into the structure of our society, how can we expect it to be integrated within theatre?'.

In these post-pandemic times, there is an urgency for ensuring such transformative actions are implemented. Reporting on a theatre survey undertaken during the pandemic, the *Guardian* revealed that 'more than 60% of women across all roles in UK theatre are considering leaving the industry, with 85% worried gender inequality will worsen post-Covid'.[26] Those worries about gender disparity have been confirmed: the post-pandemic trend towards smaller – solo or duo – casts; safe, box-office revivals; and increased financial hardship for freelancers, have indeed rendered the situation for women theatre makers more precarious. As **Sue Parrish** points out: 'in the recent National Portfolio awards no women's professionally producing theatre companies were included'.

And yet, there are cautious notes of optimism among the contributors.

Melissa MacNaught in *The Beatles Were A Boyband*

Clean Break's **Anna Herrmann** argues that 'change will come', that 'new ideas do emerge', citing the example of the newly formed, Arts Council-funded, Women in Theatre Lab, dedicated to the support of women writers (**Polly Kemp** & **Jennifer Tuckett**).[27]

**Rukhsana Ahmad**, co-founder of Kali Theatre Company, 'remains[s] positive about the future' of the company and its nurturing of women of South Asian descent who are now 'progressing into the mainstream'. **Sarah Brigham** finds strength in 'some wonderful female role models': 'it is often their example that gives me hope in the future of our industry'. Director **Imy Wyatt Corner** is 'hopeful that with the appointment of Indhu Rubasingham at the helm at National Theatre there will be some necessary and important pressure on the industry to shift us towards change'. And playwright and dramaturg **Kaite O'Reilly** advocates the 'daily practice' of remaining optimistic and hopeful for change'.

Fifty years on from the landmark women's season in 1973 at Inter-Action, the fight for a feminist future in the industry goes on. In March 2024, prompted by Jennifer Tuckett's detailed research, a group of women in theatre which included **Kelly Burke, Polly Kemp, Cheryl Robson** and **Jennifer Tuckett**, met with Arts Council England to discuss the ongoing under-representation of women in theatre. The outcome was that ACE agreed to consider setting up a gender advisory board, and to look at issues around childcare and new writing commissions.

Feminist Theatre is a history of survival and resilience: of creating, representing, and embodying experiences that malestream culture would sooner we forget. This is a feminist history that deserves to be remembered, preserved, and celebrated for future generations.

≈

**Elaine Aston** is Professor Emerita, Lancaster University. Her publications on feminist theatre include *Caryl Churchill* (1997/ 2001/ 2010); *Feminism and Theatre* (1995); *Feminist Theatre Practice* (1999); *Feminist Views on the English Stage* (2003); *Performance Practice and Process: Contemporary [Women] Practitioners* (2008, with Geraldine Harris); *A Good Night Out for the Girls* (2013, with Geraldine Harris); and *Restaging Feminisms* (2020). In 2014 she was awarded an Honorary Doctorate by Stockholm University. Elaine also served as Senior Editor of Theatre Research International (2010-12) and in 2019 was elected President of the International Federation for Theatre Research for a four-year term of office.

# NOTES

1 *Highlighted names denote contributors to this volume.*

2 These four basic demands arose from the first national conference of the WLM, Ruskin College, Oxford, 1970. Initially conceived as a women's history workshop weekend, this event inaugurated a series of national WLM conferences through to 1978.

3 Gillian Hanna, 'Feminism and Theatre', Theatre Papers, 2nd series, no. 8, Dartington College, 1978, 1-14, p.8, p.9.

4 Ibid, p.9.

5 Ruth Little and Emily McLaughlin, *The Royal Court Theatre Inside Out*, Oberon Books, 2007, p.238.

6 Review by 'Maxine', *Spare Rib*, January 1984, p.47.

7 Ten volumes were published in total, the last in 1994.

8 Gabriele Griffin and Elaine Aston, Introduction, *Herstory 1 & 2*, Sheffield Academic Press, 1991, p.8.

9 Michelene Wandor, Introduction, *Plays by Women 3*, Methuen, 1984, p.vii.

10 Ibid.

11 Mary Remnant, Introduction, *Plays by Women 6*, Methuen, 1987, pp.7-12.

12 For example, the Secretary-General's Report, 43rd annual report and accounts, Arts Council, 1987-88, states: 'We must be able to show ... that earnings and private sector income play a larger part in turnover of arts organisations than in the past' (p. 4).

13 In a past interview with Monstrous Regiment, Gillian Hanna also explained: 'all those political groups were weeded out in the '80s because they were too uncomfortable, and nobody wanted to know. The Arts Council, although they would deny it, also seemed to feel that they didn't want to support such groups anymore'. Quoted in *Feminist Theatre Voices,* Elaine Aston, ed., Loughborough Theatre Texts, 1997, p.66.

14 Aurora Metro has recently acquired the back-catalogue of Amber Lane Press with high-profile plays *Steaming* by Nell Dunn and *Once a Catholic* by Mary O'Malley being given a new lease of life.

15 Passed in 1988, Section 28 banned schools from promoting homosexuality or literature that endorsed homosexuality as the basis for a "normal" family life.

16 Elaine Aston, '"Bad Girls" and "Sick Boys": New Women Playwrights and

the Future of Feminism"', in Aston & Geraldine Harris, eds., *Feminist Futures?*, Palgrave Macmillan, 2006, pp.71-87.

17  See Natasha Walter, *The New Feminism*, Virago, 1999.

18  Gems, qtd in Heidi Stephenson and Natasha Langridge, *Rage and Reason: Women Playwrights on Playwriting*, Methuen, 1997, p.97.

19  Helen Manfull, *Taking the Stage: Women Directors on Directing*, Methuen, 1999, p.164.

20  Ibid, p.176.

21  See Elaine Aston, *Feminist Views on the English Stage: Women Playwrights 1990-2000,* Cambridge University Press, 2003.

22  Ibid, p.80.

23  Elaine Aston, *Restaging Feminisms*, Palgrave Macmillan, 2020.

24  Fuelled by the virtually exclusive, male-authored programme planned for the Abbey Theatre's season to mark the centenary of the 1916 uprising, Waking the Feminists proved impactful in its solidarity-building campaign to address women's marginalisation in Irish theatre.

25  See Giverny Masso, ' Drama School Students Report Racism, Casting Bias and Widespread Harassment', *The Stage*, 8 March 2022, Drama school students report racism, casting bias and widespread harassment (thestage.co.uk) .

26  Nadia Khomami, 'Theatre in UK Faces Exodus of Women After Pandemic, Study Finds', *The Guardian*, 9 October 2021, Theatre in UK faces exodus of women after pandemic, study finds | Theatre | The Guardian.

27  The Lab is inspired by the New-York based WP Theater Lab and Australia's Women in Theatre Programme. The former started out as the Women's Project in 1978, founded by Julia Miles. Now called WP Theater, the company has survived economic and organisational setbacks and gone on to produce over '600 Off-Broadway plays' WP History | WP Theater.

Shelley King in *River on Fire*. Photo: Suki Dhanda

# ASIAN WOMEN'S THEATRE IN BRITAIN: A PLAYWRIGHT'S TALE

## RUKHSANA AHMAD

For me, a feminist is someone committed to the betterment of womankind with an understanding of their material circumstances, their socio-economic context. Someone who is willing to battle for the rights and safety, hopes and opportunities, needs and desires of *all women*, in a collective sense … recognising disadvantage, underlining inclusivity, and always putting the group's interests and aspirations over and above those of the individual.

My mother, who was denied a college education, because there was not enough money to pay for the girls in the family to go to university, was passionately committed to educating all four of us, girls, and drummed into us from a very early age the importance of economic independence for women. She was a key influence; but I must admit she never looked far beyond that single, admittedly significant, feminist goal. Hidden beneath that modern attitude was her desire to find us suitable matches, very like Mrs. Bennett, (but with considerably more discretion!) and her abiding respect for every social tradition, good or bad. However, education is the key to liberation, and economic independence is an incomparable tool; it was enough in a sense… it created in me a passion for work and a desire for paid work.

Sadly, my first-class university degrees could not get me a decent job here… My time as a disempowered housewife and a harried mother was revelatory. I learnt as much about women's issues and intersectionality through my experience as a brown immigrant as I did from Simone de Beauvoir or Germaine Greer. I still agree heartily with every word I read in *The Second Sex*, even if I was often sceptical about Greer's positions, especially as she got older. But Greer, with her passion for stirring debates and raising controversy, had put feminism in the limelight all over the world. Things were happening for women, it seemed to us back then; change was afoot. The optimism and the activism of the 80s held us in thrall, and it did propel women consistently forward for a short spell of time.

For me, feminism wasn't some alien influence that I imbibed in the UK. It's always been embedded within me. Growing up in a patriarchal society, as the third daughter born to a mother whose feminism was relatively shallow, I acquired my insights through my lived reality. It's the prism through which I see and interpret the world. It's the motivation that drives my choice of subject and genre. For a woman, and a brown one at that, who believes in justice, it's the only perspective that makes sense.

In the mid-80s, when I started attending women's conferences, with a view to mobilising women for a cause that I was anguished about, I found plenty of women willing to help; they empathised with the pain and the anguish of Pakistani women who were defying a military dictator's brute force armed only with words: as poets, journalists, theatre practitioners and dancers. That is essentially at the core of feminism: the commitment to women's causes, the world over. The willingness to collaborate with other groups internationally, the readiness to lend the disadvantaged a helping hand.

Those early journalistic pieces, reflecting my outrage, caught Ravinder Randhawa's eye and she invited me to join her Asian Women Writers' Workshop, where I found kindred spirits: women who understood my writing, who got the sub-text and the inescapable smattering of Urdu/Hindi words that would suffer in translation. There were women who were political activists, notably, Rahila Gupta, who was on the Southall Black Sisters (SBS) Steering Committee. She brought news to the workshop of the murder of an Asian woman at a refuge in Brent. Horrified, we all joined the march behind SBS, to protest the violence against women. Rahila herself wrote a poem as a tribute to the murdered woman, Balwant Kaur. My tribute came months later, after I read a disturbing news item about a lock-out at a refuge for Asian women. My first full-length play: *Song for a Sanctuary* (published by Aurora Metro) was not a retelling of Kaur's story but a fictional response to her tragic death at the hands of her husband, in front of their three children …

When Monstrous Regiment, a highly regarded feminist theatre company, called for new work, I lost no time pitching my idea to them. Getting my first full-length script commissioned by them was thrilling.

Adele Salem & Royce Ullah in *Black Shalwaar.* Photo: Sheila Burnett

Until then, my work had been limited to theatre-in-education (three scripts commissioned back-to-back by Jatinder Verma of Tara Arts) followed by a community theatre piece, for Worcester Arts. The female director of my very first play had declared, smiling wryly, that no one got commissioned for the mainstage, and certainly never a woman: *that* was the AD's preserve.

I was unprepared and horribly disappointed when Monstrous Regiment told me they couldn't produce my play as they were in financial straits and were about to disband; and, anyhow, the script wasn't ready. But when they saw my distress, their sympathy was instantaneous and sincere. Like true feminists, one of them wrote to me the very next day, offering her cottage as a retreat, to enable me to rework the script and another sent it off to a BBC radio producer contact of hers, confident she'd see its potential and give it a life on radio. And, of course, she did that, meeting me with her notes at Broadcasting House.

That helping hand eased the pain and got me an entry into radio drama long before the play was staged. I had literally abandoned the script and set about translating Urdu feminist poetry into English. *We Sinful Women* was a passion project that occupied me fully whilst trying to earn from teaching creative writing at an Adult Education Institute in Putney. My play might never have been produced if the actor, Rita Wolf, had not approached me and committed herself to getting it staged, come what may. Within days, she'd organised a rehearsed reading, persuading actor friends to participate. But when she found no takers amongst the production houses, she cheerfully gave up her popular role in the TV drama (*Coronation Street)* and persuaded me to set up a company to produce it ourselves. That was how Kali was born. It was the same impulse which had driven companies like Monstrous Regiment, Women's Theatre (a.k.a. Sphinx) Shared Experience and Red Ladder in the preceding years to coalesce. Rita and I founded Kali because we noticed and felt the absence of Asian women in theatre. We desperately needed to see the complexities and trials of our lives, our stories, reflected on our stages. That we had an audience ready, and waiting, was proved by the fan mail, which included a small personal donation of £200 made by a stranger. Moved by the play, she decided we deserved and needed the support.

It took readings and workshops to get the play ready. It earned a nomination for the Susan Smith-Blackburn International Prize and the later version for Radio 4 was shortlisted for a CRE award.

Thanks to The Women's Press and Virago, some of my work was drawing interest in the 90s. An agent at Curtis Brown wrote to me to offer representation and Helena Bell, traced me through Virago to commission an adaptation of a short story of mine for her Brighton-based company: Alarmist Theatre. That short play, *The Gatekeeper's Wife,* which incorporated dance and had a male actor/dancer play a cheetah, taught me more about theatricality than anyone else had done. Helena's talent as a director, her willingness to experiment with form and her commitment to the visual were just what I needed to evolve into a more visual playwright, willing to break out of the realism that I had initially clung to and my fixation on text.

Years later, for *Black Shalwar*, I remember Helena created a little ritual around the preparing and eating *paan* (betel leaf) to physicalise the protagonist, Sultana's encounters with her clients. Kali audiences loved that conceit and I learnt from it. Our collaborations led to a solid friendship based on trust and mutual respect which has been my rock over the years. We have relished working with each other

Ravi Aujla, Parminder K Nagra, Shelley King, Parminder Sekhon in *River on Fire*. Photo: Sheila Burnett in various situations: there were times when she commissioned me as a writer, and times when I invited her to direct work for Kali.

When Rita migrated to the US, I had to take over as Artistic Director and I constantly tapped Helena's experience of running a theatre company. This was particularly crucial when it came to producing my own play, *River on Fire*, originally commissioned by Bill Alexander for the mainstage at Birmingham Rep Theatre with a large cast. Kali's board agreed to produce it and we managed to source funding and reduce the cast by workshopping the script. It was an exciting sell-out production that earned me a shortlisting for the Susan Smith-Blackburn International Prize, restoring confidence and self-esteem and helping us to achieve revenue funding for Kali.

One of the most gratifying projects was working with Southall Black Sisters' Survivors' Group, probably initiated by Rahila Gupta. *Meri Kahani,* literally *My Story*, was neither group therapy, nor creative writing but simply participatory theatre designed to empower the survivors. The idea was that women should recount their stories in their own voices, discover and relish their own creativity. Inevitably, there was pain and tears, but there was also laughter, shared camaraderie, and a sense of recovery when the performances based on their stories and improvisations were finally staged at Watermans…

By popular demand, we returned to work again with SBS in 2,000 and delivered *Meri Kahani 2,* on a larger scale with a team of actors and directors who paired up with the survivors to help them shape their stories. SBS supplied the space, a co-ordinator, and a therapist this time to help dry their tears. With both projects, our emphasis was on process, rather than the product.

It was Kali's hunger for scripts and my clear recognition that theatre writing was almost impossible without professional support and training that made us turn the company into a nurturing and caring training ground for Asian women writers. In 2003, I had to step down as AD since I couldn't fit in a full-time job and my own writing assignments, alongside my family commitments. It was a very busy time for me, working with Radio 4 and World Service Drama, with occasional forays into screenplays. We were delighted to find and appoint Janet Steel, a commendable director, who steered the company very ably for fourteen years to ever greater success.

The all-female board have informed the policy and held on to the vision and the feminist mission of the company. Over the last 30 years, Kali has produced well over 50 shows (plays and rehearsed readings) representing women who'd never attempted a play before. To mark our 30th, our current Artistic Director, Helena Bell, decided to publish 30 monologues from these productions in a volume entitled: *Thirty*, published by Methuen (2021).

Not every playwright who has ever written for Kali is a card-carrying feminist, but a vast majority of them are. No one has ever tried to change its orientation as a progressive feminist company dedicated to serving Asian women who wish to write for the theatre. Helena has expanded and refined its focus by identifying and developing more female directors and dramaturg associates. A quick reading of some of the plays included in *Thirty* gives one an idea of the rich and diverse talents unearthed by the company.

Predictably, most of our plays feature female protagonists, though, of course, as a company, Kali isn't hostile to men. In my most recent play, *Homing Birds* (published by Aurora Metro), the main protagonist is a troubled asylum seeker. My lovely dramaturg Suzanne Bell helped pull the two females into the forefront; especially the Afghan politician, delivered beautifully by Suzanne Ahmet.

Personally, I have worked happily with male radio producers (directors) although the most supportive at BBC Drama was a female feminist: Anne Edyvean. In theatre, I hugely enjoyed working with Chris Banfield on: *Mistaken: Annie Besant in India* (published by Aurora Metro), which toured the regions and was loved in India too. Admittedly, our producer was a strong feminist, Vayu Naidu.

By the turn of the century, the tide was turning against feminism. As reactionaries in the US determined not to let women rise, they began to push back by attacking political correctness. I remember watching David Mamet's *Oleanna* with increasing frustration and horror. People spoke of post-feminism, as if women had already achieved equality! Trump's election and anti-abortion success followed. Who knows what the impact of populism will be in the long term? But we do know that great theatre offers the kind of communal experiences that can transform attitudes and become a catalyst for change. And I am certain that without feminism, women's causes would not have progressed. I wonder if the "Me Too" movement could have happened before Eve Ensler's *Vagina Monologues* enabled some conversations?

I remain positive about the future of Kali though. I feel we have seeded some very able and talented women who are addressing topical issues fearlessly and progressing into the mainstream. They will write the kind of break-out plays that will continue to portray the transformations of not just their fictional characters but will have an impact on the real world too...

≈

**Rukhsana Ahmad** has written and adapted several plays for the stage and the BBC, achieving distinction in both. *River on Fire* was a finalist for the Susan Smith-Blackburn International Prize, *Wide Sargasso Sea* for the Writers' Guild Award for Best Radio adaptation. Her plays include *Song for a Sanctuary* (shortlisted CRE award) (Aurora Metro), *Mistaken: Annie Besant in India* (Aurora Metro), *Homing Birds* (Aurora Metro) and *Queen of Hearts*.

Fiction: *The Hope Chest* and *The Gatekeeper's Wife and other stories*.

Translations: *We Sinful Women; Contemporary Urdu Feminist Poetry* (The Women's Press, 1991). And Altaf Fatima's novel *The One Who Did Not Ask,* (Heinemann UK, 1995, Lightstone 2023.)

Screenplays: *Amal's Story* and *Maps for Lost Lovers* (based on Nadeem Aslam's novel)

Podcasts: *Trial by Fire* and *Last Thursday*.

Rukhsana co-founded Kali Theatre Company with Rita Wolf and is currently a trustee. She's the founding chair of SADAA, a former Fellow of the Royal Literary Fund, and a patron of the Ruth Hayman Trust.

www.rukhsanaahmad.com

*Pleasant Land* devised by the company with words by Nathan Powell.
*L to R*: Martha Godber, Taja Christian, Linh Huynh
Photo: Chris Webb

# DERBY THEATRE
## SARAH BRIGHAM

Feminism, and specifically feminism in relation to theatre, is more than just representation and access. It is most importantly about agency. Giving women, all women, not only equal access but also the power and the agency to effect change.

When I first took over the Artistic Directorship of a regional theatre I realised very soon that I had a careful balance to strike. The theatre was struggling financially and feedback from audiences told me they wanted me to programme plays they knew and loved – the problem was many of the titles suggested were written by white, male writers. How could we encourage an appetite for new writing and set alight a new commissioning process for female writers, always thinking intersectionally?

We began with our *RETOLD* series. Every time we programmed a "classic" we also commissioned a female writer to re-tell the story from a female perspective. So Caroline Horton took on the story of veteran's wife Penelope alongside our version of *The Odyssey*; Jane Wainwright looked at what it was to be working class and female in *Jinny* which played alongside *Look Back in Anger*; and Athia Sen Gupta reimagined middle class suburbia for one mixed race girl who was the granddaughter of Abigail in *Abigail's Party*.

Alongside this, we have supported and nurtured a whole host of female artists. As I write this, both Abi Zakarian and Nicola Werenowska will bring new plays to our mainstage next year. And we have commissioned and supported companies such as Milk Presents who take a radical look at gender from a queer perspective.

As a female chief executive of a building, I take the responsibility of opening doors to my female colleagues very seriously. For seven of my ten years at Derby Theatre, we had an all-female leadership team, and for a long time, there were more females employed full-time on our technical team than there were in our education team. This, of course, fluctuates and we have in no way introduced quotas or expectations in this area but through a working environment which respects things like caring responsibilities, which offers strong female role models and asks 'what can we do to help?', these things enable women the chance to succeed and thrive.

Sadly, this isn't the case everywhere. I have personally come up against a lot of sexism in my career, often interlaced with some prejudice against my broad and dulcet northern tones, and the disability I live with. Whether it's being told I am too overwrought (a passionate speech was too much for this particular individual), or that I'm not quite ready yet, (I had double the experience of the man who got the job), or just having my ideas spoken back to me, as if they were new. Every woman you speak to has had experiences like this, but I'm also lucky to have had some wonderful female role models to follow in the footsteps of. It is these women I go to first, when looking for advice and guidance, and it is often their example that gives me hope in the future of our industry.

In terms of my own female identity and the impact it has on my creativity, it does, of course, intersect with my class, my disabilities, my upbringing and so much more. My work changes and develops every day as I gain more experiences, become more aware of things I want to talk

*Jekyll and Hyde* adapted by Neil Bartlett from R.L. Stevenson. *L to R:* Polly Lister, Tife Kusoro, Hilary Greatorex. Photo: Grant Archer

about, and as the world around me changes and I have new things to say about that.

Defining how my feminism influences my work is difficult, but it's a rage at the injustice of the patriarchy which often drives me. Last year, for example, I worked with Neil Bartlett to reinvent the classic *Jekyll and Hyde,* using it as a vehicle to explore the roots of #MeToo. I have also mentored and supported a great number of female and non-binary artists and at the moment, I am taking time out to mentor a young female working class artist who can't seem to get a leg up in the industry. I hate injustice and as a feminist I see it everywhere, so I allow that desire to fight it, power a lot of my choices and my work.

The industry has a long way to go and I include myself in that – I don't always get it right. You just have to cast your eye over most theatre season announcements to see that equality and equity have not been achieved. We need to be ever wary of declaring "Job Done" until the workforce, artist commissions and positions of power are balanced and held equally by women – all women – working class women, Black women, women from the global majority, disabled women, trans women, queer women, – brilliant, skilled and audacious women. Until then, the industry hasn't achieved what it vitally needs to, and that won't happen until we have a fairer and more equal society … so there's a lot to do. We'd better get busy.

≈

Photo: Graeme Braidwood

**Sarah Brigham** is originally from Hull. She trained at Bretton Hall and first worked as an actor before starting her directing career. She joined Derby Theatre in 2013 as Artistic Director and is now also Chief Executive. Highlights of her career at Derby Theatre include commissioning the series of *RETOLD* plays, a new series of plays by female-identifying writers, launching In Good Company, the flagship talent development programme for the Midlands and developing Derby CAN, a programme which gives agency to under-served communities and unheard voices.

Directing credits include *Jekyll and Hyde, Robin Hood, What Fatima Did, Abi, Pleasant Land, Look Back in Anger, Jinny, Great Expectations, The Odyssey* and many more. Sarah has pioneered new work for families at Derby Theatre which integrates British Sign Language and audio description. She recognises and thanks all of the companies, and in particular, women who have supported her and whose shoulders she has the privilege to stand on.

Mercedes Ruehl and Eric Walton in *The Dinner,* Sag Harbor, New York.

# INTERVIEW WITH MOIRA BUFFINI

**What does feminism mean to you?**

After my dad died when I was four, I grew up in a female household. My mother did everything for my sisters and me. She was not only the breadwinner, she made our clothes, furnishings, tiled the floors, used power tools and taught us that you must never rely on a man, as 'anything might happen to him'. So I grew up with the knowledge that women were supremely capable. It was a privilege to have such an example. I went to an all-girls school too – another privilege – so there wasn't really any testosterone in my life until I was sixteen. It's hard to separate my feminism out from the rest of me. It's quite simply who I am. On those rare occasions when someone has asked me 'are you a feminist?' I feel like I'm being asked something that's obvious to the eye, like 'have you got teeth?'.

**How has feminism influenced your work?**

Again, it is who I am. I never made a conscious decision to write feminist plays. But feminism is such an energising and positive force, shining a light on injustice, seeking greater balance. I know there are divisions within feminism but it is broad enough to allow us discourse. The stories that interest me all have women at their heart. Women always lead the action in my work.

I never read feminist theorists much until quite recently. I consumed my feminist ideas from theatre and novels. I was lucky to have the example of Caryl Churchill and Timberlake Wertenbaker as playwrights when I was young, then later discovering a whole world of other female dramatists from Ana Caro and Aphra Behn onwards who were never performed. It made me think hard about who gets to be in the literary canon – and how charged that canon is.

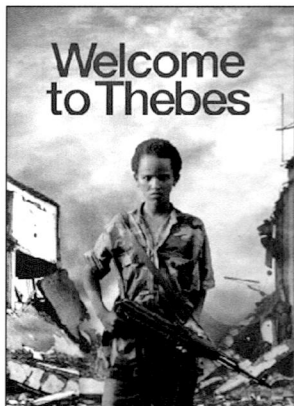

## Has the content of your work changed over time?

Yes, and the form I have written in. Change is the breath of life. I've also moved from theatre to film to TV and back. Most recently I've written a novel. I'm restless. I never want to do the same thing twice.

## Do you feel that women have achieved equality in theatre?

The answer to that can never be yes, not in this world. No, women have not achieved equality in theatre. Even in this relatively progressive part of the world, women, especially women of colour and working class women, struggle to be taken seriously and to find sustainable career paths. Older women drop out far sooner and more frequently than their male counterparts. Pay is not equal and the critical gaze of our national press is still biased towards white men. However, I would say that big improvements have been made in the decades since I began, when I could count the other female playwrights being occasionally produced on my fingers. More recently, #MeToo, #Time'sUp and #BlackLivesMatter have all led to seismic change across the creative arts but things, as we know, can only too easily slide backwards.

## Have you experienced sex bias while working in theatre?

Frequently, and visibly, when I was younger. I started out as an actor and harassment was so common I couldn't even name it. We have got better at calling out bias and putting systems in place to reduce it, but it hasn't miraculously vanished. Bias is still there and incredibly hard to confront. All too often, it works with an invisible hand.

## What would improve the opportunities for women working in theatre today?

Theatre is public and can be brutal. It's also financially precarious. Its creative workforce is made up of freelancers working short contracts. The weakness in that system was shown up by the Covid pandemic when our fragile infrastructure crashed. I can't speak for theatre buildings but I would like to make some suggestions of how female playwrights might better be supported. Playwrights are theatre's engine. We create work for all our colleagues – yet we generally work in isolation and come into buildings only when our work is in rehearsal. We need to be a strong part of these buildings and their literary departments, otherwise new work can't flourish. Playwrights, in all their diversity, should serve on theatre boards and be on the payroll in new work departments. A greater inclusivity of playwrights could be funded by the TV industry. UK theatre is a unique training ground for film and TV writers and they poach playwrights constantly. They should pay into it.

I have had to negotiate pregnancy, early motherhood and menopause in rehearsal rooms and on film sets. As a freelancer, I got no maternity benefits. When my children were born, there was a four-year gap in my CV. I couldn't afford to write a play until they started school. The commission didn't begin to cover childcare costs. Greater dialogue about these things and in-built financial support would see fewer female playwrights dropping out because of the impossible juggling act that life has given them in a low-paid sector like theatre. I'm not surprised to discover that another swathe of highly talented and able women drop out because of menopause. Ageism is another invisible

*Dying for It* directed by Rob Watt at the Almeida Theatre

hand that disproportionally thwarts women's careers.

**Does intersectionalism influence your work?**

Yes, I find myself increasingly attuned to it. Equality can only mean diversity. Writers are job-providers and it's both a duty and a gift to write diverse casts.

**Do you collaborate with other groups?**

A playwright cannot make work without being a collaborator. It's the primary joy of working in the theatre for me. Each new collaboration is like food for the soul and brain.

**Do we still need feminism?**

Fuck, yes. Do we still need teeth?

≈

**Moira Buffini** is an English playwright and writer. Born in Cheshire, Buffini was educated at St. Mary's College in Wales and Goldsmiths, University of London where she studied English and Drama. She trained as an actor at the Royal Welsh College of Music & Drama. Her plays include *Handbagged* (Olivier Award) at the Tricycle and in the West End; *Manor, wonder.land, Welcome to Thebes* and *Dinner* (Olivier Award nomination) at the National Theatre; *Dying for It* and *Marianne's Dreams* at the Almeida; *A Vampire Story* for National Theatre Connections; *Loveplay* for the RSC; *Silence* (Susan Smith Blackburn Prize) at Birmingham Rep; *Gabriel* (LWT Plays on Stage and Meyer Whitworth awards) at Soho Theatre; and *Blavatsky's Tower* at the Machine Room. Buffini is co-creator and lead writer of TV series *Harlots* and her films include *Jane Eyre, Tamara Drewe, Byzantium* and *The Dig.*

Her first novel, *Songlight,* will be published in 2024.

# INTERSECTIONAL FEMINISM AT WORK: EQUITY WOMEN'S COMMITTEE

## KELLY BURKE

**What kind of work do you do?**

I'm an actor, writer, and theatre maker, whose practice centres on women's voices and their capacity for destabilising existing power systems. I also sometimes wear an academic/activist hat. My MA was in gender theory and the arts, and I specialise in equalities access and advocacy within the industry, where I've spent the past ten years as an activist for the performing arts union, Equity. I've chaired Equity's Women's Committee for the last six of those.

**What does feminism mean to you?**

I believe feminism is inherently intersectional and goes beyond the sex distinction between women and men. Feminism doesn't operate in opposition to 'men' per se, but to a *system of power* in which women are structurally disadvantaged in their access to (and quality of) work, pay, and career longevity.

bell hooks calls this system of power the 'imperialist, white-supremacist, capitalist patriarchy', identifying how deeply our Western systems of oppression are intertwined. This means gender equality can't be achieved simply by putting women into positions of power within our existing structures and institutions as long as those institutions remain racist, ableist, classist, transphobic, etc. – because we know that other kinds of discrimination will impact women at those intersections first and hardest. Gender equality is inextricable from other forms of equality: it's all or nothing.

To see the impact of this in the arts, we have only to look at the Covid lockdowns and how support for the self-employed was distributed based on *profit*. Inevitably, this gave more support to white men, whose earnings have always been higher, and penalised anyone who had spent time away from work (eg. those on maternity leave), had less work (eg. older women), or had badly paid work (eg. disabled women, who are too often pushed into fringe and low-pay spaces in order to work at all). In 2021, the TUC published the terrifying statistic that 44% of the industry's women of colour (whose profits are less than men *and* white women's) were forced out of the industry by the pandemic. If this doesn't speak to how little we resource certain artists, how little we value certain bodies, and how intersectional our advocacy must be, what does?

**What is the Equity Women's Committee, and what are the key issues in trying to bring about better working conditions for women in the arts?**

The Women's Committee's remit is to advise the union on the core issues facing women in the performing arts, to identify how gender discrimination operates in the industry, and to advocate for those things that would make meaningful change.

In my time on the Committee, our primary areas of focus have been:

**1. Sexual Harassment**

Combatting sexual harassment involves meaningful accountability procedures, and requires challenging existing power dynamics on sets and in rehearsal rooms. It also takes men being proactive about putting a stop to bad behaviour.

Kelly Burke at the TUC Women's Conference 2023

#MeToo peaked in 2017, but I don't think anyone was surprised when, after an initial flurry of guideline writing, the industry quietly slipped back to business as usual. The pandemic intensified the divide between the resources allocated to men and those allocated to women. London theatre panicked and reverted to a largely white, male canon with small companies led by TV stars. This has meant fewer women working — though statistics tell us that the more women are in a workplace, the safer women are in that workplace. And basic workplace safety is essential for equality.

## 2. Intimacy Coordination and Consent

Consent is a also core part of workplace safety. In the past years, the Committee (with particular thanks to activist Jennifer Greenwood) has been pushing for intimacy professionals to be engaged when staging sensitive and sexual material.

Almost no one in the industry would expect actors to choreograph their own fight scenes: there is a consensus that that work should be done by professionals who know how to create the illusion of realism while keeping actors safe. It is not really surprising that fight scenes (which largely impact men) are resourced with external professionals, while sex scenes (which largely impact women) are often left to actors to block with no safeguarding, consistency, or choreographic language in place. To achieve gender equality in our workplaces, we must reframe intimacy in performance as something which requires consent, consistency, and attention to both physical and mental safety.

## 3. Employable Bodies

Even in 2024, we are haunted by the imperative that our female leads be slim, young, and beautiful. Preferably white, cis, and straight-looking. Certainly able-bodied. This criteria by which our industry assesses bodies as employable is both outdated and actively damaging.

In 2019 the Committee did an extended piece of work with Dr Sara Reimers of Royal Holloway University on aesthetic labour: how the time and expense of making oneself 'presentable' for work is unevenly distributed, inevitably impacting most heavily on women and women of colour, and requiring a great deal of vigilance around the physical body. Body size, and its intersections with everything from race to class, is an area of our industry in which discrimination is actively permitted under the guise of 'artistic freedom'. We need to rethink how we understand employable bodies if we are to responsibly represent the real world on our stages and screens.

## 4. Maternity and Childcare

There can be no workplace equality until there is meaningful provision for child (and other kinds of) care. The majority of this unpaid labour falls on women, and not only weakens CVs and interrupts the career progression enjoyed by male colleagues but, because maternity and care inevitably impact lifetime earnings, compromises women's pensions and ability to age with dignity and security.

## 5. Age

The problem of low earnings and lower pensions is compounded by the fact that women 'age out' of the industry much earlier than men, whose careers hit their prime at a time when women's see a dramatic ebb. This has not substantially improved in the wake of #MeToo or the pandemic.

Added to this, people going through the menopause are dramatically under-supported in the workplace. Basic provisions like access to water, regular breaks, ventilation, breakout spaces, and advance and/ or flexible scheduling not only support those experiencing menopause but also make workplaces healthier overall.

## 6. Resourcing

Ultimately, women have less work, less well-paid work, and less time than our male colleagues. Our working lives can be so precarious that we often lack the time and resources to *find* the resources that would make them easier. This spans everything from not having the energy to find out how to report

Kelly Burke in *Zelda*, 2018

sexual harassment, to not understanding the nudity clause in one's contract, to being unable to access mental health support.

Most recently myself, activist Abigail Matthews, and the Committee have been working on a resource called the Equity4Women Toolkit, which aims to put as much of this key information into people's hands as possible within a few clicks. It's true that knowledge is power: the more we're aware of our rights, the better we can support and advocate for ourselves.

## 7. Gender Discrimination

In the past few years our language around gender has shifted enormously. We have come to realise that 'gender discrimination' extends beyond cis women and encompasses all the ways in which our society gives power to cis male bodies at the expense of any others. It is vital to have a coalition of these voices in order to practice thorough gender equality work.

For example: the Women's Committee is the part of the union structure that advises on industrial issues around the menopause, hormonal health, and childcare. These are issues that not only impact cis women, but many trans men and non-binary folks as well — and we would be failing in our advocacy not to take these marginalised members' experiences into consideration. The Committee believes that our remit to combat gender discrimination means we need the voices of our trans, non-binary, and genderqueer colleagues in the room as part of our feminist coalition. At the time of writing we are still struggling for support and understanding from Equity on this essential point… and so the work continues.

As a final note: it is so often the case that, when it comes to equalities work, we inevitably ask those among us who are the most disadvantaged by the system to do the heaviest lifting in order to change that system. This is as true within union and arts structures as anywhere else, and I salute — with great love and admiration — those women on the Committee who, over the decade I have been there, have been unanimously fierce, generous, and committed. I owe particular thanks to vice chairs Elaine Stirrat, Abiola Ogunbiyi, and Amelia Donkor — and to our long-standing Committee mothers, Jean Rogers and Sue McGoun.

## What would improve things for women working today?

Ultimately, achieving gender equality in the arts requires attacking the problem from two directions: we need change at the top and change at the bottom. Change from the top is slow and often reluctant. The money and power in the UK theatre still disproportionally rest in the hands of men (at the time of writing, the National Theatre has just appointed its first female artistic director in 60 years). We need our artistic directors and producers and programmers to put attention and, crucially, resource towards equality work. Those with privilege and resource must be proactive in doing the work of inclusion, rather than leaving it to our marginalised workers to fix the problem of their own marginalisation.

Change from the bottom involves making workers, particularly women and intersectional artists, aware of their rights, empowering them to advocate for themselves. It can be difficult — even dangerous — to speak out or to push against the system. We all have a different capacity for resistance at different times, and resistance will look different for different individuals. We must each do what we can when we can. We must share the labour of being the one to speak out, to do the research, to hold the necessary space. And sometimes… sometimes survival inside an antagonistic system is resistance enough.

Our funding bodies and institutions remain so invested in the status quo that at times it can be difficult to imagine any way else — or any way out. But theatre makers are world-builders. Theatre helps us imagine what *can* be possible. Bringing our intersectionality, our feminism, and our stories into theatre spaces transforms those spaces and helps us shape a different future, one audience at a time.

≈

**Kelly Burke** (MA Gender, Media and Culture, Goldsmiths; BA Acting, RADA) is an actor, writer and theatre maker. Originally from the US, Kelly has spent the past 17 years in London making work which focuses on the obstruction — and expansion — of women's voices. Much of Kelly's work uses the 1920s-30s as a lens for analysing contemporary crises; productions include *Love for Sale, Natalie Barney's Last Salon, a whale is its own house*, and the award-nominated play *Zelda.* Kelly's MA work focused on the role of the physical voice in intersectional feminism, and the voice's capacity for troubling existing power structures. Between 2016-2023, she chaired Equity's Women's Committee, where she consolidated the union's response to #MeToo with that of other industry bodies and headed up work on rights awareness, resourcing marginalised workers, and embedding meaningful equalities practices into both the union and the wider industry.

# THE PERSONAL WAS VERY POLITICAL
## CLAIR CHAPWELL

My millennial son and his friends grumble often about baby boomers and our advantages in the property market. "The best thing for me as a boomer was never about the property," I always say. "The best thing about being our age was that in the 1970s and 80s, everything was changing, everything was being questioned. And we were making plays and music about it."

Small theatre groups were putting the issues on the stage and setting them to music. The personal was very, very political. I came to London as an American student in 1973 and walked into a three-month theatre festival at the Almost Free Theatre in Soho. Soho, at that time was a run-down, abandoned area of town, unrecognisable from the pricey place it has become. Gay Sweatshop and the Black Theatre Co-op were born at that festival and so was the Women's Theatre Group.

"Come along on Sundays," was the open invite after those shows to the women in the audience. "We want to launch as a permanent company. Bring your ideas." And so we did. Our show about girls and contraception toured schools. After one show, someone from the Arts Council approached a member of the cast. "Why don't you apply to us for funding?" he asked. Simple as that. We did – we got it – and suddenly we were paid, although, it was much more possible to be part of a profit-share group back in the day. I was living cheaply: squatting, riding a bicycle and shopping in charity shops. Labels were not yet a thing.

After touring schools and community centres with shows about women's issues (equal pay, working conditions, sex discrimination), I left the Women's Theatre Group, and in 1978, read the book that changed my life. In Susie Orbach's *Fat is a Feminist Issue* phrases jumped out at my hungry eyes: *diets don't work… 95% of all women gain the weight back.* And finally, and most radically, *stop weighing yourself.*

I knew that if this book was important to me, it was important to most of the women in the country. I wrote to Susie and asked permission to use ideas from her book which she graciously gave. *Time Out's* theatreboard was full of ads to start groups and invitations to free workshops. My ad said: WOMEN INTERESTED IN PUTTING TOGETHER A PLAY BASED ON 'FAT IS A FEMINIST ISSUE' WRITE TO CLAIR.

Daily, I was deluged with replies, everything from a simple line: "I am interested in your idea" to pages upon confessional pages of desperation about out of control eating. Next, we held auditions, and a group of eight women emerged. We spent the summer telling stories and improvising and I wrote a funny musical show called *Baring the Weight.* Our performances were followed by enthusiastic, impassioned discussions. Confessions, applause, tears. We offered compulsive eating groups based on the model in Susie's book. We toured everywhere. We leafletted Weight Watcher's meetings. Theatres, student bars, community centres in London, Leeds, Liverpool, Glasgow, Belfast, Boston and Amsterdam.

Spare Tyre settled to a group of three. Katina Noble, Harriet Powell and I moved on from body image to a range of subjects: mothers, men, money, whether or not to have children, sexuality, ageing (in our thirties!). In 1987, Virago published *The Spare Tyre Songbook* with some of the songs from our shows such as:

'Eat it – if you want to'

'Yippee – Pregnancy!'

'A Million Billion Lemmings Can't be Wrong'

There was financial encouragement for the work from trusts, and Ken Livingstone's Greater London Council, which funded radical arts work all over London. Our kind of work was flourishing. In the mid 80s we began to be invited to run 12-week drama and music projects for young unemployed people. Participants would learn acting, singing and drama skills, and make a musical play with us. The performers would then tour schools with their shows. A local "proper theatre" would offer an evening where they could perform it: Riverside Studios, The Cockpit, Theatre Royal Stratford East. We ran 12-week sessions along the same lines for older people: either active elderly or those in care homes, women fleeing domestic violence, a schools project on the developing world for Oxfam, The Pink Project for LGBT young people.

Throughout the 1980s the UK was awash with feminist theatre. Pick your issue. Theatre companies sprang up with names like Sensible Footwear, Cunning Stunts, Scarlet Harlots, Monstrous Regiment, Beryl and the Perils, Theatre of Black Women, Clean Break, Sadista Sisters, Charabanc, The Chuffinelles and Lip Service.

I thought I'd remembered most and did a quick check with the invaluable website 'Unfinished Histories' compiled by Susan Croft – there are 87 women's theatre groups that make the list of women's theatre. All with inventive, sometimes angry names. Some have survived for a half century, notably Clean Break, whose work is extraordinary. It has evolved and evolved beyond its original beginning of two women ex-prisoners into a multifaceted, building-based organisation.

But by the end of the 80s, that decade and a half of rage, those wild theatrical groups, had begun to disappear. Many things were happening. Audiences were looking for new forms of theatre and stand-up was arriving, amplified and outrageous and often apolitical. Funders were becoming more demanding. Bigger theatres were beginning to absorb some of the ideas, and larger audiences were now seeing some of the politics in a more conventional (and comfortable) context. Small groups often only last so long – exhaustion sets in. And finally, that curious notion: post-feminism had arrived. Women were now equal, (really?) free to make their own choices and they didn't want to see any more plays about it.

I left Spare Tyre after 27 years, and many changes of direction over the years. Ultimately, I was given the opportunity to have a very satisfying closure. For Spare Tyre's 40th anniversary, I was asked to redirect that original show *Baring the Weight* from 1979. I was delighted though on rereading, it was hugely dated. Never mind!

I decided to keep the show set in 1979 and then create a second half, set in 2019, in partnership with a young woman and a mixed cast of women with a wide age span (24-75)

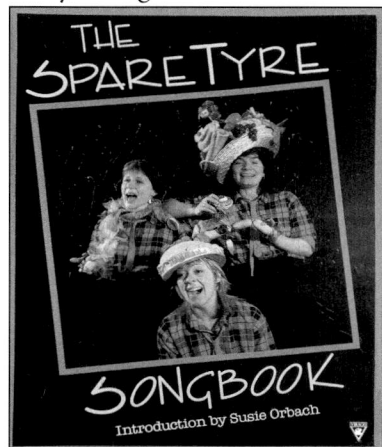

*L to R:* Katina Noble, Clair Chapwell & Harriet Powell

Jacqui Lofthouse in *Baring the Weight,* New Diorama Theatre, 2019

Clair Chapwell in *Baring the Weight,* Croydon Warehouse, 1979

who could brief one another on what life and body image was like for them. In one rehearsal, three of the women in their twenties explained why their friends were considering labiaplasty. The looks of shock on the faces of the older women, as they absorbed the knowledge, was powerful. It was a sudden realisation of the pressures on the younger women. I'll never forget that day.

Before I had started working on the new play, I had asked Susie Orbach for a steer, as she had given me so much support the first time round. She waited a long time before she answered, and then she just looked very, very sad. "Everything for women is so much worse now," she told me. "Everyone is making money out of making women feel bad about themselves."

I reflected back to my younger self – the young, twenty something who had decided that Spare Tyre was going to take down Weight Watchers single-handedly. But we did feel we could change things. A friend in community arts in the 70s was explaining to my son what his organisation had done in the 70s: "We worked locally, to use the arts to make people's lives better, to change things for people." My son looked bemused: "I don't know anyone who thinks they can change anything."

The joy of that era was feeling that you *could* change things. And so many of us from that era carry on doing work that continues to change things and people.

≈

**Clair Chapwell**
Since Spare Tyre, Clair has worked on a variety of projects commissioned by NHS Islington and Age UK writing film and theatre scripts about a range of issues affecting elders and was awarded a Churchill Fellowship in 2013 to explore theatre outside the UK for LGBT elders.
She created the Bolder Voices choir for many years which sang original songs of age and rage.
Clair facilitates an online writing group with Jacksons Lane Arts Centre called "Lockdown Lunch".

Rosie Wakley *(left)* and Alison Child *(right)* in *All The Nice Girls*, 2014

# BEHIND THE LINES

## Lesbian Love in the Limelight

# ALISON CHILD

In 2014, I set up Behind The Lines Theatre Company with Rosie Wakley to tell the stories of women who had been left out of the history books. That gave us plenty of scope. We focused on queer women, who had worked in the first quarter of the 20th century, in particular the hugely successful 'male impersonators', Ella Shields, Hetty King and Vesta Tilley as well as the women who comprised the popular British variety double act, Blaney and Farrar.

Our productions were small-scale, hour-long pieces designed for fringe venues and festivals. We performed at L Fest, the LGBTQ History Festival, the Birmingham 'Shout! Festival, and the International Women's Festival in Eressos, Lesvos. We took shows to the Brighton Fringe and the Edinburgh Fringe and we performed at PRONI in Belfast and the Chapter Arts Centre, Cardiff, and toured Shrewsbury, Gloucester, Salisbury, Bournemouth, Blackpool and Aberystwyth among many other UK towns and cities. Our research took us to Paris, Johannesburg and New York.

Being relegated to backroom spaces by men with bigger egos and more grandiose productions at some mixed-gender queer festivals did not surprise us. We knew about the role of the patriarchy in the theatre. Rosie had done her theatre apprenticeships backstage in the 1980s as a carpenter, stage manager and production manager at (respectively) the Royal Opera House, the National Theatre and English National Opera. My background performing in student theatre with the Cambridge Footlights and at the ADC, the Marlowe and on the European Theatre Group Tour had surrounded me by dauntingly self-confident young men taking their future success for granted.

Rosie and I were both in our fifties by the time we were in a position to do that vital thing of generating our own work. In my case, family responsibilities had cut me off completely, or so it felt, from professional theatre opportunities. I became an educator for 30 years.

Though not recognised by applause and awards, the creative work that goes into being a parent, a partner, and a teacher, can't be ignored and has to be celebrated. It's an inventive, fraught juggling act, that's sometimes collaborative, sometimes very much a solo show.

Coming out as gay in 2013, I met my tribe – queer women whose independence from men suddenly made feminism a liveable reality. It gave me a context and a future. Setting up Behind the Lines grew organically from the energy and excitement of this time. Rosie taught me never to regret what might have been, and to know that nothing you do is ever wasted.

Our work has been generated by us. Our mission became 'to make queer work for non queer-identifying audiences.' We sought to be visible lesbians presenting relatable stories (such as the romance between Gwen Farrar and Norah Blaney) for audiences who perhaps would never consciously choose to see an LGBTQ-themed show. We achieved this with some sleight-of-hand at the Edinburgh Fringe. When out with our publicity flyers, we'd encourage the most conventional-seeming older people we could find, to come in for a sing-along of favourite songs from the music hall. We were close enough to see the colour drain from individual faces in the opening minutes of the show ("All The Nice Girls Love a Sailor" as they had never heard it before.). By the end of the piece, as we brought

Alison Child in *Deep in The Heart of Me,* 2016

our characters forward to 2014, to take advantage of the new legalisation of same sex marriage in the UK, our audience was enthusiastically swept up in the story and applauding the outcome.

Enlightened residential care homes booked us to perform, knowing that our show could provide a point of recognition for residents whose sexuality and life experience might have been marginalised or made invisible by the conventional assumptions of caregivers and fellow residents. At one performance, in the packed communal sitting room of a care home in Kent, the audience were rapt, but, when we got to our romantic final scene, an elderly woman who had been positioned close to the action had only just woken up. Rosie's character proposed marriage to mine and the woman pricked up her ears. "Do they know they're both girls?" she called out in alarm throughout the play's closing moments. On that occasion we'd certainly achieved our goal of reaching a non queer-identifying audience.

We toured extensively between 2015 and 2019, supported by the Arts Council and the National Lottery Heritage Fund. Our work to re-imagine the Blaney/Farrar double-act culminated in the publication, by Tollington Press, of my biography of the pair. The book was very sympathetically edited by the founder of Tollington Press, Helen Sandler, whose commitment to queer stories is reflected in the work she does with Jane Hoy to bring forgotten women to life theatrically with Queer Tales from Wales and Aberration Cabaret.

The book brought opportunities to perform at the V&A Museum, the London Metropolitan Archive, and for Polari Literary Salon at the Southbank Centre. *Tell Me I'm Forgiven: The Story of Forgotten Stars Gwen Farrar and Norah Blaney* was shortlisted for the Polari First Book Award.

Researching Gwen and Norah gave me an insight into the changing opportunities for women in British theatre in the 20th century. In their heyday in the 1920s and 30s, Gwen and Norah wrote, composed, acted, sung, produced and directed in London and New York, managing their own careers, on their own terms. World War II saw the demise of their unique partnership. Gwen died. Norah married a man and outlived Gwen by 40 years.

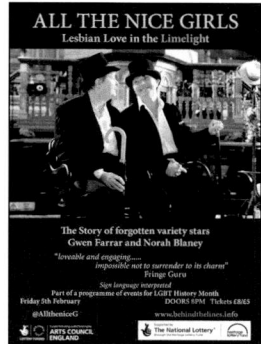

Through feisty reinvention of herself, in the 1960s, after decades of obscurity, and newly widowed, Norah found roles with the Royal Shakespeare Company and in the West End, in the premiere of Noël Coward's *Waiting in the Wings* and in David Storey's *Home*. It wasn't just being older that made reviving her career a supreme effort for Norah. Women performers, many of whom had enjoyed thriving careers in the period between the wars, were side-lined by a new generation of male writers, directors and producers subjecting women to stereotypical casting on TV, radio and film, as well as in the theatre.

Of course there were remarkable outliers in the 1950s and 60s like Joan Littlewood and Anne Jellicoe. In 1968, Joan Plowright, on behalf of the fledgling National Theatre, commissioned a play from each of four women novelists including Maureen Duffy, who was also a member of the Royal Court Writers' Group. But it wasn't really until the early 1970s and the foundation of The Women's Theatre Group, Monstrous Regiment, Gay Sweatshop etc. that things began to change for women in British theatre. Other chapters in this book will detail the history of that remarkable movement. In this essay, I can simply provide a small snapshot of the experience of two late bloomers, belatedly enjoying the chance to express ourselves as writers and performers, relatively recently, at least proving, 'It's never too late.'

Rosie decided on her 50th birthday to invent a drag king alter-ego for herself and so was born Ronnie Rialto, lounge singer extraordinaire. The Sappho International Women's Festival in Skala Eressos, Lesvos provided a spectacular setting for Ronnie to strut his stuff. I first met Rosie/Ronnie there in 2013. Our 2016 show, *Deep in The Heart of Me* was our first semi-autobiographical piece, marking a break from writing about historical women. Partly set on Lesvos, the show found a natural audience among the Festival-goers but, the following year at Edinburgh Fringe, we were able to deploy our old marketing techniques and appeal to a wider demographic. Describing the show as "a 'Shirley Valentine' tale with songs from the rat pack" we were able to attract audience members who little expected to see a conventionally-married woman meet a butch lesbian drag king crooner on a Greek island holiday. Once again, the authenticity and romance of the story won over the initially sceptical crowds.

Our connection with the Sappho International Women's Festival produced at least two more serendipitous outcomes. We were introduced to Maureen Duffy (whose commission by Joan Plowright had led to the performance of her play *Rites* at the Old Vic in 1969). Maureen had been the first out gay woman in British public life in the 1960s and had devoted her life to writing and activism, campaigning for authors' rights and animal rights. She re-discovered the 17th century playwright Aphra Behn with the biography she wrote of her, titled *The Passionate Shepherdess,* in 1977. Much of Maureen's writing has been influenced by figures from classical Greek literature and history including the 6th-century BC lyric poet Sappho, who was born on Lesvos. We adapted and filmed Maureen's 2010 play, *Sappho Singing*, with a screening in 2020 at the Coronet Theatre, Notting Hill. Clare Summerskill interviewed Maureen on this occasion and tickets sold out so fast that a second sitting was added to the evening's schedule by popular demand. We are very proud of our connection to both Maureen and to Clare, each of whose work we admire and whose support we greatly value.

The International Women's Festival also introduced us to Nadine Benjamin who agreed to become Behind The Lines' patron in 2021. Nadine is a leadership coach and professional opera singer. Initially turned down by conservatoires and told to stick to singing jazz, she worked privately with singing teachers and has built a stunning international classical singing career. In 2023, she won the Best Opera Performer Award at the Black British Theatre Awards for her outstanding performance in *Blue* at the English National Opera.

Rosie Wakley in *Deep in The Heart of Me*, 2016

In 2017, we brought a play that had impressed us in Edinburgh to Brighton for a short sell-out run at the Marlborough Theatre. *Scene* by Lola Olufemi and Martha Krish was a remarkably mature play by two students that followed the interracial queer relationship of Ayo and Flo, played by Sam Crerar and Laura Cameron. Krish and Olufemi decided to write *Scene* after noticing that there was a lack of shows that talked about race at their university, and those that did addressed racism from a white person's perspective. Interviewed for an article in *The Independent* newspaper, Krish said: "We were students at Cambridge and we felt like lots of the theatre we saw there didn't reflect back to the audience to make them think about their own lives." Olufemi added, "We had all of these ideas and we were, like, what would it mean to put all of these conversations about race that happened in different arenas into the sphere of a personal relationship, and how does that complicate the questions we wanted to ask?"

Krish summarised the play, "What does it mean to confront race with someone that you love? What is that and how do you get round that – do you get round that?" We were delighted to introduce this play and this production to a wider audience. Supporting younger artists became a conscious strategy when Rosie and I cut down on Fringe performances and touring. Low-budget life on the road became physically challenging for the two of us as we entered our 60s. We want Behind The Lines' work to continue in ways that feel new and relevant.

*L to R:* Rosie Wakley, Alison Child, (producers), Martha Krish, Lola Olufemi (writers), Laura Cameron, Sam Crerar (actors) in *Scene,* 2017

In Lesvos, where we now spend half our time, we organised a reading with emerging playwright Carol Vine. We responded to an invitation from filmmaker Rachel Dax (who we'd also met through the Sappho Women's Festival) to perform at Lezdiff at Chapter Arts Cardiff in 'The Stories of Their Lives' for LGBTQ+ History Month in 2023.

Much has changed since we started in 2014. Women-loving-women are far better represented in films, on TV, and in theatre, so that our initial mission now seems less pressing. Our teenage selves, in the 1970s, for whom lesbianism was completely taboo, would have led different lives if today's role models had been available.

As to the future, at the time of writing, the looming threat of AI, programmed largely by men for dubious commercial purposes, seems to cast a dark shadow over the future of theatre and humanity itself. Population displacement, biodiversity loss, the scarcity of resources – all symptoms of the environmental and climate crises – pose unprecedented challenges.

What is urgently needed is a revolution, inspired by feminist values of inclusion and empathy, and the notion, coined by George Monbiot, of 'private sufficiency and public luxury.' A universal basic income, to compensate for the enormous job losses to come, affordable housing, high quality, free childcare and a generously-funded arts sector. Theatre makers, working creatively with populations newly-released from the drudgery of the working week, could provide new narratives – stories that humanity desperately needs to stay resilient and alive.

≈

**Alison Child** was born in Surrey in 1963. She graduated from Cambridge University with a degree in History and a P.G.C.E. in Education, English and Drama. She taught in Essex, Kent, Buckinghamshire and Sussex. In 2012, she began writing short plays and joined the Royal Court Introduction to Playwriting Course in Autumn 2014. In the same year, she founded Behind The Lines with Rosie Wakley and spent 2015-2019 writing, producing and performing small-scale theatre pieces at festivals and at the Brighton and Edinburgh Fringe. In 2019, Tollington Press published her book *Tell Me I'm Forgiven: The Story of Forgotten Stars Gwen Farrar and Norah Blaney* (shortlisted for the Polari First Book Award and the Society for Theatre Research's Annual Theatre Book Prize).

Nicola Grier in *Playhouse Creatures* produced by Sphinx

# HOW FEMINISM HAS INFLUENCED MY PLAYWRITING
## APRIL DE ANGELIS

Without feminism there would be no women playwrights. Aphra Behn, writing in the 17th century, argued that her plays were judged more harshly than those by her male counterparts because she was a woman. Men could get away with more, she said, especially when they were writing about sex. To say this, she had to have a critical analysis of patriarchy. In other words, without feminism there would be no women writing. Women have always had to write against the grain, for example, by having an active female protagonist – allowing women to be in conversation with each other, not always on the topic of men, to tell stories where women are explored in depth and not merely as an adjunct to a male character. That is a way of saying that I have always been in a relationship with feminism, as a woman and as a woman writer, and I wouldn't have written a word without it.

The first play I ever wrote called *Mumchance* (ie. something performed in silence) was at university. I wrote it in response to a play produced by our drama society at Sussex, which was an adaptation of an Ian McEwan short story, where for one minute, a female mannikin comes alive and speaks. My thought was 'is that all the woman in the play is allowed?' So I wrote *Mumchance*, a story about domestic violence, (which went to the Edinburgh festival in 1981) in response to this plastic, inanimate, woman who was given a minute's airtime.

It's hard to imagine but at the time, apart from Caryl Churchill, there were NO women playwrights, just a lot of men called David, who ruled our stages. The breakthrough of second-wave women writers was a revolution. I wrote my next play, a gothic piece called *Breathless* about a pair of Victorian women, a mistress and servant, who are obsessed with science and who mummify the patriarch of their household ('pull the brain out of the cavities provided by the cribriform bones'). Here perhaps I had swapped the inanimate body of the mannikin for that of the male mummy! This play won a playwriting competition set up for young women writers and was my first professional production.

I was, by then, an actress in a women's theatre company called 'Resisters'. I switched to writing for them and wrote two plays. *Women in Law* – about the prejudices faced by women in the criminal justice system. One character was a hard-boiled woman detective (think Sam Spade). The second play was called *Ironmistress,* whose heroine, Martha Derby, the owner of an ironworks, was a real historical character. I gave her a daughter, Little Cog, who the mother was forcing into a traditional woman's role. This play was performed at the Oval House Theatre in Kennington and was, I suppose, a breakthrough play in that I was called into the Royal Court Theatre for a meeting and given a commission. Around this time, I also adapted *Fanny Hill* or *Memoirs of a Woman of Pleasure.*

One of the debates at the time in the feminist movement (has it ever gone away?) was about pornography. Did it by its very nature always degrade women? Pornography, literally 'The Story of a Whore', strangely always disappeared the whore's story. No narrative was allowed to impede its voyeuristic nature or interrupt smooth consumption by the user. I decided to bring back the true story of the whore, writing a counter

Frances Cuka, Nicola Grier and Geraldine Fitzgerald in *Playhouse Creatures* produced by Sphinx. Photo: Hugo Glendinning

narrative to Fanny Hill. This play was revived by Bristol Old Vic Theatre in 2016 with the brilliant Caroline Quentin as 'Old Fanny'.

*Playhouse Creatures* was a commission from Sphinx Theatre and their artistic director Sue Parrish. Weirdly, I had never even considered when women might first have set foot on our stages. The power of silence! At the time, there was precious little research on the subject. I discovered many things, such as Nell Gwyn wasn't a random orange seller/king's mistress but a brilliant comic actress who took the stage by storm. Elizabeth Howe's wonderful book *The First English Actresses* had been published around this time and was invaluable. *Playhouse Creatures* was an attempt to bring a hidden history of women to light, and I'm happy to say that it is still being performed internationally.

Feminism has been the powerhouse behind everything I've written. *Jumpy* (Royal Court/West End) looked at the relationship between a mother, Hilary, a second-wave feminist and her clash with her non-feminist teenage daughter, Tilly. *The Village* (Stratford East), an adaptation of *Fuente Ovejuna* relocated to rural India, told the story of Johti, a rape victim, who led a village revolt against her rapist and survived triumphant. *My Brilliant Friend*, a two-play marathon and adaptation of the Ferrante Quartet (NT, Olivier) featured *two* female protagonists and their struggle with class and politics in post-war Italy. *GinCraze!* (Royal Derngate) is a musical which looked at the struggles of working class women in gin-soaked 18th-century London. In all these plays I have put women and their stories centre-stage because that is the major gesture of feminism.

The climate and ecological emergency when seen through a feminist lens points to the patriarchal/capitalist/colonial rape of the earth. *Extinct,* (Stratford East) was a monologue I wrote during lockdown which detailed the terrifying climate breakdown we are in at present, which disproportionately affects the global south. It concerns a journalist with Bangladeshi heritage who revisits her grandmother's home, only to find it disappearing into the rising waters. Women, it turns out, suffer the effects of climate breakdown disproportionately too.

If you're a writer, you are a thinker, and you have to be thinking about the world which means being political. Feminism has always been my politics, my way of thinking through issues, but if being a woman writer means being a feminist, then it was obvious that I would be one in order to write at all.

Looking back over the 37 years I've been lucky enough to be writing plays, it's perhaps instructive to think about how, as a woman, I have fared in the industry. I benefitted from women and women's organizations advocating for equality in programming. This we know has never been achieved, and has stayed stubbornly around 30 percent. To translate this, it means that a male writer has over twice as much chance of being commissioned as a woman writer, has twice as many choices, twice as many productions. Over a lifetime, this surely impacts on the career of a woman writer but it's hard to concretise an argument about something that didn't happen, it remains shadowy. Add to this, the fact that 80 per cent of all adaptations are given to male writers, who also happen to get productions on bigger stages.

It's true, on the whole, that women artistic directors tended to commission me: Sue Parrish at Sphinx, Nadia Fall at Stratford East, Theresa Heskins at Stoke. However, there are brilliant male directors like Dominic Cooke who commissioned me at the Royal Court Theatre and also Max Stafford Clark before him. I recently had a (male) artistic director tell me, pointedly, 'you worked with Max!' as if I had committed a crime. He seemed to have no conception of the fact that in 1990, there were no women running the major venues, and hardly any of the smaller. Women's history, it seems, gets disappeared on a regular basis. Also why blame the woman?

One has to be careful when drawing conclusions from one's own experience, not to conveniently plonk all your failings in the misogyny basket, but I'd say it's broadly true that women's voices struggle harder to get heard for the same reason that women generally do – we are not taken as seriously as men. The accolades come more easily to male writers and that includes critical acclaim. A recent example is Penny Skinner's *Lyonesse* which opened at the Harold Pinter Theatre, in the West End. It's a powerful play that hones in brilliantly on the way women's lives are constantly stymied by convention and male entitlement, leaving no room for women to find their own voices and modus vivendi. Why is it called *Lyonesse,* shrieked one male critic? Because *Lyonesse* is a mythical lost land and a homonym pointing to women's potential power. An apt metaphor for the wastes that patriarchy always attempts to make of women's independent power to shape their own existence and the world.

Women writers have to have each other's backs and support each other. It's been salutary to see the growth in women writers over those years, including writers from the global majority. Theatre is definitely a less white and more female place and is the richer for it. However, beneath the success story there runs a counter narrative of continuing male supremacy, and now with cuts in the arts and in arts education, with theatres switching to executive producer models and abandoning their artistic directors, closing their doors and producing less shows, the outlook is bleaker than at anytime I can remember.

How are upcoming writers to make their way?

THE FUTURE is the climate crisis. Unless we deal with that NOW there won't be any more theatre. Basically, we need an eco-feminist revolution. But that could be interesting.

≈

Photo: Andy Woods

**April de Angelis** is an acclaimed writer whose extensive theatre work includes *Infamous* (Jermyn Street Theatre); *Kerry Jackson* (National Theatre); *Saving Grace* (Riverside Studios); *Gin Craze!* (Royal & Derngate Theatre); *My Brilliant Friend,* a two-part dramatization of Elena Ferrantes' epic family saga (Rose Theatre Kingston, National Theatre); *The Village* (Theatre Royal Stratford East, 2018); *Frankenstein* (Royal Exchange Manchester, 2018 *Gastronauts* (Royal Court Upstairs, 2013); *Jumpy* (Royal Court 2011 & Duke of York's Theatre 2012, Melbourne and Sydney 2015); an adaptation of *Wuthering Heights* (Birmingham Rep, 2008); *Wild East* (Royal Court 2006, Young Vic 2019); *A Laughing Matter* (Out of Joint at National Theatre, 2001); *A Warwickshire Testimony* (RSC, 1999); *The Positive Hour* (Out of Joint at Hampstead Theatre, 1997); *Playhouse Creatures* (Sphinx Theatre Company at the Haymarket Theatre 1993 and revived at the Old Vic Theatre, 1997 and again at Chichester Festival Theatre in 2013); *The Life And Times Of Fanny Hill* (The Old Fire Station Oxford, 1991; revived at the Bristol Old Vic, 2015); *Flight* (Glyndebourne Opera, 1997) and *Crux* (Lyric Theatre, Hammersmith and national tour, 1989), was published by Aurora Metro.

Nicole Sawyer *(left)* Tania Rodrigues, Shala Nyx in *The Croydon Avengers,* 2018
Photo: Barnaby Aldrick

# INTERVIEW WITH SUZANNE GORMAN

## What does feminism mean to you?

Feminism to me is:

- A recognition of the historical and current patriarchal structures that oppress women and girls.

- Engaging in a multifaceted struggle to achieve equality of choice and opportunity.

- Amplifying female voices.

- Greenham Common Women, Pussy Riot, #MeToo, Tonic Theatre.

- Taking centre stage and feeling you belong there.

- An ongoing process.

- An awakening that made me question every portrayal of women on TV that I grew up with.

- Throwing away my white stilettos in favour of (fake) Doc Martens in 1980s … and then realising it's my choice, I can wear what I like.

## How has feminism influenced your work?

I began exploring feminist theatre whilst studying at Dartington College of Arts. For my dissertation I examined the journey of the female self and experience through western theatre – I was young and up for a challenge! I discovered three fundamental insights about women in theatre that have influenced my approach to theatre-making ever since:

- We were physically absent!

- The representation of women and female characters on stages from Greek to Shakespearean times was constructed almost entirely from the male view. We need a female lens in theatre.

- Feminist Theatre of the 70s/80s used the artform to challenge the constructed idea of the female self by striving to put the real and complex experiences of women on stage as subjects at the heart of the work. We can use theatre to make change!

These insights propelled me to wholeheartedly embrace feminism. In my final year of college, I proudly presented *Psychosexually Yours,* a devised piece which explored sexuality and objectification. It put on stage both the Oedipus myth and Freud's psychosexual development theory as signifiers of patriarchal oppression. I set the second half in a matriarchy. There was a set of a hanging giant gold bra and knickers and a pumping soundtrack of KLF and Donna Summer's 'I Feel Love'. In my eyes, it was textbook feminist theatre, something that was going to both bring down the patriarchy and launch me into a stellar theatre career in one fell swoop. Of course that wasn't the case.

But I wasn't going to give up. When I graduated, I set up a theatre company with two friends. We were aware that opportunities for complex female roles were few and far between, so we had to create them ourselves. I remember being on the dole and rehearsing in a freezing room above a pub in Twickenham. I spent most of my time in a coat, hat, gloves and scarf. We called ourselves 2:2:1 Against. This should have been a sign of our ultimate fate, but I suppose we naively thought we'd ultimately win. We created a play called *Queen of Kings,* about Cleopatra and Boadicea meeting Barbie and Action Man, exploring social conditioning/gender roles, and toured it to some fringe venues. Despite winning the Best New Play Award at a small pub theatre, we reached small audiences and had to face the fact that none of us had a clue about how to run a theatre company or had any connections to the theatre industry, so, our feminist theatre company 2:2:1 Against folded.

## Does intersectionality influence your work?

It was in the 90s that I became aware that the majority of theatre, including the feminist theatre that had inspired me, had little to no representation of people like me: Anglo-Indian/South Asian and working class.

My response was to explore race, class and culture, as well as gender identity. Initially, I tackled this problem head on by putting myself on stage. *Rites of Spice* and *The Cell Net* were two one-woman shows I wrote and performed. They highlighted the history of the Anglo-Indian community in the British Empire and explored the fractures in identity of growing up Anglo-Indian in Sheffield. I began to recognise the multitude of voices and stories that were missing from our theatre stages and started to develop a theatre practice that aimed to:

- Make visible those who have been absent from our stages.

- Deconstruct unhelpful assumptions about individuals and communities who have had their stories too often told through the white, male, middle class gaze.

- Give a platform to voices that are traditionally underrepresented in theatre.

- Empower theatre makers who have lived experience so that we can find authenticity and truth.

- Offer multiple stories and representations of women's lives.

I am Artistic Director of Maya Productions, a theatre company that strives for racial justice in the arts. To achieve this, recognising how gender, class, disability, sexual orientation, and other characteristics intersect to create privilege and oppression is important. We consult, share and work in collaboration with others to support access and inclusion.

#### How has the content of your work changed over time?

When creating my performance art inspired one-woman shows, I never thought that over 20 years later I would be working on two highly accessible musicals and getting excited and stressed about bubble machines and the spillage of guacamole on stage. My latest show, *Súper Chefs* by Betsy Picart with music by Ariel Cumbría (2023), is a bilingual musical exploring food, family and gender roles. The humour in my work back then was darker. Now I'm enjoying it being fun, silly and joyful. It's a different kind of play, but still delivering messages loud and clear.

At the core of my work is an exploration of the themes of migration, identity and displacement. That hasn't changed. What has changed over time is my process and the form I use to explore the themes. I enjoy finding the form that fits the story.

'*Moonwalking in Chinatown*' by Justin Young (2007), took inspiration from Lisa Goldman's *Hoxton Story* (2005). It was a promenade performance through the streets of Soho and Chinatown with a mixed professional and community cast of over 25 people. Developed through creative community workshops for Soho Theatre, it shone a light on three generations of British Chinese women and their relationship to the Chinese Autumn Moon Festival. The piece blurred the lines between reality and the world of the play. It inspired both audiences and passers-by to reconsider how these women and this community is presented to us through theatre and the arts.

In 2010, I became an adopter of digital work. *Tales of the Harrow Road* by In-Sook Chappell (Soho Theatre) was a project working with Arabic-speaking, Bangladeshi and other women living in the Paddington area of London. Not only was a play produced but the reach of the work was extended by the creation of an interactive web map and a soundwalk around Paddington that gave audiences the opportunity to tap into many local women's stories and experiences and invited them to record and upload their own too. Finding new ways to extend the reach of a piece of theatre became part of my process.

The model of practice we use regularly at Maya Productions has this extended collaboration at its core. Before embarking on a piece of work, community and arts partners with a vested interest in the topic will form a steering committee. A writer is then commissioned and supported from the outset to engage participants. A research and development process will involve participation projects inspired by the play and its themes. The play is shared at each stage with participants and other audiences, who give feedback.

This process enables the writer to think and work in new ways. It builds relationships and trust between artists and audiences. It opens up a dialogue that can take work in surprising directions. When you put characters on stage who are rarely seen, traditionally viewed from a particular lens, and often stereotyped, it pays to ensure that the theatre you are presenting is based on truth and authenticity.

Cinthia Lilen in *Súper Chefs* by Betsy Picart, 2023. Photo: Hector Manchego

Throughout my career I am proud to have witnessed firsthand the changes theatre can make. For example, a participant who was touched by her story being transformed into a play, which, in turn, greatly moved the audience. Or seeing the difference it made to female students watching the character of Aisha in *The Croydon Avengers* by Oladipo Agboluage (2018), a play about young refugee superheroes, and being really excited to see a strong female Muslim character on stage.

In some ways I'm coming full circle. After years of directing, I'm once again writing. *Benny and the Greycats* (with music by Mike Gorman and Riz Maslen) is a new musical that tells the story of a family of Anglo-Indian railway workers and musicians who migrate from South India to Sheffield in the 1960s. It was inspired by my family heritage. My uncles founded the Madras jazz group in India in the 1950s and then played in pop combos in Sheffield clubs in the 1960s.

At each stage of development, we have shared the work. Additionally, a brand-new arts and heritage project *Routes to Roots* has emerged alongside that highlights the migration stories of more South Asian communities in Bradford, Croydon and Sheffield. I've been witness to moving stories, powerful poetry and inspiring visual arts from women and girls through live performance that now will be documented and archived through oral history podcasts, film and an exhibition. Theatre making change in action!

*Benny and the Greycats* itself has gone on a journey. Originally focusing on the young men in the family, the central character is now Mabel, a middle aged, working class mother. This shift in focus is influenced partly by the many inspirational women I have met through *Routes to Roots,* and in part by my need as a feminist to put the female experience front and centre. Unlike my early shows *Rites of Spice* and *The Cell Net,* this time I hope to be able to take up the space on a much larger stage.

**Do you feel that women have achieved equality in theatre?**

For much of my career I believed that if you were passionate, determined, worked really hard, and made good theatre, you would succeed regardless of gender, race, sexuality, class, disability etc. This was despite the fact that I had felt the oppression of patriarchy, made feminist theatre, and had lived experience of the racism that pervades in our society.

Although the theatre and arts industry has cultivated a reputation for being an open and liberal sector, welcoming those on the margins of society, the belief that the sector is meritocratic and will reward talented and hard working individuals with success is harmful because it puts the focus on the individual at the expense of analysing the structures that enable or disable others.

Despite the progress we may have made, women have not yet achieved equality. The theatre industry is built on traditional structures that disproportionately reward and enable the progression of white, able-bodied, middle class men. This, in turn, puts at a disadvantage those of us who do not share those characteristics. It means that I've been subject to external and internalised bias around sex, class and race such as:

- Lacking confidence at times, suffering from imposter syndrome.

- Struggling to find a sense of belonging.

- Having my process as a director questioned in a way I don't see happening to male directors i.e. different standards.

- Seeing the 'main stage' as a sacred place that was out of my reach (unless I'd directed at least 30 plays, and had 50 5* reviews).

- Being invited to take on certain leadership responsibilities without being given any support to step up i.e. being set up to fail.

- Working in environments where the default artist was male and the idea of a female artist was considered a risk.

- Being patronised.

- Being informed, as a new mum, how much show budgets had to be reduced every time someone got paid maternity leave.

Overcoming these structural inequalities is not possible as an individual. It takes deep and long-term sector change.

### What would improve opportunities for women in theatre today?

As a Clore Fellow I undertook a research paper. 'Where Am I?' highlighted the importance of Black, Asian and Global Majority Background role models and leaders for workforce diversity and inclusion. The findings can be applied in relation to gender and other characteristics. Role models provide connections between underrepresented communities and work on stage. They spark inspiration – if you can see it, you can be it. They can support the creation of inclusive environments, inspire a sense of belonging, and support others to be confident and ambitious.

In order to improve the opportunities for women working in theatre today, we need to close the pay gap, recognise the fragility of the freelancer life, fund more female-led theatre companies, and build inclusive working environments with these characteristics:

- Trustees and leadership teams committed to a review of policies and procedures that discriminate.

- Equality is seen as the responsibility of everyone. Training is given to increase awareness of discriminatory practices and inspire allies for inclusion.

- An offer of flexibility in the way people can work.

- An ability to enable progression through giving trust, support, knowledge, encouragement, permission, access and active coaching/mentoring of individuals.

- Visible championing of role models and leaders to inspire others.

## Do we still need feminism?

More than ever. Issues around body, consent, ownership, safety and choice are ever-present for girls and women, here in the UK and globally.

## Anything else you want to add?

If it hadn't been for other women in theatre supporting, guiding, and mentoring me, I would have left the industry long ago. Thanks to all.

≈

Photo: Hector Manchego

**Suzanne Gorman** is Artistic Director of Maya Productions, where she has directed *Súper Chefs, Machinal, The Croydon Avengers, In Time, Barefoot Gen* and *Babel Junction* and is developing a new Anglo-Indian musical *Benny and the Greycats.*

Suzanne previously led the Education Department at Soho Theatre, directing over 15 new writing productions and pioneering the company's ground-breaking site-specific and digital work with communities. She has held Associate roles at Derby LIVE, Sheffield Theatres, Theatre Royal Stratford East, Immediate Theatre and Barbican, and worked as project manager at BBC Arts for Performance LIVE.

A Clore Fellow, Suzanne's research project 'Where Am I?' highlighted the importance of Black, Asian and Global Majority Background role models and leaders for diversity in the performing arts. She supports workforce inclusion through research projects, coaching/mentoring, training and facilitation. She is also a trustee at Immediate Theatre.

*Favour* by Ambreen Razia. Photo: Suzy Corker

# CLEAN BREAK
## ANNA HERRMANN

I have proudly worn the label 'feminist' since my early teens, as I began to make sense of the world around me. It is a central tenet of my world view, which understands the existing system of patriarchy as a core oppressive force and seeks to dismantle and reorganise society to meet women's needs and realise all women's rights to equality, freedom, and opportunity. My version of feminist is a collaborative, collective endeavour, and I have practised this feminism for the past two decades, and been free to do this in a women-only space, away from societal expectations and organisational structures that I found limiting – a space where I felt safe away from the male gaze, and a space where, alongside other women, we could reclaim, reimagine and make real, the values and ethos intrinsic in feminist.

Clean Break was founded in 1979 by two pioneering women, Jacqui Holborough and Jenny Hicks, who met in prison and whose experience of injustice and imprisonment led them to form a collective of women on their release, using theatre to tell their own hidden stories, to engage audiences in dialogue, and to challenge public perception and prejudice around why many women get caught up in crime. Their role as theatre makers was a form of activism – seeking change in society. Alongside the plays they wrote, devised and produced[1], they campaigned for the closure of women's prisons and partnered with other newly-formed women-led charities (Hibiscus and Women in Prison to name two that are still in existence to this day) seeking justice and better treatment for women in prison. This fusion of theatre and activism remains a huge driver for the company as we journey through our fifth decade, many years after the founders moved on. Wrapped around each play we produce, we

---

[1]     you can find more information about Clean Break's history in our digital timeline www.cleanbreak.org.uk/timeline/)

campaign for change – through amplifying the work of our sister organisations and hosting panels and speaker events (e.g. our 2022 production of *Favour* by Ambreen Razia platformed the important work of sister organisations Muslim Women in Prison and Children Heard and Seen). The enduring harm that prison causes women, and their children, is better understood now than it was in the 1970s and the benefit of a gender-specific approach seems to be an argument that has been won in principle, but sadly change in policy and practice is far slower.

Women are less than 5% of the prison population in England and Wales[2], which means their needs are often overlooked and sidelined. Despite numerous reports on the failures of the system and clear recommendations on the way forward e.g. Baroness Corston's[3] report in 2007 identified "the need for a distinct radically different, visibly-led, strategic, proportionate, holistic, woman-centred, integrated approach", alongside many individuals and organisations campaigning for alternative community-based approaches, we continue to use prison as our foremost solution. Understanding that past trauma and oppression are the root causes of many women's entry into the justice system, (including poverty, racism, mental ill health, addiction, sexual violence and abuse) hasn't prevented the ongoing use of imprisonment or propelled us as a society to invest in better solutions to the injustices that women experience at the hands of the system.

Women with this lived experience are at the heart of Clean Break. The use of the exemption in the 2010 Equality Act (Schedule 9, Part 1) has safeguarded our women-only status, and provides the legal framework within which we provide theatre making opportunities for women in prisons, in women's centres and in our own women-only studios in north London (which we purchased in the mid-1990s). Here, women join a regular programme where they can participate in theatre, playwriting and creativity, learn new skills, find confidence, access support and therapy, build new networks and use their resilience and voice for self-expression, recovery, and personal and collective transformation. We have established a women only creative community which provides a temporary oasis from life's harsh realities, and a space to organise and

---

2    In 2022, there were 76,226 men and 3,216 women in prisons in England and Wales    https://www.statista.com/statistics/283475/england-and-wales-prison-population-by-gender/

3    https://webarchive.nationalarchives.gov.uk/ukgwa/20130128112038/http://www.justice.gov.uk/publications/docs/corston-report-march-2007.pdf

build hopeful futures. Alongside this direct work, for four decades the company has kept the subject of women and crime on the cultural radar by commissioning and (co)producing multiple groundbreaking plays written by inspirational women playwrights – many of those at the forefront of British theatre writing – Alice Birch, Tanika Gupta, Lucy Kirkwood, Morgan Lloyd Malcolm, Chloe Moss, Winsome Pinnock, to name but a few.

Many of the plays have been performed in women's prisons, enabling prison audiences to see their lives reflected compassionately on stage, alongside on our national stages including Royal Court, Royal Exchange, Donmar Warehouse, Sheffield Theatres, The Bush, and most recently in Summer 2023 at the National Theatre Dorfman stage. Leading up to our 40th year in 2018, we made a conscious decision to make bigger work for mainstages, recognising that the continued placement of ourselves in studio spaces was part of our organisational limiting beliefs, and that we wanted to lead with increased confidence and ambition to take up space and move our stories out of the margins. We celebrated our 40th birthday in the Great Hall of the Old Bailey under the eye of the penal reformer Elizabeth Fry, and this symbolic moment has stayed with me, as a reminder of our responsibility to take up space boldly, and not to be intimidated by the structures of power, but to continually strive to disrupt and reimagine.

Frustratingly, women playwrights still face immense barriers getting their work put on. Clean Break is no longer told by potential theatre partners as it once was, 'sorry, we had a women's season last year', however women writers continue to be seen as a greater risk, are programmed less than their male counterparts, and for shorter runs. The 2021 Women in Theatre Forum report[4] painted a stark picture of ongoing inequality in theatre, with women underrepresented in every sphere – with caring responsibilities preventing women from accepting work, few women in leadership positions, and Black Womxn in Theatre noting that Black women feel completely erased and are still struggling to get in the door. This is clearly not good enough. The fact that childcare continues to be a structural barrier to gender equality 50 years after the second wave of feminists demanded 24-hour childcare, illustrates perhaps how little progress we have made. Tonic Theatre has shone a light more recently on

---

4    https://sphinxtheatre.co.uk/wp-content/uploads/2021/01/Women-in-Theatre-Forum-Report-11121.pdf

a much less spoken about barrier facing women, that of the menopause[5], with their recent research identifying its negative impact on women in theatre, exacerbating gender inequality in senior roles and adding to the gender pay gap.

Clearly, the need to overcome structural barriers facing women's careers, to programme more women writers on our national stages, remove gate-keepers and to continue to amplify women's stories feels as urgent today as it did in the past. There are some amazing women artistic leaders of theatre buildings around the country who programme and champion women writers, however they are a still a minority, and few unashamedly programme solely feminist work, or feel able to prioritise work by women writers. We need to see more of this. The current financial barriers and risks to theatres post-Covid mean that the system itself is incredibly broken to support initiatives perceived as risky. However, new ideas do emerge, like the recently announced Women in Theatre Lab,[6] and change will come.

For Clean Break, the evolution of our feminist practice over recent years has been the deliberate weaving together of our participatory work with our public-facing work, reconnecting with our foundations, valuing lived experience in the creation of our produced work and recognising the need for clearer pathways for women with lived experience of the criminal justice system into the theatre industry as actors, writers, designers, directors, stage managers. We have worked harder to ensure that women with different backgrounds, particularly across race, class and lived experience, are represented in our team, on stages, behind the scenes and on our Board of Trustees. Post Covid and the global reckoning after the murders of Breonna Taylor and George Floyd, we have undergone a root and branch review of our own organisation. Learning from the work of Black feminists, Kimberlé Krenshaw and Patricia Hill Collins and under the skilful guidance of a women-led anti racism consultancy, darvaja[7], the company now has a clearer understanding of intersectionality, and recognises the ways in which we have failed to lead with an active pursuit of antiracism. We have a road map ahead to support this work, and are holding ourselves accountable, creating new roles, prioritising career progression, reaching out beyond our networks, and delivering on a

5    www.tonictheatre.co.uk/menopause-the-change-in-the-industry/
6    Exclusive: scheme to tackle under-representation of female playwrights (thestage.co.uk)
7    www.darvaja.org/

strong commitment to listening and sharing power differently. As a white leader, I better understand how my own positional power can oppress and I am consciously inhabiting a feminist leadership which seeks out, listens and values different contributions and which leads with courage and kindness.

The mistreatment of women in the justice system is one of the clearest demonstrations of where feminist action is most needed in contemporary Britain. If we look in our prisons and our immigration detention centres we can understand fully that structural inequality continues to discriminate against women from working class, migrant and global majority communities. These are the same women excluded from theatre. We can't dismantle systems without everyone engaged. Those who came before us, those who we'll never meet, those by our side, and those to come are all part of the same struggle. Clean Break exists to prioritise, stand in solidarity with, and strive for freedom and equality for all these women, using theatre as the vital means to tell stories, nurture hope, change hearts and minds and create new futures.

≈

**Anna Herrmann** is Artistic Director/Joint CEO of Clean Break. Anna has been working in the field of theatre and social change for over 30 years, in the UK and abroad. The majority of that time has been in the women's sector for Clean Break, which she joined in 2002 as Head of Education. She became the Joint Artistic Director / Joint CEO in 2018, and Artistic Director in 2022. Anna is co-author of *Making a Leap: Theatre of Empowerment: A Practical Handbook for Creative Drama Work with Young People* (Jessica Kingsley Publishers) and has written for other publications on the work of Clean Break. She has an MA in Arts Education from Royal Central School of Speech and Drama, where she was awarded an Honorary Fellowship in 2022. She also has a PG Cert (Distinction) in Race and Ethnic Relations from Birkbeck University. She is a visiting lecturer on Applied Theatre courses at universities across the country and between 2006 and 2018 was a trustee of Leap Confronting Conflict; a UK based national charity specialising in youth and conflict. Anna sits on the Steering Group of the National Criminal Justice Arts Alliance and is also a trained coach and mentors artists in participatory settings.

# THE WOMEN IN THEATRE LAB
## POLLY KEMP & JENNIFER TUCKETT

The Women in Theatre Lab was founded in 2023 as a UK version of the US's influential Women's Project (now WP) Theater Lab and Australia's Women in Theatre Programme. It builds on co-director Polly Kemp's work as Director of ERA 50:50, the equal representation for actresses campaign whose supporters include Emma Thompson and Phoebe Waller-Bridge, and co-director Jennifer Tuckett's work as Research and Literary Director at Sphinx Theatre, where Jennifer created the influential *What Share of the Cake* Report (2019), *Women in Theatre Forum* Report (2020), and *Women in Theatre* Surveys (2021 and 2023), which were all covered as exclusives in *The Guardian* newspaper. Jennifer also co-created the one-off programme Sphinx 30 for Sphinx's 30th anniversary in partnership with Sphinx and 15 leading theatres, as well as her work as Director of University Women in the Arts, the mentoring organisation to help improve the transition for women from studying the arts to working in the arts.

**Polly Kemp:**

ERA 50:50 emerged in response to influential reports, including Geena Davis's 2015 study, Elizabeth Freestone's 2012 research, Purple Seven's insights, and the momentum surrounding the release of the film *Suffragette,* coinciding with the centenary celebration of women's voting rights. Despite the wealth of research highlighting the inequality faced by actresses, our own experiences contradicted the narrative of progress. As we aged, it seemed that equality was regressing.

The organisation sprang from a pivotal moment when actress Elizabeth Berrington sent a single text to her phone contacts, leading to a cascade of responses and emails. Subsequently, a meeting was convened at the Soho Theatre, some time before the #TimesUp UK movement. Attended by experienced actresses, the lively discussion covered topics such as the scarcity of substantial roles, disparate fees compared to male counterparts, and experiences of sexual harassment. Out of this frustration, a mandate to effect change emerged.

We initiated discussions with key figures, engaging in productive meetings with individuals such as Anna Serner, the CEO of the Swedish Film Institute. Drawing insights from successful strategies that had fostered gender parity in the Swedish film industry, these exchanges proved invaluable. Additionally, Oona King, a Labour Peer and head of diversity at C4, played a pivotal role in assisting us as we approached major broadcasters, contributing her expertise to refine and shape our ideas.

Our inaugural event aimed to present the actress's perspective to the industry without being unfairly characterised. Held at BAFTA, the evening featured presentations of facts from research, including findings from the BFI, supplemented by personal stories. ERA 50:50, reliant on voluntary contributions due to budget constraints, saw its role as amplifying existing research, notably the work done by Jennifer Tuckett. With Olivia Colman graciously hosting, supported by the hardworking actresses who had put the event together, we presented impactful findings, such as:

- Only 17% of crowd scenes in films feature women

- Men predominantly write 65% of roles for men, while women write 52% of roles for women

- Female-led films operate with 20% lower production budgets but achieve 33% higher box office returns

- On-screen, women are often paired with men 20 years their senior, contrasting real-world relationships

- Women aged 42–65 receive just over 20% of the words allocated to their male counterparts in modern screenplays

The event left a lasting impression on the invited audience, prompting several organisations to incorporate gender parity into their future policies. Saskia Schuster, at the time Commissioning Editor of Comedy at ITV, influenced by

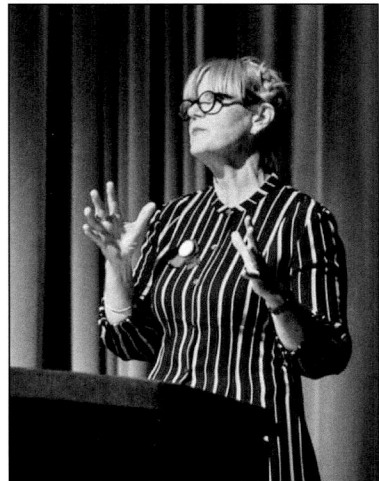

Polly Kemp at an ERA 50:50 event

the event and the findings from WGGB, subsequently initiated Comedy 50:50, a female comedy initiative for writers to network and get better access to opportunities.

**Jennifer Tuckett:**

I first met Polly via the December Group, which was a group of leading women in theatre who came together to campaign for Arts Council England to consider the under-representation of women in theatre in their next 10-year strategy. I was working at Sphinx as their Research and Literary Director at the time, where I wrote four research reports from 2018-23, all of which were featured as exclusives in *The Guardian* newspaper. This led to some good outcomes including being in the Fair Work review by the Scottish government, being discussed in the House of Lords, with Lord Neil Mendoza, the Commissioner for Cultural Recovery and Renewal, and with Sir Nicholas Serota, Chair of Arts Council England, and being used in other countries including India and Australia.

Via that research, I discovered some shocking findings such as, in the early reports, only 0.64% of NPO funding going to women's theatre companies, only 31% of NPO Artistic Directors in theatre being female and in control of only 21% of NPO funding (suggesting they were Artistic Directors of smaller NPO theatres generally) and, in the later reports, statistics such as that over 60% of respondents to the Women in Theatre Survey had considered or were considering leaving working in theatre post-pandemic and that respondents felt the situation for women in theatre had gotten worse since the pandemic. The Women in Theatre Survey in 2021 was the largest recent survey of women working in theatre in the UK so this finding felt important.

As Polly and I kept talking together, it seemed to us there was the need for a UK version of US and Australian support models which had had a big influence in terms of supporting women in theatre and addressing gender inequality in those countries, for example the Australian Women in Theatre programme had helped lead to gender parity in the country's most funded eight theatres and the Women's Project (WP) Theater Lab had been described by the Pulitzer Prize winning playwright Sarah Ruhl as "Long live WP, beacon of hope for women writers and directors. This theater gave me a community in which to thrive when I was an emerging playwright, and more recently, a home in which to experiment. I celebrate its past and look forward to its future!" The key to these programmes seemed to be they focused on being an ongoing pipeline of support – providing advice, toolkits and mentoring for women in theatre – for example Australia's important *Women in Theatre* study that took place in 2012 and which helped turn the tide of gender inequality in theatre in that country had recommended development programmes as a way of improving gender equality in theatre. Inspired by the US and Australian models, we came up with the idea of creating the Women in Theatre Lab, which also builds on past one-off projects we had been involved in such as the programme TellHerVision which Polly had created and run with actress Joanna Scanlan to support women writing for television and the one-off programme Sphinx 30 which I had created for Sphinx's 30th anniversary (30 female playwrights were provided with seed commissions, with 15 female playwrights being selected by theatres, plus ten from an open call and five selected by Sphinx). It seemed to us that these programmes had shown us there was a need for a UK version of an ongoing paid pipeline of support for female playwrights from ideas to first drafts to full commissions and productions. This would be similar to the US model of the Women's Project (WP) Lab and Australia's Women in Theatre programme. And, so, when Sphinx was unable to continue the Sphinx Lab after Sphinx 30, which I designed and led on whilst Sphinx

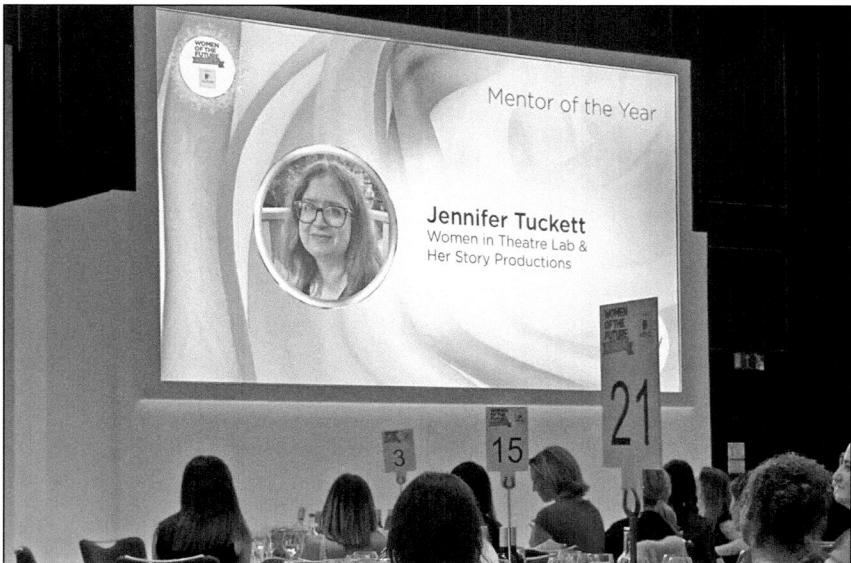

Jennifer Tuckett was a finalist for Mentor of the Year
at the Women of the Future Awards 2023

oversaw the showcase element of the Sphinx 30 programme, the UK's Women in Theatre Lab was born.

By a coincidence, shortly after having these conversations with Polly, I was invited to speak about my research into women in theatre at the Jermyn Street Theatre, where I met the Artistic Director Stella Powell-Jones. Stella and I soon realised we were very much on the same page in terms of our thinking about the need to support women in theatre and to improve gender equality, so Jermyn Street Theatre came onboard as our partner theatre. Jermyn Street Theatre has previously produced work by many notable female playwrights including April de Angelis and Timberlake Wertenbaker. I think the Women's Project (WP) Theater in America and the Women in Theatre programme in Australia both show it is really important for projects of this nature to be based at a theatre building from which to provide ongoing support.

Our next step was to recruit a group of leading women in theatre who would be happy to advise female playwrights on the programme. These include the UK playwrights April de Angelis, Timberlake Wertenbaker, as well as Australian playwright Suzie Miller (who wrote the hit *Prima Facie* starring Jodie Comer), and who will talk about what can be learnt from her experience of working in Australia, and American playwright Dorothy Fortenberry, who was a writer and Executive Producer on *The Handmaid's Tale* and *Extrapolations* (starring Meryl Streep), and who will talk about what can be learnt from her experience of working in America.

We also recruited leading women in theatre who would be happy to advise on business skills, including Stella Kanu, CEO of Shakespeare's Globe Theatre, another big supporter, as well as Lesley Gannon of The Writers' Guild, Jermyn Street Theatre's Artistic Director Stella Powell-Jones, Titilola Dawudu, Associate Dramaturg at the Bush Theatre and co-founder of Black Womxn in Theatre (with Stella Kanu), BAFTA-winning actress Joanna Scanlan and Emmy-winning actress Doon Mackichan, co-creator of *Smack the Pony* and author of the book *My Lady Parts.* More general supporters of the Lab also include actress Gemma Arterton, theatre director Matthew Dunster, and Executive Director of the Jermyn Street Theatre, David Doyle.

The structure of the Women in Theatre Lab is inspired by the US and Australian models, as well as by my own research which convinced me of the need to include advice and mentoring on craft and business skills. We also provide seed commissions (and later on full commissions/productions) in partnership with theatres, and a showcase at the end of each project.

While I was Director at University Women in the Arts, the mentoring organisation to improve the transition for women from studying the arts to working in the arts, I went back to complete post-graduate study at Cambridge University where I conducted the world-first major mixed methods study into how to improve the transition for women from studying the arts to working in the arts. As part of my studies, I came across research, for example from the Australian academic Dawn Bennett, of recurrent findings that demonstrated the importance of career advice from women leaders in their fields, skills toolkits, mentoring, women writers being included on reading lists, discussion of gender issues such as unconscious bias, and networking with peers to gather a support group to assist with improving gender equality.

The under-representation of women in theatre continues to exist and there is a danger that it is being dismissed as an issue that has already been resolved. Similarly, the increase in gender inequality post-pandemic is being ignored. Lesley Gannon of The Writers' Guild said in our *Women in Theatre* Forum report: "We have lots of conversations with women writers across a whole range of different areas and the consistent

Jennifer Tuckett and Titilola Dawudu at University of Women in the Arts

message we were getting was that women's work was simply not getting commissioned, not getting put on, that they were finding it increasingly difficult... Because as much as we were hearing this from our members, we were being told repeatedly that things were getting better."

Similarly, in the *Women in Theatre* survey update which was released in 2023, respondents highlighted that post-pandemic they felt things had gotten worse for women in the industry. Quotes from respondents include "I thought there was some momentum behind the push for gender equality prior to the pandemic, but I think that has been replaced by other agendas" and "Decrease for everyone overall, which disproportionately affects marginalised groups. Theatres close off their networks, afraid to take risks, and fall back on the 'old boys' network. Not to mention the added difficulty of childcare". So it seems there needs to be change from policy makers, as well as support from initiatives such as ours, particularly, I think, in terms of childcare, which the pandemic shone a light on in terms of how the majority of childcare responsibilities continue to fall on women.

Some of the suggestions from the *Women in Theatre* surveys to address this ongoing discrimination include for the Arts Council to make childcare part of access support and to consider a fund that freelancers can apply to for childcare costs. Other recommendations include the creation of a central hub of guidance like Australia's Creative Equity Toolkit website which would be helpful for arts organisations to get advice on areas like preventing unconscious bias and for the government and the Arts Council to investigate more thoroughly why women continue to be under-represented in order to bring about sector-wide change. Actions that theatres could take immediately include offering unconscious bias training to staff, looking particularly at problem areas like leadership or discrimination against women over the age of 40, or investigating why commissioning female work continues to be viewed as a greater risk.

In the meantime, Polly and I (and our partners and supporters) hope the Women in Theatre Lab will be one way to provide an ongoing paid pipeline to support female playwrights from ideas to first drafts to full commissions and productions in a similar way to US and Australian models which have had a beneficial effect. Our vision is to support a generation of women in theatre who can lead, challenge, disrupt and change British theatre to be a more diverse and equitable industry in the future.

I recently attended the UN Commission on the Status of Women which said, post-pandemic, it will now take 300 years to reach gender equality without action. Based on my five years of research, we – myself and the partners on the research – wrote to the Culture Secretary to request a government inquiry into the under-representation of women in the arts but have received no reply. However, we secured a meeting with Arts Council England, bringing together the leading organisations in this area, to meet with Sir Nicholas Serota, Chair, and others. I'm delighted to report ACE agreed to work with Parents and Carers in Performing Arts on the childcare issues raised by the research and to consider creating a gender advisory group. This was a historic moment and the first time ACE has agreed to take action on these issues, during the five years of research. Fingers crossed for more change!

≈

**Polly Kemp** is co-Director of the Women in Theatre Lab and Director of ERA 50:50. Polly's recent credits include *This Time with Alan Partridge* (BBC) and *The Windsors* (C4). 30 years as a professional actress includes seasons with the RSC, the Peter Hall Company and appearances in the West End include *Piaf* at The Piccadilly, *Becket* at The Haymarket Theatre and *Enlightenment* at Hampstead Theatre. Series include *The Thick of It* (BBC), *Desperate Romantics* (C4) and *Anne* (ITV). In 2016, Polly co-founded Equal Representation for Actresses (ERA 50:50) alongside fellow actress Elizabeth Berrington. She runs the Women in Theatre Lab with Co-Director Jennifer Tuckett.

**Jennifer Tuckett** is co-Director of the Women in Theatre Lab and was previously the Research and Literary Director at Sphinx Theatre, where she wrote four influential research reports on women in theatre, all published as exclusives in *The Guardian*, and co-created the programme Sphinx 30 for Sphinx's 30th anniversary in partnership with 15 leading theatres. Jennifer is also an academic and playwright and trained at Cambridge University and on Yale School of Drama's world-leading MFA in Playwriting where contemporaries included Oscar winner Tarell McCraney and Pulitzer Prize finalist Amy Herzog. At Cambridge University, she completed the world-first major mixed method research study into how to improve the transition for women from studying the arts to working in the arts. Her research has informed the Scottish government, been raised in the House of Lords, and been used as far afield as India and Australia amongst other places.

A scene from the play *Trouf: Scenes from 75\* Years* at Theatro Technis, 2021 as part of Shubbak Festival. Photo: BayremBenMrad

# INTERVIEW WITH HANNAH KHALIL

**What does feminist mean to you?**

A feminist is someone who recognises the structures that have historically oppressed and restricted women and wants to actively work against them. I find it deeply depressing when women are pitted against one another in theatre and the world in general and forced to compete for space and airtime. I will always try and amplify the voices of other women and celebrate their successes and fight for their rights and opportunities.

**How has feminism influenced your work?**

It's worth saying I never really sat down and thought "I'm going to write a feminist play" but being a woman of Palestinian heritage who started out with aspirations to be an actor it was that experience that first fired my writing. The lack of opportunities for global majority female artists, and specifically MENA artists, when I was starting out, was appalling. And what opportunities there were tended to be of the problematic kind – terrorists' wives and silent oppressed sisters or mothers with no agency. These were not the MENA women I knew! So I always tried to write interesting parts for women – especially women from the MENA region but also more broadly women from the global majority and also older women who are often overlooked.

**Has the content or form of your work changed over time? How?**

The content of my work has changed but also remained the same too, because I have inherently the same concerns about the world and I'm trying to understand things through my writing. However, as my life experience grows, that experience is inevitably ploughed into the plays. So for example, I would never have written my play *Sleepwalking* before I became a mother – it's uniquely and intrinsically tied to that experience.

In addition, I think I've become braver with form over time – take my play *Museum in Baghdad* which was ten years in the writing; if you read draft one it's a fairly conventionally structured play about Gertrude

Bell and the museum is secondary. Ten years and probably twenty drafts later, it is set in two times, Gertrude is still there, but part of an ensemble of players who explore the consequences of colonialism in a much more theatrical way, including large choruses in Arabic and English. I think an artist's work is ever changing and developing, otherwise it's pointless – if you're doing the same thing again, why bother?

**Do you feel women have achieved equality in theatre?**

No, because we have not achieved equality in the world. You just have to look at any theatrical season announcement, from the largest to the smallest theatres in the land, and the majority of the plays, directors, actors and creatives will be male. Meanwhile, in the admin offices, there may be more females than males, but you can bet they are in the less senior positions and it will be men in the Artistic Director's chair, making the decisions.

It is however worth saying that feminism doesn't mean no men – indeed there are plenty of women who fail to support, encourage, or raise up women and plenty of men who do. But the demographics of people working in theatres is telling and until it changes I don't think equality can be possible.

**Have you experienced sex bias while working in theatre?**

I was once told I was too nice. And that because I was such a nice person I'd never be able to be hard on my characters, so the plays would never be truly excoriated and interesting. I don't believe the man that said that to me would have said the same thing if I wasn't a woman.

But it's also worth saying that class bias is as real as sex bias. My background class-wise is truly weird and intersectional, but when I started writing plays I couldn't afford to do any kind of academic qualification in playwriting and I think this counted against me. I was told time and again I wrote "fascinating characters" but it was a shame I "couldn't do structure". Of course, what they meant was that I wasn't writing pieces that were structured in a conventional Western three-act style – and without proving my credentials in being able to do that, I wouldn't be allowed past the door.

**What would improve the opportunities for women in theatre today?**

I'm tempted to say quotas but I suspect that isn't the way to go. Perhaps a body to advocate for women in theatre and help create mentorship opportunities and other pathways into the industry would be useful, as they have for film and tv? I think the power of seeing other women succeed and knowing that it's possible is the most important thing of all.

## Does intersectionalism influence your work? How?

Intersectionality is key in my work as a Palestinian Irish writer who grew up in the Middle East around great wealth but then was put in a difficult financial position in my teens back in the UK. Intersectionality is where the truth and nuance of human relationships and contradictions and character lies. It's also key to understanding our, and other people's bias, and I believe that if theatre can gently reveal people's own bias to them and encourage them to address it, then it can do great good in the world.

## Do you collaborate with other groups?

I love to collaborate – it's why I'm a theatre writer. When I started out over twenty years ago now, I felt quite isolated, but gradually, by going to readings and plays and events and doing work of my own, I built a community of like-minded artists. Some from the MENA world, some not, some female, some male. These are the people who have sustained and renewed me and helped me keep the faith in the dark times. I am grateful to them, they know who they are.

## Do we still need feminist theatre? Why?

Yes, because unfortunately women are still not given the same space or rights as their male counterparts in any area of life.

## Do you think having a theatre dedicated to women's work would have an impact?

I actually think this would be a very exciting proposition on the caveat that it included all women including trans women. Also it must not exclude men. We need to keep working together and talking to each other debating and thinking and LISTENING to move forward and understand each other. And, of course, men can be feminists too.

## Are prizes important? Why? Why not?

Yes and no. Yes if they come with money which can grant the gift of writing time or a bit of safety from the terrors of the economic world. Yes if they can offer a deadline and an aspiration and ambition. No if they become too much of a focus or over relied on by gate keepers as a lazy way of finding new talent. And no if they become a writer's marker of self worth – the only real awards you need in that regard are the ones you give yourself when you complete a draft, hear it read or performed and think 'yes that's it, that's what I meant!'

**Is arts funding equitable?**

Arts funding in the UK is impossible: it is intimidating, it is inaccessible, it is elitist. I have a degree and I have never successfully completed an Arts Council funding application. I find the whole system difficult to navigate and hard to understand. I quickly get frustrated when I try to intuit what is required. I know that in person I am an excellent representative of my work and I can write a great pitch, but funding applications intimidate me and if they intimidate me, a woman who has been working in the industry for 20 years and who is neurotypical, I cannot imagine how someone with less experience of the industry, education systems in the UK, or who might be neurodiverse, would navigate them either. The whole thing needs to be simplified and overhauled. We need a kinder, more direct, personal system.

**Are there allowances made for people with caring responsibilities – either children or elderly?**

Most theatres will be accommodating to those with caring responsibilities, if you ask. But you usually have to ask. And I know that can be scary, particularly as a woman. When I had my daughter, I was afraid to tell people in theatre I was a mother, in case they assumed I would be less reliable. But actually, when I did build up the courage to do so, I was encouraged by the support and solidarity I received. I didn't expect it.

**How can we improve things for women in theatre?**

I think we can improve things for everyone in theatre with a bit of transparency. One very important period in my career was a year-long attachment at the Bush Theatre in London. As part of that attachment I attended literary meetings where we discussed plays that were being considered for production. It was eye-opening. I suddenly realised that if a play isn't selected, it's rarely, if ever, about the quality of the work. There are a million other factors including what else is in the season, cost implications, casting thoughts, production elements, directorial availability, or taste, and on and on. I found this a very useful lesson and still remind myself of it when I get knockbacks. If more theatres could talk openly about the realities of programming, I think it would be really good for artists to hear and understand that.

What's more, it's important to share the truth about our own journeys and disappointments. All too often the media (and social media) pursues the 'overnight success' story, which in my experience, is an unhelpful myth that only serves to make people struggling feel bad about themselves.

I think generally if theatres could spend a bit more time and effort in creating a safe welcoming space for their freelance artists, creating a community and making them feel valued, that would be a step in the right direction. And that needn't take too much time or money. A room that's bookable and free for people to use to work in, or a space to do so, perhaps a set night where there's a ticket offer for every show, free talks or an open door day so freelancers can talk to people in the building: these are all small things that make a big difference and will build a community of freelance artists who can support one another and feel valued. We need to feel like that to make great work.

Finally kindness. Kindness and consideration are incredibly important. We are not in competition with one another. There is room for us all and if we approach each other with kindness and try and listen to each other, then the world, not just the theatre world, will be a much better place.

≈

**Hannah Khalil** was the 2022 Resident Writer at Shakespeare's Globe and her work there includes *Hakawatis: Women of the Arabian Nights, Henry VIII* and *The Fir Tree* (2021 and 2022). Hannah's other stage plays include *A Museum in Baghdad* (Royal Shakespeare Company) which marked the first play by a woman of Arab heritage on a main stage at the RSC, *Interference* (National Theatre of Scotland) and the critically acclaimed *Scenes from 68\* Years* shortlisted for the James Tait Black Award (Arcola Theatre, London, 2016). *Scenes* has also been mounted in San Francisco, New York, France and in Tunisia in a British Council supported production called *Trouf*. Hannah has written radio plays for BBC Radio 4 and TV work includes multiple episodes of the Channel 4 drama *Hollyoaks*. She held the Heimbold Chair of Irish Studies at Villanova University and the Samuel Beckett Creative Fellowship. She is a Fellow of the Royal Society of Literature.

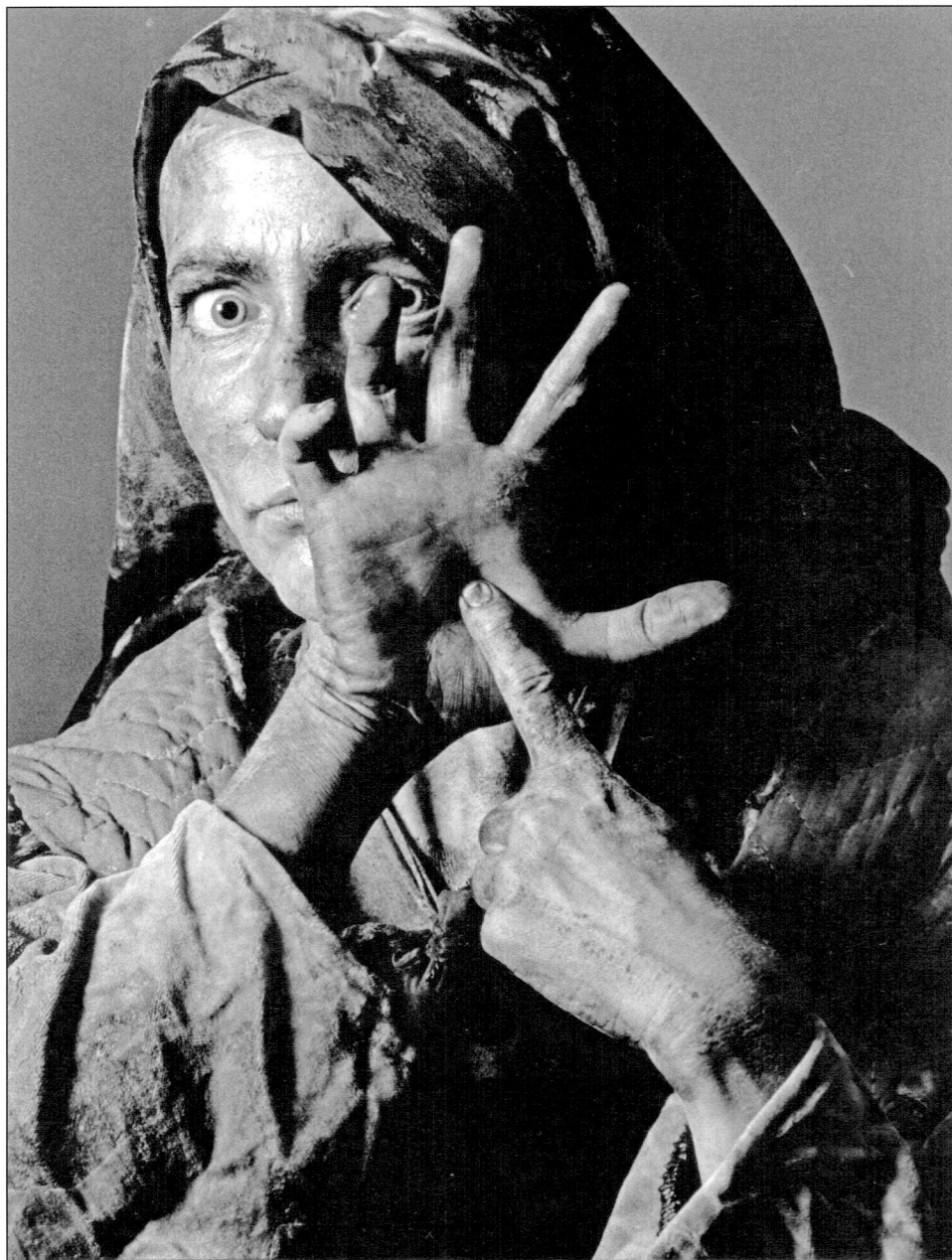

*The Porter's Daughter* in 1991. Photo: Graham Fudger

# PERSISTENCE, EXPRESSION AND EVOLUTION
## PETA LILY

Feminism keeps evolving. Inclusion and intersectionality are now vital drivers of feminism, after earlier omissions and marginalisations. While the road to equality is still disappointingly long (thank you capitalism, patriarchy and polarisation), over the decades I have enjoyed seeing the development in scope and detail of interpersonal and socio-political dynamics. I have listened hungrily to new feminist writers identifying how inequality shows up at the granular level and I have enjoyed the finessed articulation of viewpoints and concepts in all media.

My early theatre-making career was a product of 1970s' Women's Studies ('Second Wave Feminism'). Economic, class, sexual and gender inequalities were to a degree identified, but in my lived experience, I swam in and swallowed a lot of discontent that was pervasive, foggy, un-mapped out, and often used my work to explore threads of this discontent. I recognise my position of white privilege as I attempt to give this account of what I have explored in my theatre practice over four decades.

'Girls can't do anything,' my brother loved to say. My father's policy was that 'children should be seen and not heard.' Reinforcement of my worth beyond good behaviour and obedience was absent. Mine was not a free or boisterous childhood. When I was a girl, I heard of a film called *The Women* that had an all-female cast. The idea dazzled my mind with a frisson of possibility. I tried to guess the plot and could only think that it must hinge on the female characters' relationships to men … (thank you, inner patriarchy). *The Women*, written by Anita Loos and Jane Murfin (1939), should be credited for its innovation (it scores 2 out of 3 on the Bechdel test!).

The presence of women in mainstream theatre was unsatisfactory. For example, in the 'ground-breaking' play *Equus,* the female role was comprised of well-worn character tropes. I appreciated the female actor's courage, (especially with no intimacy coordination) but I remember feeling discomforted by her vulnerability and exposure. While the theatre maker in me was enthralled by the chorus of platform-shoed 'horses', this production didn't inspire confidence to audition for established theatre companies.

I arrived in London in 1979, hungry for theatre experience. Acting is a competitive career, and in London I felt that not only my gender, but my non-Britishness were additional hindrances to securing work. I had the usual uncomfortable experiences of actresses (as we called ourselves then) from the very minor (an agent saying I needed to dye my eyebrows) to the very disturbing – an encounter with a producer who was convicted decades later on multiple counts of indecent assault, which happened in 'interview' meetings, exactly like the one I had attended. It's important to remember how much was unvoiced before the #MeToo Movement. The continuing imbalance of power in the industry allows conditions whereby some will act abusively – and many on the receiving end still choose not to speak up, to avoid endangering future work prospects.

A fellow Australian had seen me in a production of *Act Without Words*, and recommended a mime teacher. More by chance than design, the creative and production team for that show were all female. Given the difficulty today of gaining permission from the estate of Samuel Beckett to produce his work, I'm surprised that we were able to do the play at all. I know of female theatre makers who, in 2022, were denied permission to perform Beckett's works because of their gender.

Making up for *Three Women*. Photo: Patrick Bouillaud

Mime training provided a way to create work outside of the system of auditioning for plays. I loved the visual, sculptural focus of the form and the humbling physical aspect of the work. Etienne Decroux said the mime practitioner needed 'the body of a gymnast, the mind of an actor and the heart of a poet'. We were given a military physical fitness programme which I followed with deep commitment. In 1982, I discovered Robert Mapplethorpe's images of Lisa Lyon, the pioneer female bodybuilder who was exploring, as the *New York Times* said: 'new archetypes of femininity, different from the Marilyns and the Twiggys that had come before.' Louise Lecavalier of Quebecois dance troupe La La Human Steps with her stunning athleticism and blurring of gender norms was another thrilling inspiration. The practice of mime gave me a voice without words – a way to express, innovate and be visible, an agency in the creation of work and a stronger sense of physical self. It encouraged a sense of self-creation versus a self-sense diffused and dissociated due to shifting, internalised lenses of objectification, expectation and stereotype. A fellow mime school student said, 'I feel sorry for you, because you're ambitious and you're a woman so you are not going to find it easy.'

I was a co-founder of Three Women Mime and for a short while we used the tagline: 'Britain's first all-female mime company'. Mime is a niche form and vulnerable to populist derision. Done badly, or taken out of context, it can be ludicrous. It was a first that no one apart from we three (Tesa Schneideman, Claudia Prietzel and myself) noted or celebrated. However, we won an award in Edinburgh and were invited to perform at the London International Mime Festival, and festivals in Barcelona and Denmark. We toured the UK small-scale theatre circuit and with the British Council to Germany. We also made the cover of *Time Out* (1982).

We wanted to enjoy innovating and subverting the form of mime and we wanted to explore and express women's perspectives and issues. And to have fun doing that in an accessible way. I am a believer in the nudge-power of the Absurd and the subversive and unifying powers of humour.

The Arts Council of England put great emphasis on the importance of marketing and audience building – the word 'feminist' was considered alienating, so we never used it, although I did mention I was a feminist in a *Time Out* interview. In this new century, I discovered that Camden People's Theatre ran a Feminist Theatre Festival and in that moment, I experienced a strange combination of celebration and chagrin at lost possibility.

Three Women created shows composed of short pieces. We dealt with negative self-image, motherhood, eating disorders, domesticity (*The Housewives' Circus*) and more. In one early piece, a screen masked our upper bodies while we used our legs from mid-thigh down to show multiple interactions including a little girl defeating a flasher and a mother struggling to walk because of a chain of small shoes dragging after her. In the days before children's books routinely featured assertive girl characters with agency, we re-wrote a classic tale: Bra-barella. We used undergarments in inventive ways and subverted the trope of a woman's fulfilment by the arrival of a prince. We satirised old-school corporate manhood in *Businessmen*. A show called *Follies Berserk* took a look at unhelpful female stereotypes in entertainment. Some pieces used the abstract and grotesque rather than levity – there were two different pieces dealing with rape: *Ask Any Woman* and *Walking Home.* One audience member said these pieces helped him understand his girlfriend's problem with catcalling. Some pieces mixed up flavours: one portrayed a woman doing a striptease while wearing a baby harness and followed through with the baby's limbs being twisted off and discarded.

A special collaboration with director Hilary Westlake produced a piece called *Wounds* about sexuality, and with 'archetypal references to the symbolic wounds of femininity', as *The Guardian* reviewer said in 1983. They also praised the work for its 'nonverbal wit and pungent comment' and said we used mime 'as a dramatic weapon.'

In 1983, I decided to become a solo performer. I continued experimenting with different ways to combine movement, text and poor-theatre design, and to subvert or retell stories and share overlooked points of view. Wanting to write about success, I turned to Shakespeare's *Macbeth* and wrote *The Porter's Daughter* (1991). I wanted to question what is valued, and I wanted to show a female protagonist who was abused but who survives. Then for Fife Youth Dance (a remarkable initiative by Royston Muldoom and Tamara McLorg), I created *She Is Moving* for a group of 18 young women with imagery of traditional roles of care-taking evolving into an expression of united presence and strength.

A series of changes in my life and living circumstances and a cessation of funding support greatly reduced the amount of work I created post 1996. I abandoned theatre making completely for several years and turned towards the corporate field, but I returned. My autobiographical trilogy,

*Topless* (1999), *Midriff* (2002) and *Chastity Belt* (2011) respectively dealt with divorce and breast cancer, reaching midlife and challenging the role of 'good daughter', ageing, violence and war.

As a solo artist, my work lacks a dimension of diversity, but when teaching or directing ensembles, I aim to use best practices of inclusion and intersectionality. In my speciality work on the Dark Clown (a genre I developed to stretch the expressive range of the Red Nose Clown and to provide a way for Clown practice to deal with dark content), I focus on oppressed humanity and humanity in extremis. A few Black course participants have reported that they have found the Dark Clown work to be a useful support as they approach their examination and theatrical expression of colonial trauma.

I have always made work out of problems and obsessions, while aiming simultaneously to entertain. My latest performance work is *Parker Dee: Sensitive Guy* – both a digital project and a live, sung drag show with a story arc. This deeply flawed, yet well-intentioned character, with his online videos such as *Manspreader, Mansplainer* and *Sissy my Cis* is my current exploration of issues such as the complexities around consent in contemporary feminism.

≈

**Peta Lily** is well-known for her solo works: *Wendy Darling* (cited in *The Road to the Never Land* by R.D.S. Jack); *Beg!* (cited in *Feminist Stages: Interviews with Women in Contemporary British Theatre* by Lizbeth Goodman and Jane De Gay); *Chastity Belt* features in Lois Norman's award-winning documentary *She is Juiced* (Tate Britain 2017). Early work is cited in: *Mime into Physical Theatre: A UK Cultural History* by Mark Evans and Simon Murray.

She teaches at RADA and RCSSD and leads independent theatre workshops. She has written three plays: *The Porter's Daughter, Random Oracle* and *Blame.* Lily has developed a new genre: *Dark Clown* cited in Jon Davison's *Clown* (Readings in Theatre Practice) Palgrave MacMillan 2013. Award-winning documentary maker Robert Golden made a short film about the work titled *Peta Lily's Dark Clown: Taking Laughter to the Limits.* Lily's latest project features a drag king persona Parker Dee.

Roberta Livingston alongside fellow performer Jessica Manu on the set of *Where The Bugaboo Lives* at the Little Angel Theatre

# INTERVIEW WITH ROBERTA LIVINGSTON

**What does feminism mean to you?**

Choice. To choose the life you exactly want to live. From being a stay-at -home mum to a full/part time career gal to doing it all. For me, feminism is being free from the restrictions of what a woman's life 'should look like'. I feel equality can be lived when we live our chosen paths free from judgement and outdated expectations. It also means ensuring female theatre makers are getting the same opportunities as their male counterparts.

**How has feminism influenced your work?**

I've gravitated to a lot of brilliant stories where the main protagonists have been male and I always ask why couldn't this character be a woman? And usually it's because many believe male characters are the default option. I was raised by a single mother and had a very close relationship with my grandmother so matriarchy is all I'd experienced growing up and I feel that hugely influences my writing. So naturally when I create stories, my main protagonist is always a woman. I'm consciously trying to push women's stories and experiences to the front.

**Has the content of your work changed over time?**

Yes because as I'm getting older I simply have less f's to give. I'm trying not to concern myself too much on what 'theatres want' but what I want. I always come from the perspective that as an avid theatre-goer, if I feel there is something missing from these stages, I will write those stories myself. An artist who constantly tries to please others is only disarming herself. As women, it is instilled in us quite early on to please people and I say we quit that BS. In saying that, I'm still trying to master that myself. When I'm writing I still get that little voice in my head that says "maybe that's too much" or "maybe theatres won't like that" so I'm trying to ignore that voice and stick to my truth.

**Do you feel that women have achieved equality in theatre?**

I think there are women who have climbed mountains to achieve tremendous accolades in theatre, some of these pioneers have written in this very book. I think we've come a long way but we've still got a long, long way to go. Especially in terms of women of colour, our trans sisters, queer women and women with disabilities. For me, equality can't be achieved until I'm seeing those women in particular get their flowers. This equality needs to start from the ground up, not just the actors, writers or directors but also the designers, artistic directors, executive directors, I think theatre has relied heavily on tokenism and disguised it as equality.

**Have you experienced sex bias while working in theatre?**

What I find interesting is how I've been fortunate enough to participate in writers groups and various schemes for emerging theatre makers and I've noticed the careers of my male peers have accelerated considerably faster than my female peers and I think that says a lot within itself. Don't get me wrong, a lot of my male peers are incredibly gifted but it's just an interesting observation I've noticed.

**What would improve the opportunities for women working in theatre today?**

I think gatekeepers and those who make executive decisions in theatres need to look over their programming and observe whether it's serving female theatre makers at our fullest potential. I also believe a genuine higher belief in our work could make a shift, there are plenty of men out there who have written sub-par theatre and we are told to believe that it's "good" work. Also allowing space for us to fail will help, we are so petrified of failing because only a certain amount of women actually get through the door and we don't want to blow our chance.

**Does intersectionalism influence your work?**

As a Black woman, I'm constantly exploring the intersection between my race and gender so naturally that shines through my work. This intersectionality inspires me to think of stories Black women are not necessarily placed in, and it encourages me to think outside the box, and present people with the unexpected. The downside to that is that I've met some resistance because it isn't the so-called Black trauma play that a lot of theatres tend to love and yes those types of plays are important in portraying the struggle we face but my artistry right now, is focusing more on other ways we can centre Black stories.

**Do you collaborate with other groups?**

Whether that's writing or performing, I've been fortunate enough to collaborate with many female-led companies from Polly Creed's company Power Play, to Sarah Brigham's Derby Theatre. From working with these women and so many others, it has revitalised my faith in what is possible for female artists in theatre. In fact, the show I did at Derby Theatre was a family show that had been done many times before, however this particular production was going to be special. For one reason, the show was going to have integrated BSL and the second being, I was the first woman to play the lead role of the character that had always been male. At the time I wasn't aware that there had been any reservation of me playing a male role but I'm glad my director, the incredible Emily Howlett, stuck to her guns, as when the audiences, particularly the children, came to see the show, they didn't care that I was a girl playing a role that was intended to be a boy. They just came for a good story. That experience will stay with me as it not only taught me how to be an effective creative leader like Emily Howlett but it also taught me to always consider how I can make theatre more accessible to communities such as the D/deaf community who are often overlooked too.

**Do we need a dedicated women's theatre?**

I think that could be a valuable resource for female theatre makers to feel supported, safe and unapologetic in their processes. The same way Talawa Theatre Company was created to address the imbalance of Black work in British theatre, the same could be done for women. I think

In NT dressing room during the run of *Small Island*

it'll help a lot of women who haven't reached their full potential and are seeking a place to find it.

## Do we still need feminism?

Without a doubt. The events that have occurred over the recent years from #MeToo to Sarah Everard have categorically highlighted that we still need feminism. If feminism isn't implemented into the structure of our society, how can we expect it to be integrated within theatre? We are still being overlooked and under-appreciated. There is plenty of work to be done but I have faith that the women who have contributed to this book and beyond will be at the forefront of making the changes we yearn for. Plenty of incredible women have already started this work, we just need to make sure it continues.

≈

Photo: Olivia Spencer

**Roberta Livingston** is writer and performer of Caribbean heritage from East London. As a performer her credits include *Dear Elizabeth* (Gate Theatre), *Small Island* (National Theatre) and *Where The Bugaboo Lives* (Little Angel Theatre). She is the co-founder of Speaks of Rivers a Black female-led theatre company dedicated to telling stories for young audiences. As a writer she has written for Talawa Theatre Company, The Mono Box and Radio 4. She has also participated in writers groups with Tamasha Theatre Company and the Almeida Theatre. She's a recipient of the BFI Young Audiences Content Fund and participated in BBC Writersroom London Voices.

# ECOFEMINISM IN THEATRE
## BIBI LUCILLE

Four years ago, I had a boyfriend. We were walking home from a night of heavy drinking in London when he brought up the topic of the news – something he often liked to discuss and I often liked to avoid, as I found the emotional strain of daily news too much to bear on a regular basis. Despite this, perhaps to provoke a reaction, he mentioned it anyway:

'Did you hear about the oil spill in Brazil?'

Against my better judgement and partially wine-fuelled, I burst into tears. My partner then spent the next hour comforting me as I sobbed about the state of the world, the unfathomable indifference and complete disrespect that humans have for Mother Nature and the inevitability of our eventual demise. There was something deeply disturbing about the image of powerful men digging holes into the earth, destroying all the life it had created and halting all the life that was yet to be lived – all for the sake of corporate greed. The constant attack on the earth felt like the ongoing abuse of women's bodies.

There is no question that the earth is inherently female: to birth life, to create climates that cultivate sentience, the cycles and seasons that align perfectly with a woman's uterus. Women and the environment are so deeply connected that the injustice of a patriarchal society creeps seamlessly from one to the other. Despite its intimidatingly 'woke' name, ecofeminism offers a way of understanding these links and fighting against the injustices that bleed both women and Mother Nature dry.

Three years ago, I wrote *Meat Cute*, a one-person tragi-comedy about a woman who desperately fights for the rights of animals and the environment by using the one feminine quality she knows how to weaponise best – sex. For as long as humans have gained consciousness, the female body has been labelled an asset. Whether this asset is something to be shamed and covered, or celebrated and displayed, a woman's anatomy has existed as a commodity for exploitation.

In recent years, there has been a dramatic shift in western pop-culture. In the 50s, we saw a celebration of female modesty in the arts, with 'tasteful' gowns and barely a kiss in a Humphrey Bogart romance. As rebellious hippies and the birth control pill took hold of the West in the 60s, women enjoyed greater sexual freedom, with less risk of unwanted pregnancy. This has allowed women to compete more equally in the workplace with men but it has come with emotional and psychological stress.

In productons of Michaela Cole's *Chewing Gum Dreams* and Phoebe Waller-Bridge's *Fleabag,* messy, selfish and morally confused young women take to the stage. In *Fleabag* we see the protagonist's selfish nature leading her down a dark path. Celebrated for its candour and sagacious substance, the 'messy woman' became its own fresh trope. The beauty of this trope was down to the sheer rawness of being a woman and laying bare the darkest parts of our natures that have been shunned for too long. Fringe theatre has provided a platform for women to show that the essence of womanhood had nothing to do with our bodies, but lays in all the dark corners we have tried, for centuries, to hide.

In music, performers such as Madonna, and Lady Gaga, decided to reclaim ownership of their bodies and use these 'assets' to obtain power and fame. I have always been fascinated and somewhat thrilled by the idea of fictional characters weaponising and manipulating the very thing that oppresses them. Lena, the protagonist in *Meat Cute,* refuses to be shamed for her sexual attractiveness and, in turn, uses it on behalf of her mission to convert men to veganism.

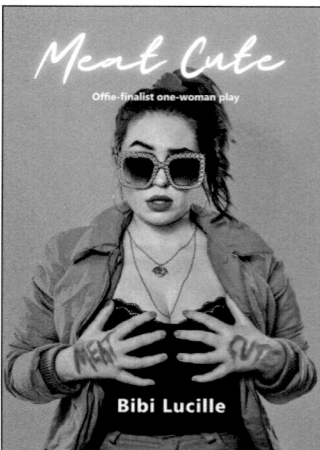

When writing *Meat Cute,* I felt the wonderful catharsis of writing a woman without a filter. Someone who was complex and strange and completely unafraid of her own sexuality, but essentially someone who was desperate to just be *good.* As Lena is revealed as a deeply flawed person, she attempts to stay true to her ethics and is plagued by the female burden of empathy. Lena represents the idea that merely existing as an empathetic woman is to suffer, as we are forced to navigate an indifferent society. By the end of the play, she has given up and

Bibi Lucille performs *Meat Cute*

sits in front of an oncoming truck full of live farm animals, all heading towards their inevitable death. Her instincts to care for other sentient beings and fight against injustice are what eventually drive her to insanity, as we have seen many times before in the history of women.

As of late, the trope of 'female rage' and the fight for justice have found a home in theatre, with many artists using the platform to address moral quandaries and try to influence how we should treat our fellow humans. Most female rage that is depicted in art is fuelled by frustration for a lack of empathy or understanding in the other characters they encounter. It is not uncommon to watch a story where the woman is being psychologically poked and prodded, which is what drives them to an eventual outburst. Nature and the environment are no different. As the earth has been continually goaded, it has fought back. With sea-levels rising and the climate changing, Mother Nature is flushed and losing her patience. Men continue to dominate her land, strip her of precious oils and make her a commodity. This behaviour can either break a woman, or turn her into a monster.

The need for action has been shunned by government and industry, with many young men remaining cold and removed from the pressing issues of climate change. Suppressing their worries, they fight a losing battle, as these can only lead to anxiety and misery. The continuing exploitation of fossil fuels for short-term gain offers no solution for future generations. This is where the arts can help. Theatre creates windows in which we can glance into a person's life, understand the bigger picture and feel hopeful of change.

Growing up, the small theatre I trained in felt like a place untouched by reality. Men and women were equal, nobody cared how old you were, and humanity was the god we all collectively worshipped. Going out into the 'real' world was where my dream of the theatre shattered. Working under the constant duress of a (much older) male director proved to me that feminism barely touched the surface of the arts and how desperately it needed to change. Nearly a decade later, society has shifted and my naivety has subsided, allowing me to clearly see the warning signs of an un-feminist production. Occasionally, I find myself feeling the comfort I once had as a teenager, where the men and women I encounter in stage work are equally as horrified by the patriarchy and injustice that breeds in the arts. But nothing is black and white. Some productions are still plagued by hierarchical gender-fuelled structures, whereas some exist in equality and praise fairness. Feminism will always be needed and although there are many theatre companies which respect equality, diversity and inclusion, there are more which do not.

The fight for feminism and the fight for sustainability and climate change mitigation are so intrinsically linked, it's important for artists to understand the great need to fight for both. The continuing abuse and attack on our planet is a feminist issue and requires us to fight against widespread injustice and corporate greed.

Bibi Lucille performs *Meat Cute*

Theatre helps us to accept and celebrate all human emotion, creating the perfect platform to rally for change and social justice. As artists, we must offer the shoes for our audience to walk in, so we can encourage empathy and lead with love.

≈

**Bibi Lucille** is an award-winning actress, having won the Starnow award for Rising Star and the Women of the Future award (2021) for her contribution to Arts and Culture. She studied acting at Questor's Youth Theatre in Ealing before beginning her professional career at the age of 19 with a lead role in Noel Coward's *This Was a Man* in the West End. She returned to Leicester Square Theatre for a lead role in *Lipstick and Scones* before a month-long run at the Edinburgh Fringe. Other roles include Lady Anne in *Richard III* (Baron's Court) and Jane Watson in the UK tour of *Hound of the Baskervilles* (London Mayor's Choice 2018).

Screen credits include: *All Inclusive* which won first prize at the 48hr Sci-Fi Film Festival and garnered Bibi a 'Best Actress' nomination at the Pastel Film Festival. She then went on to star in Popstar! TV's *Purgatory* and Amazon Prime's *Trust.* She gained a cult following from the indie web-series *I Am Sophie* which won first prize at the BAFTA and Oscar-qualifying Flicker's RIFF film festival.

Following the pandemic, Lucille began writing her first play, *Meat Cute* (Aurora Metro). Following its debut at The Chiswick Playhouse and Camden Fringe, the play gained critical acclaim and became a finalist at the Offies Awards.

Aida Leventaki, Caroline Strange, Mary Mallen in *Belfast Girls* at the Francis J. Greenburger Mainstage, Irish Repertory Theatre, New York, 2022. Photo: Carol Rosegg

# THE THIRD WORLD OF IRISH WOMEN

## Feminist Theatre in Ireland, Past and Present

## JAKI MCCARRICK

Four members of the Women's Social and Political Union (WSPU) – Mary Leigh, Gladys Evans, Lizzie Baker and Mabel Capper – travelled to Dublin from the UK in July 1912 to carry out a violent campaign in support, as they saw it, of their fellow militant suffragists, the Irish Women's Franchise League (IWFL). Their activism included: throwing an axe at the head of Prime Minister Herbert Asquith, who was visiting Ireland at the time to discuss the twice defeated Home Rule Bill with Irish MP John Redmond – whose head (or ear, to be precise) the axe actually reached – and an arson attack on Dublin's Theatre Royal, during a packed show with Asquith in attendance. The women were arrested and subsequently jailed for a number of years. Rather than welcoming this militant support from their English sisters, the Irish suffragists were appalled by their actions. As Sharon Crozier-De Rosa states in her essay on the differences between Irish and British feminism, *Divided Sisterhood? Nationalist feminism and feminist militancy in England and Ireland*, the IWFL's disapproval of the WSPU activities in Dublin was due to two key factors: the fear of unsettling already strained Unionist and Nationalist relations, and because most of the militant suffragists in Ireland were in support of the Nationalist cause and were horrified at the prospect of a further defeat for Home Rule.

In their formation, the Irish suffragists would have taken their cue not just from the Pankhursts and the WSPU but also from the activities of the Ladies' Land League, founded by Anna Parnell, sister of Charles Stewart Parnell, three decades before. The Ladies' Land League assumed the functions of the Irish Land League once its founder Michael Davitt and other leaders were imprisoned in 1879. This organisation grew rapidly and had over 300 branches, including several in the US.

Dr Tina O'Toole states that the group "may be seen as a paradigm shift: the moment when 'New' possibilities for Irish women begin to emerge."[1] As Crozier-De Rosa explains, the connections between Irish and British feminists were strong but with the crucial difference of Irish Independence:

> Indeed, to observers at the time, it surely seemed that both campaigns were inextricably linked. Both movements were, of course, embedded within the left-wing political cultures of their respective countries. The WSPU grew out of the British Labour movement … the IWFL was located at the radical end of the left-wing spectrum, advocating as it did, not only radical feminism – but Irish nationalism.

WSPU leader Emmeline Pankhurst was a staunch supporter of keeping the Union together, which was completely at odds with the hopes of Irish feminists (such as Hanna Sheehy Skeffington and her husband Francis – who was executed in 1916). The IWFL was further encouraged to militancy by the activism of Countess Markievicz, the first woman to be elected to the British Parliament, though she did not take her seat. De-Rosa states: "Markievicz's main aim was to cajole Irish women into arming in support of nationalist politics." Hence, as suffrage and nationalism in Ireland are intertwined historically, in many respects Irish feminism is of a different order to feminisms elsewhere, which in turn are determined by the societies from which they emerge.

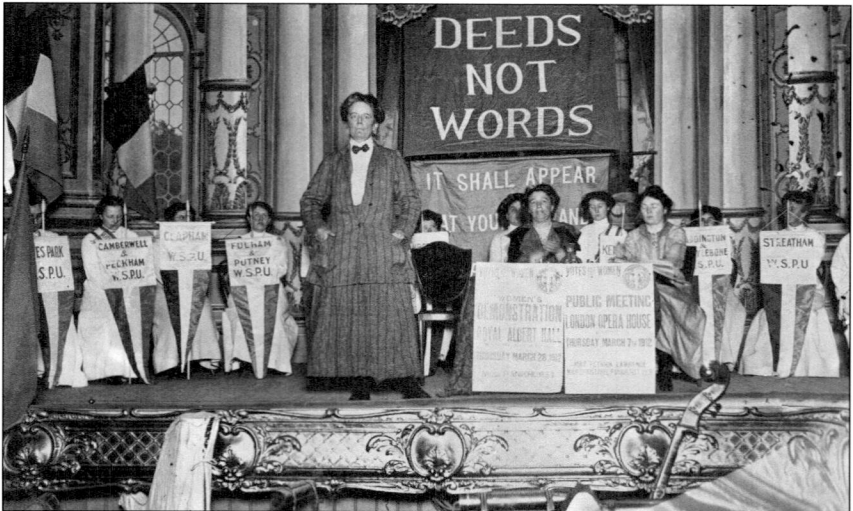

Ethel Smyth *(centre)* at a meeting of the WSPU in 1912

---

1 Following the freeing of the male leadership, the Ladies' wing of the Land League was disbanded in 1882.

What the Irish suffragists were not to realise was, that as soon as the liberation of Ireland from the Empire (minus, crucially, six counties of Ulster) took place, after decades of activism, from the Ladies' Land League to militant suffragists to the organisation Cumann na mBan (an all-female Republican paramilitary group) of which my own grandmother was a member, within two decades they and all Irish women would be pushed as far down the pecking order of Irish society as is possible to be pushed. Their militancy would be ended, their status diminished, their activism barely recalled, their enormous contribution to Independence neglected, and in some instances erased, and all of this was sealed into the De Valera Constitution of 1937 (whereby, for instance, married women could not work for the civil service or any public or semi-state body). The full contribution of the Ladies' Land League, for example, whose work involved the tireless writing of pamphlets, newspapers, raising funds to look after prisoners' wives and families, has not yet been fully examined (the records of the Ladies' Land League were – rather conveniently one might say – lost in a fire in Dublin in 1916). Addressing this neglect of such important work, Faith Binckes and Kathryn Laing, authors of a monograph on writer and one-time elected Secretary for the London branch of the Ladies' Land League, Hannah Lynch (*Hannah Lynch (1859-1904): Irish Writer, Cosmopolitan, New Woman*) state:

> Countering the neglect of the Ladies' Land League both in the immediate aftermath of its demise and subsequent histories of the period, recent studies agree that it was an extraordinary and highly significant organisation. It has been described as 'a crucial first link in a chain of female political agency which stretches forward into the early twentieth century to connect with other feminist nationalist and suffragist organizations such as *Inghinidhe na hÉireann* and *Cumann na mBan*.

Hence, to all intents and purposes, the nationalist project in Ireland betrayed the women who helped achieve it and, in turn, all Irish women, for the best part of a century. The English suffragists might well have said, I told you so, if it weren't for the fact that the WSPU itself disbanded in 1914 in order to support the war effort and British nationalism (the Empire) abroad. Although suffrage continued in the UK after the war.

Thus followed in Ireland many decades of the much-documented subjugation of women by the colluding forces of State and Church, which would claim complete dominance over the female body and the female in society generally. This system of control has been referred to as "the Taliban" by author Rosita Sweetman, and also by Fr. Roy Donovan, a priest from Limerick (while bemoaning the lack of female representation in the clergy) – such is the chokehold it has had over Irish women's lives for so long. There isn't the space here to cover all the horrors inflicted during this period upon Irish women but they include: abuse meted out in institutional structures such as the Magdalene Laundries, mother and baby homes, industrial and reformatory schools, mental asylums (what James Smith refers to as Ireland's "architecture of containment"[2]), as well as interventions such as forced adoptions and forced seizure of children. Irish women have had no abortion rights and no rights of divorce until relatively recently. By now, most people will have heard of the Bon Secours mother and baby home in Tuam, Galway, in which 796 children are believed to have been buried in a septic tank. The last mother and baby home in Ireland closed its doors as recently as 1996; hence many of these abuses are in living memory for a number of Irish women.

This is the context in which Feminist Theatre in Ireland must be seen. It has been witness to a committed, loyal activism swiftly followed by the State's betrayal and decades of neglect and oppression. What do I mean by *Feminist* Theatre? This F word, like the people it vouches for (women), would seem not to have a fixed, permanent value. It is a variable word that changes with the times and is required to perform different functions as the times change. That is its strength: it can accommodate change and multiple circumstances. Feminist Theatre, then, takes different forms in different places, and in Ireland – nationalism, colonialism, post-colonialism, economics and the entire history of the country are in its bloodstream.

Lady Gregory

At the formation of the Irish Literary Theatre in 1899, which later gave rise to the Irish National Theatre Society (and then the Abbey) in 1904 – women playwrights were both active and visible on the Irish stage. Lady Augusta Gregory *(left)*, who founded and ran the Abbey with Yeats for 25 years (often her contribution is overlooked) wrote over 19 plays and many translations, most of which were staged. Her play *The Workhouse*

2   James Smith, Ireland's Magdalene Laundries: and the Nation's Architecture of Containment (Notre Dame, Indiana, 2007)

*Ward* for instance, performed at the Abbey Theatre in 1908, is an expertly plotted one-act play with Pinter-like rhythms and recalls Synge in its musicality. In his essay *The Stifled Voice*, Christopher Murray writes: "In the beginning, even before Lady Gregory began as a playwright in 1902 … to be a woman was no obstacle to success in the Irish Theatre in the early years of this century, when the theatre movement was but part of a broadly based cultural revolution in which women played a significant part. Thus, one could name Winifred M. Letts, Geraldine Cummins, Susanne Day and Joanna Redmond … Lady Gregory is, however a special case." In the years immediately after Independence, there were plays staged in Irish theatres by women such as Teresa Deevey, Mairead Ni Ghrada, Mary Manning, Christine Longford and later, Maura Laverty. While Laverty's plays *Liffey Lane* and *Tolka Row* are reputed to have saved the Gate Theatre from closure, records show that Laverty was usually the last to be paid by directors Michael MacLiammor and Ernest Blythe, and that she had to chase them for payment.

The decline in female voices on Irish stages begins in earnest from the late-1930s onwards. After Maura Laverty's plays at the Gate, this theatre did not stage a single play by a woman for 30 years. The Abbey proved no better. It seems that after 50 years of suffrage and campaigning for Independence, Irish female dramatists (and Irish women generally) found themselves in a much worse position. Nonetheless, from the 1950s onwards women's voices – while still glaringly absent from the main stages in the country – were beginning to be heard on the margins; in town halls, small theatres and bars.

In his seminal new work, *Theatre and Archival Memory: Irish Drama and Marginalised Histories 1951–1977*, Barry Houlihan pays close attention to some of these marginalised Irish women dramatists, and to plays more generally that have been crucial to the development of Irish theatre but more usually excluded from the canon. He refers to Dan Rabellato's argument that the 1950s was a far more vital and creative period in UK theatre than is generally considered, and suggests the same may be said for Irish theatre, despite the many social and state-imposed constrictions of this time.

Houlihan considers three plays by Irish women, which either received marginal productions in the post-Emergency[3] period, or whose receptions were fairly vicious: *The Millstone* (1951) by Carolyn Swift,

3 In Ireland, "The Emergency" is the name given to the years of World War Two, in which Ireland was neutral.

*An Triail* by Mairead Ni Ghrada (1964, 1973), and *A Pagan Place* by Edna O'Brien (1972, 1977), adapted by O'Brien from her novel of the same name. I will touch on just two of these works here.

Carolyn Swift's play *The Millstone* – which to date remains unpublished – was the first production for the Pike Theatre, and opened in September 1954. It concerns the forced adoption of children from mother and baby homes in Ireland, mostly to the US, an issue that remains extremely contentious in Ireland. In the second act of the play, a character states:

> These children become the property of the state – the Free State … a bloody labour camp, that's what this country is. We've been manufacturing world labour for a hundred years solid. Every goddamn factory here is foreign, employin' cheap Irish labour. They put 'made in the Republic of Ireland' on the stuff and we're away, we have an Irish industry. Do they think we're gob loons or something? Kathleen Ni Houlihan (Ireland) Ltd?

Such lines brought Swift much criticism in an already censorious time in Irish arts (with books banned and "watch committees" sent to observe the moral standards of theatre performances), though the attention confirmed The Pike Theatre as the locus of cutting-edge theatre in the country, a reputation it had until its closure in 1957. Despite the opprobrium Swift received from critics and audiences alike, Houlihan states that:

> Swift continually pushed the boundaries of Irish dramatic repertoires, and through her artistic vision for a new and modern Irish Theatre, one that was influenced by international cosmopolitan thinking and form.

Of her play *A Pagan Place* – staged at the Abbey in 1977 – Edna O'Brien said, "in terms of overall perception, I think in high echelons women are still regarded as being a bit lower down the table. The male voice is perceived differently, and regarded higher by both men and sometimes women." This play, about a young nun who recalls her youth in Ireland, including a sexual assault by a priest, was also received negatively by Irish critics, while garnering a warm reception at the Royal Court in London a few years before. Houlihan states that these neglected dramatists and "their collected body of work … presents an alternative national drama that subverted constitutionally prescribed domestic roles for Irish women."

The 1980s and 1990s provided an improved landscape for women's theatre writing, with works by Marina Carr, Emma Donoghue, Gina Moxley produced in Dublin. In Northern Ireland, plays by Marie Jones

Poster for Opening Night, 1904

(Charabanc Theatre Company), Anne Devlin (whose play *After Easter* I saw and loved at the Almeida Theatre in London), and Christina Reid, also made their mark. While this was a creative time in Ireland, it was also a period of mass emigration as a result of a recession that lasted for two decades – until the arrival of the infamous "Celtic Tiger". I myself left Ireland for London during this time.

When the TLS asked me to review Charlotte Headrick and Eileen Kearney's *Irish Women Dramatists* in 2015, I researched the commissioning of female playwrights in Irish theatre companies. According to Patrick Lonergan, Professor of Drama and Theatre Studies at NUI Galway, since the new Abbey Theatre building opened in Dublin in 1966 until 2015, there had been five plays on the main Abbey stage written by women compared to approximately 320 plays by men. The Abbey's smaller Peacock Theatre has staged comparatively more work from Irish female playwrights. These are revealing statistics but they are in keeping with statistics on the commissioning of female playwrights in the UK and US. In a feature for *The Guardian* (2015), in which she laments the lack of female writers with plays on in the West End and on the larger UK stages, Ellie Horne writes "the writing is on the wall: big spaces are for men, while the smaller spaces associated with risk are where the work of female playwrights is far more likely to be seen." So, clearly, while mainstream Irish companies have a lamentable record in staging the work of female writers – so too does the UK. In a later 2020 study, conducted by Sphinx Theatre Company and playwright Jennifer Tuckett, the gender gap in UK theatre had not improved. And while it would seem gender parity in American theatre has improved, again this is not a fixed situation.

The Waking the Feminists campaign that formed in Ireland in 2016 acted as a vital pressure group, and urged Irish theatres to stage more plays by women. While the immediate reaction to this campaign was lively and positive, it remains to be seen if Irish theatre companies will listen on a more permanent basis. After all, as Susan Sontag states in her essay *The Third World of Women*, "the liberation of women will be at the expense of male privilege." Liberation is not about equality, she claims, but *power*.

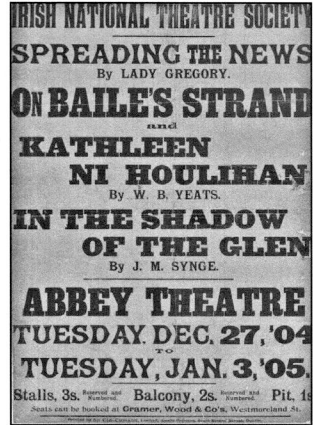

Protest for justice for survivors of the Magdalene Laundries. Photo: William Murphy/Flickr

While there are many excellent Irish female dramatists working today, many of whom have had plays staged in the UK[4] and US, their national celebration is far from the attention currently bestowed on Irish female writers of prose and poetry (Sally Rooney, Elaine Feeney, Louise Kennedy et al). Irish female dramatists simply do not get the equivalent chances to shine, in terms of productions in Ireland, at least; I should know, I write both prose and plays and getting a play on (in Ireland or the UK) is infinitely harder than getting prose published.

In terms of Feminist Theatre companies in Ireland, along the lines, say, of London's Sphinx Theatre Company (formerly the Women's Theatre Group), with whom I worked in 2008 when they presented a reading of one of my plays at the Soho Theatre, these are mostly fringe entities and are short-lived. The most well-known feminist theatre company in Ireland is probably Charabanc, founded in Belfast in 1983 and disbanded in 1995. (Though the company claim they were neither feminist nor socialist, they have often been considered both).

Just as suffragism and militant feminism in Ireland has been historically linked to nationalism, in more recent years, some plays by Irish female dramatists have turned their gaze to the State, and are written from a stance of sharp criticism of it. Such works include: *Eclipsed* (1988), written by Patricia Burke Brogan, a groundbreaking work and one of the first pieces of Irish drama (or fiction) to expose the scandal

---

4 On a recent attachment to the National Theatre in London, I shared an office floor with another female Irish dramatist, also on attachment to the National.

of the Magdalene Laundries, *Heritage* (1998) by Nicola McCartney, the aforementioned *The Millstone* by Carolyn Swift, *Twinkletoes* (1993) by Jennifer Johnston – and a number of others. There is a century of oppression to work through, after all, and the various traumas that have resulted from this surely need extensive airing. This daring to criticise the State, the past, the position of women in society, is why I believe many theatres in Ireland have been slow to commission plays by women (I find the reason often given – "they're not good enough" to be spurious; many plays by women find excellent homes outside the country). Could it be that subsidised theatres do not want to produce work that criticises the hand that feeds them? Many plays by writers mentioned in this essay have premiered abroad; some have never been staged in Ireland at all.

It might also be argued that these admonishments of the State from female Irish writers – is what makes them feminist. While until recently, any play written and staged by a woman in Ireland was a feminist act in itself, now it would seem neglectful of theatre writers not to query the past. Today, feminist drama writing and feminist theatre (in Ireland at least) surely must critique the very State that has oppressed women for so long, to address its past and present transgressions.

Like much of the West, Ireland is now a neoliberalist economy, a system of capitalism that has also not delivered for 21$^{st}$ century women. Feminist drama today, then, must surely comment on this also. Female writers/directors/theatre makers currently operate within this neoliberalist system, which has been in place pretty much since the Thatcherite 1980s, and not to critique it in some way is to accept the status quo. What do I mean by neoliberalism? Well, a system of essentially free market capitalism, laissez-faire even, which purports to allow for freedom but in reality, for women at least, today means: a 15+% pay gap in many Western countries, costly childcare, discrimination across the board, including in the arts, unaffordable housing for many, being thrust to the margins in any kind of societal crisis, be it a recession or a pandemic.[5]

In 21$^{st}$-century neoliberalist Ireland, domestic violence figures are at

---

5 Alexandra Topping writes, "The specific needs of women are not on anyone's agenda right now … Women are being treated as "sacrificial lambs" as the UK economy contracts, with half of working mothers unable to access the childcare they need to return to work." *The Guardian,* 24.07.2020

a record high. In Northern Ireland there is a domestic violence incident every 16 minutes. Ireland has the highest domestic homicide figures in Europe. Neoliberalism today has arguably made the working classes' lives much harder and the lives of working class women harder still, while it has made the top 1% richer.

Most of my own plays are critical of the Irish State, or status quo, or some aspect of Irish society. My play *Leopoldville*, both the male and female versions, seeks to argue much the same point the playwright Edward Bond makes in his 1965 play *Saved* – that if there is brutality at the top, in the form of wars and colonialism, then you cannot be surprised by violence on the streets, from people disenfranchised from the system or who are victims of it. Like children, people learn from the society they live in. In *The Naturalists* (Aurora Metro), I interrogate the hollow promises of nationalism, which rarely delivers, as we can see from the history of Irish suffragists. In my first play *The Mushroom Pickers*, the lost and broken Republican activist Frank is the one who offers the protagonist Laura a way out of her self-suppression. My play *Belfast Girls* blames Church and State for the trafficking of women to colonial Australia in the 19th century, under the guise of helping them. In my new play *All the Stars are Bleeding*, set on the Irish border, I explore the connection between the Troubles and the aforementioned high rate of domestic violence in Northern Ireland. Most of my plays have been staged, though rarely in Ireland, and in the case of *Belfast Girls*, by primarily feminist theatre companies, such as Artemisia of Chicago, who premiered the play in the US in 2015.

There is still a long way to go in terms of presenting female stories on Irish stages. While audiences are overwhelmingly female, in Ireland we still mostly sit and watch plays by men and view their versions of women. Because of that, I would welcome more (or any!) all-female theatres and theatre companies, quotas, and anything else that will stop a slide back to a time when the voices of female dramatists on Irish stages fell resoundingly silent.

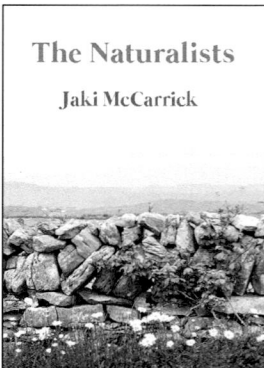

The Naturalists

Jaki McCarrick

**Jaki McCarrick** is an award-winning writer of plays, poetry and fiction. Winner of the Papatango Prize for New Writing for her play *Leopoldville*, Jaki's play *Belfast Girls* was developed at the National Theatre Studio, London, and has been staged many times internationally. Shortlisted for the Susan Smith-Blackburn Prize and the BBC Tony Doyle Award, *Belfast Girls* made its New York premiere at the Irish Repertory Theatre in 2022, and was staged again in New York in 2023 by the Irish Classical Theatre Company. In 2024 the play tours Ireland. Her play *The Naturalists* premiered in New York in 2018.

Jaki's plays have been published by Samuel French, Routledge and Aurora Metro and have been translated into Swedish and French.

Her debut fiction collection *The Scattering* was shortlisted for the 2014 Edge Hill Prize and includes the Wasafiri Prize-winning story, "The Visit". In 2020 Jaki was shortlisted for the An Post Book Awards Short Story of the Year Award (Ireland) for her short story *The Emperor of Russia.*

Jaki was Writer in Residence at the Centre Cultural Irlandais in Paris in 2013 and at the University of Leuven, Belgium, in 2022. She has written critical pieces for the *Times Literary Supplement, The Irish Examiner, Poetry Ireland Review* and other publications.

She has recently completed her debut novel *The bright, bright world* and is working on a new play.

*My Song Is Free* (1986) Maureen Morris *(back)*, Yolanda Vazquez *(front)*
Photo: Willoughby Gullachsen

# MONSTROUS REGIMENT
## MARY MCCUSKER

Monstrous Regiment Theatre Company was created in 1975 as a performers' collective by a group of professional actors and musicians who wanted to make exciting political theatre which put women's lives and experience centre stage. Between 1975 and 1993 the company produced 30 major shows, ranging in style from epic to surreal, straight play to cabaret. It was one of the most influential feminist theatre companies of its time. International in outlook, the company produced both new writing by young British playwrights and British premieres of work from Chile, Finland, France, Italy and the USA. Newly commissioned music was a feature of many shows. With financial support from the Arts Council (ACGB), it toured throughout Britain, reaching new audiences in clubs and community centres as well as mainstream theatres. It also performed at international festivals in Rome and Boston.

These words neatly sum up the 18 years when we were producing plays, starting in the 70s, when 'the Second Wave of feminism' carried us through the hard work, and on through the 80s and early 90s – the Thatcher years – when terms like "performers' collective", "feminism" and "theatrical vision" pushed up against business plans and commercial sponsorship.

### How we began

I was one of the women Gillian (Gillie) Hanna invited to a meeting in London in August 1975, to discuss the possibility of starting a new theatre company. We had all auditioned for the same small part in a show the radical theatre group Belt and Braces were taking on tour. Gillie, a member of the group, was amazed that so many talented women were interested in such a tiny part. So she decided to bring us all together. We didn't know each other, but by the end of the day we knew that like many other women in the 70s we were ready for change. Women were picking their way through the male landscape determined to live and work without being sucked into the traditional backing group smiling behind the men. And as performers we wanted parts in plays that reflected the richness of women's lives.

At that time (almost unbelievable today), there was just one woman lighting designer employed in the UK. There were very few female company managers, stage managers and technicians, and major theatres rarely produced work written or directed by women. We planned to change all that. It was simple. Men were not excluded, but there would always be (far) more women than men in the company and in any show we put on. This 'on stage' visibility principle would also apply 'off stage' to all the roles involved in producing and staging plays, including directors. And, of course, to writers – over the years we produced some plays written by men, but only a few.

At the following meetings we decided on further principles for how we would operate. We would set ourselves up as a performers' collective that prioritised new writing. This would give us, the performers, control over the company's work. All decisions would be shared, everyone would have a voice and be paid the same. Instead of an artistic director, it would be us who commissioned writers and hired directors and designers. Our work would be informed by our politics, but it would always be theatre, not agitprop. We were, first and foremost, professional actors (and musicians). Wherever possible, music would be an integral part of the shows.

By the end of 1975, the company had a name: Monstrous Regiment (in ironic reference to John Knox's 16th century pamphlet), and the writers for our first show, Claire Luckham and Chris Bond, were on board. Meanwhile, Chris Bowler, Gillie Hanna and I, had been given the task of getting funding for the company from the Arts Council and the Gulbenkian, and setting it up as a legal entity. Early in 1976, along with David Bradford, we started planning a tour for our first (and as yet unfinished) play.

## The first shows

In May 1976, just nine months after our first meeting, something special hit the stage at the Chapter Arts Centre in Cardiff. Five women and two men amidst boiling tubs of water – you could smell the laundry as soon as you entered the space. The story of the 1871 Paris Commune was being told, but this time with women laundry workers at its centre. This was *Scum*, directed by Susan (now Lily) Todd, with Andrea Montag's wonderful set that allowed the action to move seamlessly from laundry to barricades to hot Parisian streets, and Helen Glavin's stunning music.

We had said we would produce and perform work that met high theatrical standards, now we were out in the world and on stage doing just that. And more was to come very soon. *Vinegar Tom*, written for the company by Caryl Churchill, opened just a few months later, and was toured in tandem with *Scum* till July 1977, with (more or less) the same performers in both shows. Set in the 17th century world of witch trials, and directed by Pam Brighton, it again had terrific music by Helen Glavin. The songs were performed in modern dress, despite the play's setting. They were hard-hitting pieces that pinned the historical treatment of female bodies firmly to the present.

By the end of this (extended) year of touring we had clocked up nearly 130 performances at over 70 venues, spread across the country from Aberdeen to Exeter and many points between. As the figures imply, these were mostly one-nighters. This was exhausting, but also exhilarating, especially with such positive responses from audiences.

And we followed this up in 1977-78, with a tour of similar scale and pattern, and two more newly written shows, very different from the first two: Susan Todd and Ann Mitchell's *Kiss and Kill*, an experimental play about men, women and violence, and *Floorshow*, a cabaret of songs and sketches about women and work.

*Shakespeare's Sister* (1980). Hannah Beardon *(front)* Chris Bowler, David Bradford, Mary McCusker, Gillian Hanna, Josefina Cupido, John Slade. Photo: Mark Rusher

Looking back now, I feel in awe at our energy and stamina, and wonder how we managed to get so much done in so short a time (including many long meetings of the collective!). One reason is that we had such a lot of support from local women's groups and networks, drumming up audiences for us at local colleges and community centres, encouraging venues to book our shows despite being such an unknown quantity, providing accommodation and other practical help. The relationships built with these local groups and venues remained vital to us later on.

Another reason is that we benefitted from the support and advice given by women working in the arts who shared (or at least respected) our artistic and political vision – in particular, at the Arts Council, from the incomparable Ruth Marks. Amongst very many other things, she encouraged us to include funding for childcare provision in our applications to the Council, though nothing could solve the problems for anyone with children of being away from home for such long periods.

## Into the 1980s

With minor variations, we continued with this same mode of working for the next few years, into the early 1980s: around two shows a year being toured across the country (though not in tandem after the second year, and with some longer runs at particular venues), with their casts drawn from the collective (whose actual membership – around eight performers plus administrator and tour manager – changed over time, with a large turnover in 1979-80).

The shows continued to be well received by audiences, and some achieved more mainstream success, as when *Gentlemen Prefer Blondes* (1979), a musical, broke box office records at the Glasgow Citizens Theatre. The focus remained on new work, and the scope of this was expanded by drawing on Gillie Hanna's great translating skills, so that our audiences could also enjoy recent feminist theatre from France and Italy, such as *Shakespeare's Sister* (1980), a physically bold and surreal piece directed by Hilary Westlake.

Of course, as with any way of operating a theatre company, not everything went smoothly all the time. A shared belief in feminism didn't guarantee that every writer who came in to work with us was satisfied with the experience. Nor did every director enjoy being presented with the cast of the show already decided. However, we were a *performers'* collective; we brought our passion for theatre, our acting skills, and our commitment to each show into the rehearsal room, and that was usually enough to solve any difficulties.

## Adapting to changing times

Operating as a performers' collective came under a lot of pressure during the 1980s. Changes in political culture made egalitarian collectives seem less attractive, both to potential members and to funding bodies. More straightforwardly, financial constraints meant a shift towards shows with much smaller casts. The shift triggered some great creative responses including Bryony Lavery's stunning duo of *Calamity* (1983) and *Origin of the Species* (1984), written in close collaboration with the company, and *Enslaved By Dreams* (1984), a visually beautiful piece inspired by the life of Florence Nightingale, and devised and directed by Chris Bowler, developing ideas from a much earlier company workshop she had been involved in as a performer.

By the mid-80s, our collective had shrunk, in effect, to the three remaining founder members (Chris Bowler, Gillian Hanna and myself), plus the administrator and tour manager (initially Sandy Bailey and Meri Jenkins). Later in the 80s, Katrina Duncan joined this group. It was now an all-women collective. Financial stability was maintained by making the administrator the sole fully-paid position. And we adopted a more flexible approach: separate casts would be engaged (including men), dictated by the needs of each play, and actor-members of the collective wouldn't be expected to perform in every production.

This had some big advantages. It gave more freedom to writers, since they were no longer expected to write for the company's core performers, and enabled more diverse casting, extending the range of plays we could produce. For example, Jorge Diaz's *My Song is Free* (1986) was based on the personal accounts of four 'disappeared' women in Chile. We included in the cast South American women whose experiences contributed much to our production. Similar points applied to the casting of Jenny McLeod's *Island Lives* in 1988, and Debbie Shewell's *More Than One Antoinette* in 1990.

But it also meant that performers no longer benefited from the breadth of experience that we had enjoyed, provided by closer relationships with writers and involvement in all decisions. And people booking shows didn't have such a clear sense of what a Monstrous Regiment show would be like, something that well-written publicity alone doesn't provide for productions of new work.

In 1990, I conducted a review for the collective, addressing this and related issues and suggesting various solutions. We then submitted plans to the Arts Council that secured funding till 1993. As part of that process, it was agreed that an artistic director should be appointed, and Clare Venables (previously at the Sheffield Crucible) took up this position in 1991. This move was clearly at odds with our original vision. But we recognised we were now operating in very different times, and Clare had worked with the company in various roles over the years, developing a very positive relationship with us.

We very much hoped that, over time, we could merge the best of the collective's experience and commitment with the artistic stability and confidence that would be generated by such an experienced and highly regarded artistic director. But this was not to be. Towards the end of 1992, the Arts Council rejected Clare's new plans for the company's future, and she resigned, leaving the company in 1993, after directing two shows for us.

## Archives and website

Although in 1993 we'd reluctantly decided to stop producing shows, we kept the company going as a legal entity, partly in case we one day wanted to do so again – 'dormant but not dead', we said. But by the time the 2010s arrived, what seemed more important was how to keep its history and achievements alive, how to enable later generations to find out what it had actually done.

Gillian Hanna's book, *Monstrous Regiment: A Collective Celebration* (1991), had served this purpose well, but had been out of print for many years. But our Arts Council funding meant we'd always had an office and administrator, so we had a big archive of photographs, posters, flyers, tour dates, interviews, set designs, correspondence and scripts. Perhaps a website based on these could be created?

The archive had been inaccessible since being deposited at the Fawcett Library, but this all changed in 2015 when it was moved to the V&A's Theatre and Performance collection. They hosted a launch party for the new acquisition and enabled us to scan a lot of the material over the next couple of years. We also tracked down and digitised much of the music recorded at the time and the website finally went live in 2019 (www.monstrousregiment.co.uk).

The site – as well as looking beautiful – tries to give a detailed, concrete picture of all the work the company actually did, how it operated, and how its shows were received at the time. It doesn't try to engage with theoretical debates about feminist theatre and politics, or to evaluate its own contribution to these. Instead, it provides a resource for people to think about these things for themselves.

## Some personal thoughts

For me, working on that website was an exciting time. So much information and so many memories, how to pluck the right ones from years of work and friendship? And if only, back then, we'd had today's technology – there'd be a selection of videos on *YouTube* with highlights from the shows, plus backstage footage of the get-outs, with a quick guide to packing and van-loading from Gillie and me. But at least the existence of the website has enabled me here to go swiftly through the years without listing every show and naming all the talented writers, directors, technicians who worked with us. Let alone the performers! They're all there – just get online.

We were lucky that our company was launched when the second wave of feminism was powering through the decade Throughout the UK and in other countries, women were actively seeking ways to take control of their lives. We were part of that. Our desire to reflect the complexity and strength of women unconnected to the male gaze matched the feelings of the time. The audience was out there waiting before the plays were written.

This fuelled the positive responses we received. And so too did publications such as *Time Out,* in London, and the inspiring feminist magazine *Spare Rib*, which were already well established. Their articles and reviews gave new plays like ours a supportive evaluation. The responses from mainstream reviewers were often good but more mixed, and sometimes highly dubious. For example (names removed):

'The company – a feminist bunch who order up plays by women writers – managed somehow to produce something that was about people as much as women.'

'Gillian Hanna is Calamity Jane [dressed as male], who maybe partly accounts for the success of the production by persuading the playgoer to forget for considerable periods that this is in fact an all-woman show.'

The response to the plays gets smothered here by the hostile attitude to feminism or the dismissive attitude towards women. And in other, less extreme ways, our writers and their work often suffered at the time from the very fact of being produced by a *feminist* company. I sometimes thought they'd have got a better reception with a different label.

I left school at 15 and worked for nine years as a window dresser before drama school. Despite three years of night school and diplomas, I could never achieve equal pay with male colleagues. I couldn't even access the electrical tools without the permission of one of the men. When I complained, I was regarded as unreasonable, loud and aggressive. And all accompanied by the relentless understory of the grope, the ambush in a dark corridor, the hand inappropriately placed. That was all a bit of fun wasn't it? If I responded with a knee in the groin, I felt much better but was an aggressive bitch and unladylike.

I shouldn't have been surprised: when I started work as an actor, it was the same in theatre – no more subtle, and with a lot more opportunities for the predators. Feminism gave me the confidence to name the problem, and to put my anger into the bigger picture. And it was when I identified as a feminist that men also called me strident, shrill and a whinger.

Dale Spender, in *Man Made Language* (1980), starts with a splendid poem called 'Women's Talk'. Here is the last verse:

I'm sick of being bait

men denigrate our talk at their peril
but that's because they're in ignorance
of its power
our power
those precious few of us who see ourselves
as powerful
    serious
        and deadly.
Astra

Feminism has been a force for good, bringing tangible changes in attitudes, laws and actions. In the UK today, women are in important positions in all areas of life including the arts. For me, feminism always seemed a sane response to a mad situation. Has the madness gone? Women are still sexually assaulted and often stay silent, fearful of repercussions. Women still struggle to work and find childcare. Worse still, there are women across the world who are denied their basic human rights, unable to access education or work and living with the constant threat of violence.

I sit at home safely and wonder – can we find a louder and more powerful voice to bring about a change in global thought and action? This book is celebrating feminist theatre then and now. Perhaps we could turn our thoughts to how to make some visible theatrical moment at every performance in 2024 to show our support for our global sisters, something that can be translated into financial help for them?

≈

**Mary McCusker** was born in Glasgow, where she trained as an actor at the Royal Scottish Academy of Music and Drama, after working for some years as a window dresser. Her acting career began in 1971 with seasons at the Edinburgh Lyceum, Glasgow Citizens, Newcastle University and Liverpool Everyman theatres, and in 1975 she co-founded Monstrous Regiment Theatre Company. She performed in over half its shows (including Luckham and Bond's *Scum,* Churchill's *Vinegar Tom,* Lavery's *Origin of the Species* and Tikkanen's *Love Story of the Century*) and has remained a central figure in the company's management both before and after it ceased production in 1993, most recently in the development of its archive-based website (www.monstrousregiment.co.uk). Outside Monstrous Regiment she has performed leading roles in many classical and contemporary plays – from *Mary Stuart* and *Macbeth* to D*ancing at Lughnasa* and *The Steamie* – and has also worked extensively as a communication and performance trainer with professional jazz musicians, medical researchers, homeless teenagers and many others.

Cheryl and Abigail Byron in *Don't Forget The Birds* by Open Clasp Theatre Company.
Photo: Keith Pattison

# OPEN CLASP THEATRE COMPANY
## CATRINA MCHUGH

**What does feminist mean to you?**

A feminist is a person who fights for the rights of all women, inclusive of trans women and is also an ally to all those who are oppressed and discriminated against. I often think back to where this started. I see myself, the youngest of five with four older brothers, in a house that celebrated everything that is the army and patriarchal. A culture that supported entitlement to take up space and air, with bars in pubs lined with men and pints, tables circled with women and vodka and orange. Money that sat in the trouser pockets, wages given to the wife for the home and living. Of pound coins hidden in pleated skirts, food pushed and thrown across tables. Knives held and then lines crossed. The early days of my life are the foundation for my fight for the rights of women and girls, my main focus, but not my only one.

I became a lesbian at 17, hidden and full of secrets – it was 1980. I found drama through a scheme after being asked to leave a dull job. I met politics that juxtaposed with my background (my brothers were in the Falklands War) – I embraced both. At Greenham Common, I fell in love with a woman from Derry and learnt about Ireland, its history, oppression and resistance. I changed again. This is the backdrop to why feminism is threaded through, and centre stage, in my work with Open Clasp.

**How has feminism influenced your work?**

I co-founded Open Clasp back in 1998, a feminist theatre company which can't walk past injustice. We aim to Change the World – One Play at a Time. I have worked with hundreds of women over the past 25 years, sat in circles in community and youth centres, and prisons, in the UK, New York and online, and with those involved in sex work in New Zealand and Ireland during the pandemic. The workshops are democratic and aim to build power.

I write plays in response to those workshops. The design of the workshops and the plays written are through a feminist lens, not only mine but with the whole creative and staff team involved. Productions tour live and online, reaching local, national and global audiences. Hundreds of women speak to thousands, and change happens.

**Has the content or form of your work changed over time? How?**

When working with women, we don't go in with an issue, but its rare that we don't bear witness to domestic violence, rape and child sexual abuse. It's not the first thing said but it's always there. It's a constant that fills me with rage – rage at the entitlement of others to perpetrate violence and have power over another. This hasn't changed, but how we respond has. Our commissions have included theatre work to train entire police forces in how to recognise and manage coercive controlling behaviours. Our work is digitalised, a hybrid of theatre and film, and streamed, reaching a global audience. We have found strength in the inclusivity of our co-creators and other experts. The performances act as a prompt with our post-show panels, inclusive of our co-creators and members. The company is 25 years old and continues to evolve. The creative teams bring innovation, and we strive to make the best theatre we can.

**Do you feel women have achieved equality in theatre?**

I work in a women's theatre company based in a women's centre. We have success; our work is valued and celebrated. But before the pandemic I was thinking about our work versus the venue's need to get bums on seats, asking 'will feminist theatre sell?'. We offer great storytelling, unapologetically based on a truth told by women. We are award-winning and yet, because our theatre places women centre stage, we could alienate audiences. Why? The barrier that is patriarchy is alive and kicking in society, and therefore in our theatres.

Every time actors and/or creatives join our company, they share how different it feels to work with just women. They have space to be creative, feel valued and can thrive. They're not embattled and/or they don't have to find ways to convince male senior members of staff to book a production when its protagonists are women.

We are intersectional; our starting point and life journeys are different, and those involved in creating theatre need to continue to be inclusive and equitable when thinking about equality for women in theatre.

## Have you experienced sex bias while working in theatre?

At 19, I met feminists, went to Greenham Common and lived outside the law. Throughout my twenties I campaigned and marched against Section 28, against racism, to free Nelson and Winnie Mandela, those seeking asylum. I saw the power built when space is made for women to gather. I co-founded Open Clasp to make sure women's voices were heard on stage, to challenge the bias.

## What would improve the opportunities for women working in theatre today?

Institutions are influenced by society and without societal change, why would they give up their privileges? Patriarchy is ingrained, like racism and all forms of entitlement to discriminate. Over the years I have been disheartened to hear and know of perpetrators who work in theatre, often with their fist clenched in solidarity with the #MeToo movement, yet they themselves are no different from any other perpetrator out there. I expect more from those involved in creating theatre. I think those with governance responsibilities should hold people accountable for their actions and those in senior leadership positions should create an inclusive, democratic atmosphere, that builds power that enables professional growth and creativity.

View from the gallery filming *Key Change*. Photo: Mark Savage Photography

Jessica Johnson as Angie and Christina Berriman Dawson as Kelly in *Key Change.*
Photo: Keith Pattison

### Does intersectionalism influence your work? How?

It's the fabric of our work. Our productions represent who we co-create with, for example our most recent production, *Mycelial,* which was co-created with sex worker activists around the world, is inclusive of all women – lesbians, trans women of colour, Māori, non-binary, neurodiverse people, those who are disabled, trans women and Irish. Those involved in the sex work industry are diverse: it's you, me and us.

### Do you collaborate with other groups?

We work with communities of women across the globe. We partner with youth and community organisations, researchers and commissioners. Our methodology invites women to pull on their lived experiences to create a composite character. They work creatively, discuss and debate. Our co-creators respond to scripts written and attend rehearsals, comment on set and attend previews and join our post-show panels. The very nature of our work is collaboration.

### Do we still need feminist theatre? Why?

It's rare that intersectional communities of women get an opportunity to take up space and be heard. Theatre told through a feminist lens makes change happen, and we need change. So yes, we need feminist theatre.

### Do you think having a theatre dedicated to women's work would have an impact?

I think it would depend on the ethics and values of the venue/theatre. Managed well, inclusive and with investment it could be a great idea. As I said before, for creative teams that come and work with us, (a women's theatre company based in a women's centre), the environment grows their creativity and confidence, so yes it would have an impact.

### Are prizes important? Why? Why not?

When we won the Carol Tambor Best of Edinburgh Award it changed the trajectory of Open Clasp. We were striving to be recognised on a national level, but careful of how, taking time to build relationships and making sure we didn't parachute into communities. We took a risk with *Key Change* and it paid off, we got to New York off-Broadway and into a women's prison over there. *Key Change* was then commissioned by The Space and streamed across the world to 35 countries in six continents. We connected the North East to Edinburgh to New York, and then the world. The Carol Tambor Best of Edinburgh Award was for the quality of theatre created. In an unequal world, that win is important – it opened doors.

### Is arts funding equitable?

We have been creating feminist theatre for the past 25 years, working with women in communities, meeting them where they are at and creating award-winning work that makes change a reality, for the women and audiences. We have been part of Arts Council England's National Portfolio since 2012. They invest in us because we help the Arts Council achieve their aims – their aims and ours align. Our communities are those that others find hard to reach, so investing in Open Clasp means the Arts Council funding represents equity, for us. However, as I write, we hear other funders aren't funding our current project. Sex Workers' rights might be a bridge too far when we talk about equity?

In 1998, when I co-founded the company, I found it extremely challenging as a working class woman. I'd gone back to education after leaving school at 16, didn't know how to write an essay, and was now filling in funding applications and managing a regional tour. I got Bell's Palsy in the first year. We are now a six strong team of women, qualified, experienced and award-winning, but funding isn't thrown at us, we have to fight for it. If the Arts Council didn't fund us, we wouldn't survive.

**Are there allowances made for people with caring responsibilities – either children or elderly?**

Within Open Clasp yes, our staff team are supported, and freelance creative teams, are through scheduling support and contributions towards child care costs. Annual Leave is on a par with productions and the well-being of staff and creative teams is high on every agenda; it's feminist and political.

**How can we improve things for women in theatre?**

Which women and what theatre, I asked myself. One of the highlights for me is when women in prison meet theatre, create and appreciate art, theatre that speaks to them, represents their world. I think working class women and girls need access to the world of theatre – creating work, as writers, directors and producers, as well as actors on stage. The gap has widened over the years since Open Clasp began.

Over the past 25 years we have taken work outside of traditional theatre spaces, to community and youth centres, schools, and grassroots organisations. We have recently created a theatre space in the West End of Newcastle, at the West End Women & Girls Centre (our base). Therefore, we are able to make theatre accessible to those women and girls who feel alienated in the traditional theatre venues. Our hope is this will improve things for more women, particularly working class women, to access a career in theatre. There are so many stories to be told, poets not celebrated, those with innovative eyes and ears to direct and produce. We need to improve things for these women.

Our Call to Action is for audiences to see the work created.

≈

# CATRINA MCHUGH

Photo: Phyllis Christopher

**Catrina McHugh** MBE is Open Clasp's joint CEO, Artistic Director, lead facilitator and playwright. Catrina's expertise lies in working with women and writing in response. She has dedicated her professional life to making ground-breaking theatre that matters and changes lives for the better. Her philosophy is written into the DNA of Open Clasp, which seeks to 'Change the World – One Play at a Time.' Her work has been met with widespread critical acclaim: *Key Change* won the Carol Tambor 'Best of Edinburgh' Award in 2015, and was named New York Times Critics Pick when the show transferred to off-Broadway in 2016.

Writing credits include: *Key Change, Rattle Snake, Don't Forget the Birds, Sugar (BBC Arts for iPlayer) and Lasagna.*

McHugh was honoured with an MBE for services to disadvantaged women through theatre in 2017 and will receive an Honorary Doctorate in July 2024 from Newcastle University.

www.openclasp.org.uk

*Caress/Ache* by Suzie Miller at Griffin Theatre Sydney, 2015.
Photo: Brett Boardman

# INTERVIEW WITH SUZIE MILLER

**How did you begin writing for the theatre?**

I used to write in a particular way where I'd spend a lot of time thinking and then I'd sort of launch into writing a play in a kind of hot fever. When I was mentored by Edward Albee, he said that's how he writes, and so I was reassured that it's not such a bad way to do things. I think you refine your process each time you do it. Spending that much time writing it in your head doesn't mean that the first draft is the perfect draft, but I think what comes out is something that's very much what you've been drilling down on mentally for some time before it is sort of born.

I guess all writers talk about being in the zone. And if you're in the zone where the dialogue is really clicking and the characters are very much alive, they just take you with them really. There are certain projects that I've thought about for a long time, trying to get the exact right angle. Edward Albee described it as such: "What you do is you take a metaphorical dog on a metaphorical walk on a metaphorical beach up and down until it comes together and is crystallized. Then you actually let it out." That was quite a helpful way of talking about writing for theatre, because it described my process. He also said something that was really profound for me, "You can take someone that doesn't have sight to the theatre and they will still have the whole experience of the script because the script is actually meant to be spoken and it's meant to be heard. You write for an aural experience. Whereas when you write for film or television, you're writing more for a visual experience."

**Is there greater equality for women in theatre in Australia?**

When I first started as a playwright and I'd quit law to go into theatre writing, I remember being quite shocked thinking I was going from quite a conservative profession as a lawyer to a profession that was very left-wing and all about equality and freedoms and exploring concepts.

Then I started looking around the programmes and realized that the artistic directors were all white middle class men, and that very often there would not be a single female playwright in their seasons, or if there was one, there would just be one. I remember asking, "What's going on?" The response from those artistic directors was, "There are no plays of merit written by women." I knew that was profoundly wrong because they used to say that about women lawyers until they compared the grades we got at university. Women highly outranked men in terms of marks at university. So, the corporate law firms came to the conclusion that they'd be crazy economically not to employ women in as many numbers as they could because they were actually better performers.

There's no equalizer like that in theatre or in the arts where you can say "Well, I've got this mark at university, therefore I have the skillset and you need to acknowledge that or else you're missing out on something." Really, it was about the taste of those specific artistic directors and they very much favoured the sort of men that they were when they were young, which basically excluded women and anyone that wasn't white or from a certain background. In that regard, it was an extreme situation.

I kept talking about it because I'd been through that in law, and because I had a human rights voice and I understood how to talk about these things without being super threatening. I remember starting an organization called Australian Women Playwrights Online, which we called AWOL because we were just invisible otherwise. We had a lot of conversations about how it was affecting us, but it seemed that the conversation was very challenging to the artistic directors at the time. They found it very confronting that women playwrights and directors were unhappy to be excluded from the seasonal programmes, and seemed to be defensive about their own lack of insight. Because of the lack of productions women playwrights never had the opportunity to see their plays performed, or for women directors to develop their craft – and we all know that in order to develop your theatre voice and craft, you must have that. I was one of the lucky ones, I did have work on. Yet, there were never enough slots for women playwrights or directors; it was very scarce. So, it meant that women were made to compete for very small slices of the cake.

I looked at the women playwrights in the generation above me and realised that they all disappeared. These were women I'd admired. I'd gone to their shows, I'd read their work when I was at high school and they'd all moved to television. I remember panicking, thinking, is that what's going to happen to me? I'm just going to work at this for 20 years and find out that the only doors really open long-term are in television. Television's great, it pays the bills and sometimes it can be extraordinary, and I've got some great gigs in television but, if you want to be a playwright, you want to know that opportunities exist. The fact that it's so badly paid and then, even if you work for a long period and get better and better at your craft, but that you might still be invisible to the profession seemed really outrageous to me.

That's probably why I moved to London, to be honest. I remember going to a talk about why women were not being programmed in Sydney. It was so inadequate that I thought, "I don't actually have the time to wait around for theatre to catch up. I think I have to move countries to where, they're starting to have this conversation." London was just that little bit further ahead.

Australia, didn't really have quotas. It very much resisted quotas. I felt like quotas were something that were a no-brainer for me. I'd seen quotas work in law firms. When you have quotas, you bring people to the game and to the party. They sink or swim, but by the same token, you support them, and you give them opportunity and you create a pathway for women and people that aren't of the dominant paradigm. You actually allow other people to have their stories brought to life and shared.

I remember my first couple of plays. I was told very specifically by theatre companies that it was all well and good that I had female characters, but I couldn't have a female protagonist because audiences didn't tolerate it. You look back at the canon and you realize, on the odd occasion where you had a Hedda or a Miss Julie, there are not a whole lot of plays where the woman is the protagonist. That was an awful moment. I remember thinking women can easily tell the stories of men because they've actually been vigilant enough about the male experience and been subject to it for so long that they can tell those stories. But the secret life of women and their stories are not as easily told by men because there is so much silence around women's stories when they are deemed 'unacceptable'.

There was an implicit message and assumption that if you were telling a woman's story that it was somehow not a real play. The amount of times I said to theatre companies "More than 50% of the audience are women. You're telling me they don't want to see their own stories on stage?" They had frequented the theatre all their life or had come to it late in life and enjoyed it because they love storytelling. But they weren't calling out for women's stories because they hadn't been brought up to believe that women's stories were important. So, it's a whole cultural shift to actually say, with some level of confidence and without apology, "I want to write a story about a woman".

Many people of diverse races would say the same thing, telling a story from their racial background is now something that is possible, but in the past, they would have been very reticent to tell those stories because of the way they'd be received. Once women started seeing women's stories valued enough to be programmed, they really wanted more and more of them. I think that even men want more of them. There are incredible stories and issues to grapple with. I'm a very strong feminist. I've never

Heather Mitchell in Sydney Theatre Company's *RBG: Of Many, One,* 2022.
Photo: Prudence Upton

made any apology about that, even when the feminist word was the F-word, never to be spoken. I did gender and the law at law school.

In one of my plays, *Prima Facie,* I say, "Once you see, you cannot unsee." Once you see the gendered version of the world around you, in the same way that once you see the white version of the world around you, you no longer cannot see it. It's important that feminism is not just for women, but I think that the patriarchal world has actually described men in a certain way that harms them as well. I feel like no one wants to be brought up to be the provider of every other person, and no one wants to think that they have to be the kind of man that does certain things to assert control or domination. Well, maybe they do, but I'm saying there should be a choice around that for men as well. I feel like it's an invitation for everyone. This particular generation of young people are really hungry for that and really prepared to go deep with that concept of "What is gender? How does it describe me? How does it discriminate against me? How does it actually portray me on such a conceptual basis that I don't feel I belong? How does it define relationships? How does it define community values and community systems? How does it define the legal system, the medical systems and more?"

## What do you think would improve the opportunities for women working in theatre today?

Things like childcare in every profession is a fundamental because I know that when I started as a playwright, a producer who was producing my first work at the Sydney Opera House said to me as a way of endearing themselves: "I'm so glad to be working with you. I hear you're a really hard worker. The last person I worked with had a baby and my God, I'm not going to go through that again."

What they didn't realize was that I had a three-year-old and a newborn. I was silent. I thought they're going to find that out next week and they're going to be embarrassed about what they just said to me. But I was so shell-shocked that they said it that I didn't even have a response. I just thought "Oh my God, you've just told me the truth of what people think about women in the arts who have children. Because no one wants you to bring the baby to rehearsal."

I had two children while I was becoming a playwright. It was really hard. Every single cent I earned went on childcare. It's not the same when someone has someone at home looking after their children. I didn't have family and things like that because they lived in a different state. I was very aware that when I was a lawyer, I could pay for care and it didn't feel as oppressive, but when I was a playwright, it was overwhelming to have to think about it all the time. When I went to rehearsals, it wasn't a thing to talk about the responsibilities that you had at home, or if you had to go at three, it seemed like you were jumping off early rather than anyone realising that you were paying a fortune per hour for someone else to feed your children.

A lot of the awards are for young playwrights, for example under 30s, and I think women don't get there until later if they've had children. So, men have a much better opportunity at that than women who are bearing children. I think women carry most of the care load when it comes to their elder parents or other family members too. That goes really unacknowledged and we want women to write stories about that, because those are aspects of the world that we really want to know about.

I remember once I was in a studio where the artistic director said, if anyone's got children, just bring them in. There was a male playwright in that studio and I remember acknowledging how annoyed he was whenever the children made a noise. I didn't have children at the time, but I went out of my way to make sure those women playwrights felt that their children were not making anything difficult. I mean the world has children in it.

Women have internalised a lot of that discrimination and we always saw success as being someone that doesn't include and sometimes doesn't tolerate the messiness of life with children. We're using a masculine template for leadership and there are other forms of leadership and other ways to lead. I once worked with a director called Lindy Hume, who's very well-known in Australia. I wrote my first opera with her. Lindy had a really strong commitment to women being empowered in the artistic workplace – and I remember feeling so enabled by her. I had a daughter at school at the time and one of the other workers also had a young daughter and she incorporated some of our understanding of parenting into the work that I was creating. She would actually say things like "You're going to be amazing, this is going to be terrific," and "This is the feedback I have, but you go forth, you can do this, I totally believe in you." There was something so empowering about that. I realized I'd never been nurtured like that as an artist before. I thought this must be what young men get from older men who bring them into companies and mentor them as a rite of passage. I thought "No wonder they get confident quickly. This is a wonderful way of learning your trade." Also there was a woman who was composing the music for it. I watched her really step up and glow under Lindy's leadership. I thought, "I'm never going to forget that this is how you mentor women. You don't actually be a man, you be a woman, and you remember what it's like to be a young woman who doesn't think they own the space, and you let them."

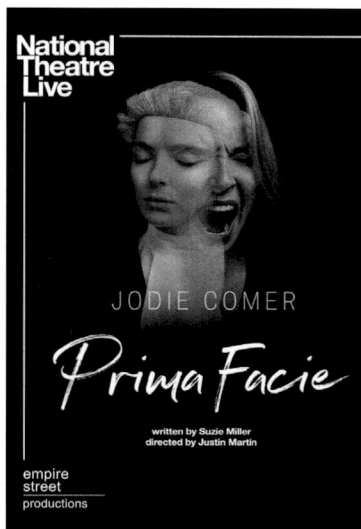

What we have to remember is the patriarchy sets women up to be in competition with each other. You don't have to stop younger people from getting great positions or worry that everyone is coming up behind you and doing really well. My view is that everyone writes a different play, so, let's make space for everyone to have their own voice.

## What's the journey been like with *Prima Facie?*

When I first wrote *Prima Facie*, it was just before #MeToo and I thought "I'm writing this play because it matters to me to write it." It's basically a one-woman show about rape that has humour in it. "No one is ever going to put this on." That's what I thought when I wrote it. I put it into a competition for national unproduced work and it won that. And then the Griffin Theatre (national unproduced writer's theatre) put it on in Sydney.

I'd had work produced at the Griffin Theatre a number of times before, but there was just something about this piece that we didn't expect. It just really hit a zeitgeist but even aside from that, it created a conversation. With my work, I always aim to create a conversation so that people go out for dinner afterwards and they feel the need to talk about what they've seen and what it's brought up for them. But this conversation ended up having a life of its own and even though I feel strongly connected to it, I feel like it really is its own thing in the world now.

What's also interesting from a feminist perspective is when it went on in the West End (with Jodie Comer), I had a call at nine o'clock one morning from a woman who was a senior London judge. She was actually the judge who's in charge of writing the directions to juries for the UK. She said she sat up all night after seeing the play and really grappled with what she had seen because she couldn't unsee where the law was lacking. She said she rewrote the direction to the juries based on the language in the play. Now every judge at a rape case has to read it. The play talks about how just because someone doesn't remember their evidence in a chronological order, or there are a few peripheral issues that don't add up, that it does not mean that person is lying. It might mean they're traumatized.

Then another judge, a senior woman at the Old Bailey, made it compulsory for Northern Irish judges to have to watch a film of the play before they can sit on a rape case. Then, 3,000 police officers saw it and some of them wrote to me and said, "I had no idea what I was doing all this time but I'm part of the problem and I'll never be that again."

Early in 2024 I went to New York and spoke at the UN about how art can affect change. *Prima Facie* has now gone on in 32 countries. It's kind of astonishing to me. It's just its own rolling ball, really. But I feel like it was the voice that women really needed to hear at a certain time, and it was put in a way that they could hear it. If they'd ever been the victim of a sexual assault or if they'd ever grappled with these problems, they could tell someone to see the play or read the play. On opening night in the West End, a professional producer came up to me and said "I just want you to know that I saw the play, I loved it, but I'm also one-in-three." That was a line from the play. And I thought, "She's just told me she's a sexual assault survivor." I remember thinking "To say I'm one-in-three now is a thing that people can say without having to say all the hard words. You can just acknowledge it and then move on."

I like to give my characters a surname that is after a famous female playwright, just to keep women playwrights more visible in the world; the feminists amongst us will pick it up. Every now and then someone would ask, is she called Tessa Ensler because of Eve Ensler and *The Vagina Monologues?* That's a little Easter egg for the sort of women who are thinking about other women playwrights and just giving them a nod.

Then I met up with Eve Ensler in New York and we did a roundtable at the Algonquin with some women who work very closely in the area of sexual assault. It was an incredible discussion with really strong women, strong feminists. That group was enlightening for me because I don't work in all of those organisations but I could see other issues that arose and they could see how they could use the play in different forms with some of the young people that they work with to build confidence and discussion.

**You've worked internationally. In terms of feminist theatre, what would you say are the differences?**

In Australia, we had an organization called Playworks, advocating for women playwrights. It was a great organization. It was phased out because there was a view that their work was done. All of us who were part of that organization sort of rolled our eyes and thought "Well, the job is done, is it? We're not even close." I had to leave Australia because there were not enough possibilities and access to the stage to remain there.

When you start to look at big budget musicals and plays that are looking to transfer, I don't think many women are given the opportunity as directors or as playwrights to lead those because the producers rely on the voices that have currency.

I'm in a very privileged position at the moment. I'm highly aware of it that, at the moment, I can actually have those meetings and make those calls because of the success of *Prima Facie*, but I could just as easily have not had the success of *Prima Facie* and still be where I was before that, which is trying to knock on those doors.

What is interesting is that when you have had that success, people then revisit your old work and realise that some of it is extremely good. Works that I cherished for years that didn't make it big, are now in retrospect being collected because people have thought, "What else did she write?" I knew those works, at the time, were ones I really would have stood by very strongly and advocated for, but you need that groundswell of people going, "You're already a proven entity before we can take those risks." Particularly with women. Even with the Olivier Awards, there are so few women playwrights who have won, or women who have won any of those awards. You look back over the winners and it's quite a shock. I hope that there's more prize-giving that actually elevates women to a standard where producers know that there's someone they can bank on.

I also worked in Canada and it was more outspoken there, because they were talking about access to stages for indigenous people and women. The advocacy of women in America is strong, because they've been funded by private philanthropists and have more of a platform because of that financial input. That culture of philanthropy is so different to the culture that we have in Australia or the UK.

I think it's incumbent on women, as we get older, to think about how we can support women coming up to have access to stages and theatres and ways to financially contribute, or ways that you can mentor or have a conversation with them. It's a very small gesture, but maybe when a big company approaches you to give a talk, you can say, "I'd really like you to make a donation to this organisation, rather than pay a fee." I feel like companies are prepared to do that because they write it off anyway. There's such a big divide between where the corporates are at and where the theatre is. They don't realize that most theatre companies who put on a play are "run on the smell of an oily rag," as they say in Australia. They're shocked when you do a fundraiser and you get a small amount and they go, "Is that all?" And you go, "Well, that's big for us, you know." They're used to such big amounts of money.

**Do you think feminist theatre is still necessary today?**

Absolutely, of course. I think it's a fundamental perspective and portal to the world showing what women have struggled to achieve and what they continue to struggle to achieve. I also think it's about the lived experience of half the population. Women are managing the next generation and trying to manage their own careers, juggle relationships and caring responsibilities, as well as trying to advocate. There's a sort of assertion now that we have every right to be here.

Jodie Comer with her Tony Award for Best Actress 2023 for her role in *Prima Facie*

The current generation of young women is amazing. I want us to continue until women theatre makers can no longer recall a time when they did not have a space which they felt entitled to. I think what we are going to see in the next 20 years is going to be very exciting feminist theatre if we actually fund it and give it appropriate development time and productions.

≈

**Suzie Miller** is a contemporary international play-wright, screenwriter and novelist. Based in both London and Sydney, Miller's work has been produced around the world winning multiple prestigious awards, including the Laurence Olivier Award for Best New Play 2023, for her smash hit one-woman play *Prima Facie*, which had a sold-out season on London's West End and on Broadway in New York. Miller is educated in science and law, with a doctorate in drama and mathematics. She practised human rights law before writing full time and is currently developing major projects in theatre, literature and screen.

# INTERVIEW WITH ANN MITCHELL

**How did you start in the theatre?**

I'm an only child and was born just before the beginning of the Second World War. I grew up in the East End. During the war years cinema was very important to everybody. My mother loved the cinema, and we went three times a week and once on Sundays to the People's Palace to see foreign films. Much of my education and imagination took place in the dark. I knew from a very early age that I wanted to be an actor. From about the age of five. I used to act in plays that I'd written and directed on the gym steps. I don't think there was any question that I was going to be an actor but no one in my family had any connection with such a world. I knew nothing about how to become an actor, but I was lucky enough to meet a woman who was an actor and had seen me in a school play. She was very helpful and encouraged me. From her, I learnt what a tough and wounding profession it could be.

I was brought up by three very strong women: my mother, my auntie and my grandmother. Although my family had no idea what it meant to be an actor, they did understand that it could be very difficult. They encouraged me to find something to fall back on, so I took shorthand lessons and languages at the Regent Street Polytechnic, now Westminster University.

At this time, I also went to Saturday morning classes run by Maggie Bury – an actor with Joan Littlewood's company at the Theatre Royal, Stratford East. These I loved so much. I watched all the shows at the theatre and so that was how I was introduced to theatre by Maggie and Joan Littlewood and her company. But it was always an ambition, a hope if you like.

Then I met my first husband when I was about 17. I got married and had a baby when I was 20. During the 50's there was enormous pressure on women to be married. Especially women from a working class background. Saturday morning classes had ended. Theatre Workshop were in America, and they'd become enormously successful, much to Joan's displeasure. I think she wanted to keep the work in the East End. One day I had a call from Maggie Bury – by this time I had my son – saying "We are starting a drama school, the East 15 Acting School, and we would like to offer you the first scholarship". I remember to this day – and that was 60 years ago – a mixture of surprise, thrill, gratitude, and fear that there was no way I could do that with a young baby. But my family – my mother, my auntie and my grandmother worked everything out so I could go to drama school, for which I have been eternally grateful. So, that's how I got into East 15. I'd auditioned for RADA when I was about 16, which is far too young: I didn't get in. Then I auditioned for Drama Centre and didn't get in there, but there I was, being offered the first scholarship. It's something I'm very proud of to this day. At the time, I lived in Baron's Court. I used to meet my mother on Stepney Green station and hand over my baby. Then I would collect him in the evening. I was lucky enough at the East 15 in the two years there, to play all the leading roles in the productions and never once did I experience any envy from the other students. It was an extraordinary experience – we had classes in the mornings – and performed in schools in the afternoon.

**You worked with Monstrous Regiment and Glasgow Citizens on leaving East 15. Was there a conscious aim to engage with feminism and the politics of the day?**

No, not conscious in the sense I think you mean. Certainly, it would have been subconscious. I was brought up in a socialist family. My beloved stepfather was a Jewish tailor. He was a trade unionist and fought at the battle of Cable Street. Although he didn't live with us until I was 11, he was an enormous influence on my life. He was a wonderful man and father and taught me a great deal about socialism. I have always been politically motivated. Also, if you've been brought up by three strong, working women in the East End, you're bound to have some feminist blood in your veins.

To my mind and experience, Glasgow Citizens wasn't a political company. What it had in abundance was an extraordinary artistic aesthetic. It was phenomenal. Three amazingly talented, committed men who arrived in Glasgow with a trunk of the most remarkable plays to put before a Scottish audience. They were Philip Prowse, Robert David MacDonald, and Giles Havergal. I wouldn't say they were political. Not in the sense I think you mean. Where they were political was in offering 50p seats, we had free dress rehearsals when a lot of the homeless men and women, often heavy drinkers, came in to watch for free. That was a wonderful alarm for us because as the seats bumped up, we knew we were boring. You had to up everything to keep their attention. Yes, the actors all got the same money. They were democratic and came down to London and had open auditions which were almost unheard of then.

**You've played a lot of roles that could be described as strong women. Tell me about some of those, particularly in theatre.**

Yes. Many. Mother Courage I based on my grandmother. My grandmother couldn't read or write. It was never mentioned or commented on in our family. We protected her as she protected us. She was a cleaner, a laundress. She grafted. She was six foot, much taller than the rest of my family. She had enormous physical strength and a very loving heart. She died as I was playing Mother Courage on stage at the Citz.

Hecuba was at the RSC, Peter Hall directing *Tantalus,* the 12-hour play written by John Barton. I was ten hours on the stage. It was exhilarating. We rehearsed for nine months in Denver, played in the US for three months, then toured for nearly two years. I try to bring the strength and courage and wit of the women I grew up with in the East End to the stage. Working class women have so often been stereotyped and it was always my mission to bring something unexpected to a role, modern or classical.

Ann Mitchell in *Gunfight at Dry River* directed by Daniel Simpson (2021)

And in a way say, "Oh here's what you think of working class women, well have a look at this, and fuck you!"

I think when parts are labelled 'strong' you have to bring a complexity to that, to any role. When there is a strong role, look for the vulnerability and vice versa. I've done other marathons – for the RSC and other companies – nine hours, Edward Bond's *The War Plays*, eight hours *Angels in America*. It's very tiring but a wonderful connection with the audience who've stuck it out! Yes, so many strong, complicated women. And I've tried to honour them.

They've pulled off the job and gone into hiding

Lynda La Plante's

**WIDOWS**
series two

Will they get away with it?
or will the past come back to haunt them?

**Lynda La Plante changed the game in television in terms of the depiction of women. Can you talk about working with her and your character in *Widows* – Dolly Rawlins?**

I'm eternally grateful to Lynda for writing the role of Dolly. I understood the character from the moment I read the script. And I certainly think that after *Widows* more opportunities were given to women to lead series. Of course, there had been some before but there was nothing quite like the impact *Widows* had. It was phenomenal at that time. The story of how Lynda and I met is one I cherish. She didn't know my work and had, quite rightly, asked around. I think it was someone at the Royal Court who reassured her that I was a very strong actor. We never really met properly until we started filming. On day two of filming, I noticed this amazing looking red-head lurking, hiding round corners but being very discreet. On a set you very quickly know who everyone is. You make it your business. I wondered who she was, but forgot to ask and got on with the job. After the second day's 'rushes', a huge bouquet arrived on the set for me with a note from Lynda saying "You ARE Dolly." It gave me the encouragement I needed to try and bring it home. We've been friends since *Widows* and I love her dearly. Her generosity is such that she wrote *She's Out* for me.

**Do you think theatre is lagging behind television in terms of the portrayal of complex women?**

There are, of course, great roles in the theatre. Classical and a wealth of fine modern plays so I don't think theatre lags behind television in that sense. But I do think it lags behind in diversity. Partly, to be fair, in a television series, there are more characters and more opportunities for a diverse cast. I would like to see more diversity of all kinds in the theatre. At the moment, adverts are among the most diverse of anything you will see on television or film. They're ahead of the game. They have to be; they need to know who's buying! I welcome every step to make television, films and theatre reflect the people of this country. For people to see themselves – where you come from, what you look like – up there on the screen or stage is important.

**You've had plays written for you by people like Pam Gems and Robert David MacDonald. What was that like?**

Thrilling! It's a great honour and also a great responsibility. Robert David MacDonald wrote Eva Braun for me in *Summit Conference*. I asked him "Why me, Robert? Why me to play Hitler's mistress? And he said, "because I look for the opposite." Other writers have written for me too and it's always so exciting and challenging. A kind of validation. I'm very grateful to all of them. I'm also always really excited and challenged to play a 'real person' like Ayn Rand or Mary Stuart. You have to pick out exactly what you think are the right qualities and juxtapose them with something else. It can't be mimicry.

**How has feminism informed your work as an actor and director? Does it inform the choices you make?**

Yes. Yes, it does. Most definitely. It always has and it always will. You mentioned something about unlikeable characters. What do you mean by that?

**Women have been constrained by having to be likeable characters, so having women as unlikeable characters is somewhat of a shift. Is that something that you see?**

Very definitely a shift. Although when you go back to the great film stars of the 30s and 40s and see how dark they played – and played with relish. After the war, women had to go back into the homes. So, fashion and roles were dedicated to that, were pushed back to that.

**In the 80s, there was a move to create a women's theatre. Do you think it's still important to have a building dedicated to women's work?**

Yes. I think not just for showing women's work but the whole building to provide training not just for the artistic side but the administrative side. An outreach section to reach out to young people and take the plays, readings etc into schools, women's prisons, women's refuges etc. A building where all can come but the focus will be on the education, classes, opportunities for children and older women, whether that be artistically or in other capacities. Those that look after the building and the personnel given opportunities to join classes, discussions on women's experience. And where men are welcomed to join and participate in some activities. We have to educate men and have allies.

**Are prizes important?**

I think they're often very important for the community where the writer, director, actor, choreographer etc comes from. To see other races, sexes, genders get rewarded other than those from the Establishment is important. To witness people from your community being acclaimed can be inspiring, "She/he did it maybe I can too."

For the individual, I'm not so sure. Apparently, there's such a thing as the Oscar's curse! For myself, awards don't seem to have made any difference to getting work. I had a tough time after *Widows* as far as television was concerned but I was offered wonderful opportunities in the theatre. I already had a track record in the theatre and theatre producers like to use actors who are known to a television audience.

**You did the RSC after *Widows*? There was a period at the RSC when they gave more opportunities to women?**

At that time, the Women's Liberation Movement had an effect – not so much on casting – there are only so many female roles in Shakespeare, but at the time when the late Buzz Goodbody, who was a great supporter of the WLM, was working, there was a time when more opportunities for women writers and directors were being discussed. Buzz's untimely death was a fatal blow. And it has taken many years since for a woman to be considered as artistic director. I think during that period there was a drive to move away from the type of middle class, white actor the RSC cast and were associated with.

**Who do you feel changed that sort of casting ghetto?**

Working class actors, Black and Asian actors, gay actors became angrier and more vocal about the barriers for us against playing leading classical roles. I felt very strongly for other actors from those communities that they hadn't had the opportunities I'd had in the theatre. Mine had come not from the RSC but from the Citizens Theatre. Thank God when I go to the theatre now, there is no longer an all-white cast. Hallelujah! Years later when I played Hecuba in John Barton's 12-hour marathon *Tantalus* directed by Peter Hall for the RSC in Denver, it was a very diverse cast. The chorus and soldiers, who were the backbone of the production, were from all over America. It was a mix of American and British leading actors and a very diverse cast. It was wonderful to work with so many lovely young people.

**Do you think we still need feminism today?**

More than ever. The gap between men and women is wider than it's ever been, and the suffering seems greater to me. I've never understood how the critics of feminism can't see that it's always been about equality and being given a fair chance and that can only be good for the whole of society.

**What is your experience as a woman director?**

I directed with Monstrous Regiment, which was an extremely nourishing experience. There was support for me and the work I wanted to do with the actors. They were very open to that. Working with some male actors, I found more difficult. Not always, and working with women was not always inspiring. Both men and women bring a vast array of emotions and sometimes their issues to the work. In a company like Monstrous Regiment, which had a history and philosophy behind it, you get the opportunity, as a director, to go deeper than when you're working with a cast that's been brought together just for one project. With a company that has worked together, know each other, has battled out their difficulties, perhaps with each other, then they're more able to be free and comfortable with each other and are open to new ways of thinking about a play, a role. I was allowed to work with the company in ways that were different for them. I've directed with Clean Break too, with ex-prisoners and I very much enjoyed my time working with them.

**Do you think the situation in terms of funding women's theatre seems to have gotten worse?**

I think the situation for theatre funding overall has gotten worse. In a situation like we're facing now in the UK, the Arts will be the first to be cut. It's difficult for women, women's theatre, women's groups not to be crushed by it, to keep going. You sometimes are allowed to create something special but not to build on it. We have to fight the same fights over and over again. We will always need a female perspective to be spoken, sung, danced, marched. We need it more and more. This is a broken world. We have to embrace a female perspective as well as embrace men as our allies, which we've always done.

≈

**Ann Mitchell** is a leading British stage and screen actor. In 2016 She was awarded an Honorary Doctorate for Services to Drama from UEL. She came to prominence in the 1980s when she starred as Dolly Rawlins in the crime series *Widows* as well as the sequels *Widows 2* and *She's Out*, all written by Lynda La Plante. Mitchell has performed significant major roles at all the theatres throughout the UK and has guest-starred in most of the outstanding TV series since the 60s.

For her film work she has been directed by Ken Loach, Ken Russell, the great Terence Davies and many more. She played Cora in *EastEnders* from 2011 to 2016. Her roles include Hecuba, Mrs. Warren in *Mrs. Warren's Profession,* Mary Stuart, Eva Braun, Mother Courage, Ayn Rand in David Hare's *Ayn Rand takes a Stand* and many more, for which she received much critical acclaim including her Olivier Award nominated performance for *Through the Leaves*.

Sue Hill in *Sea Cry Saga,* a co-production with Creation Theatre.
Photo: Meier Williams

# INTERVIEW WITH REBECCA MORDAN

**Can you tell us about Scary Little Girls?**

It's hard to believe that the company is 21 years old now. The reason I started Scary Little Girls so early on was that I'd had a really great feminist upbringing. My mother was a Greenham Common campaigner and then I had a really empowering, amazing time at university. I went to Sheffield, where I was a big part of the Women's Committee. It's still one of the only universities with a women's officer, largely because of the campaigns that we ran at the time.

Then I went to Bristol Old Vic Drama School and I had the most horrendous time there. They had a policy of taking very few women, three or four per group, mainly to keep their employment stats high. They didn't want the fact that the industry doesn't work very well for women to affect their rating of 100% employment in the first year out.

It was basically three years of #MeToo kind of stuff, with teachers joining in the bad behaviour, lots of institutional problems. When women would finally be broken by these guys and go in tears to tell the principal or the vice-principal, they would do absolutely nothing. Their attitude towards women was just awful. We'd managed to get into this school, up against at least a thousand other women, (whereas the guys there were up against maybe a couple of hundred other guys), paying thousands of pounds to be there and you hear them say, "Well, if you don't like it, why don't you go?" Many women do leave but then they've actually beaten you. Just leave the industry if you don't want to be sexually harassed and touched and called disgusting names and bullied the whole time.

Because the men knew they were able to get away with this kind of behaviour, in one improvisation class, with the teacher there, this guy bent me over backwards, held me by my neck, physically holding me, and acted out violently anally raping me. It was horrible. There were a lot of issues at my drama school, and it made me quite aware of what the industry might be like.

So I set up Scary Little Girls to create better parts for women and better employment standards for women in the theatre industry. I wanted women watching our work to see themselves on the stage. None of this unofficial 'women can only be one age, one size' or whatever. It was about seeing talented women representing many different women's stories.

**What does feminism mean to you?**

Feminism means deconstructing patriarchy. It means liberating girls and women. I don't think it means equality exactly, because I don't really want the right to be as bad as the blokes are, and run society as badly as the current one is. Patriarchy and capitalism are terrible systems to be in at all. Feminism means liberating ourselves, thinking outside the box, chucking away all the boxes really, and thinking, "what could we be if we weren't affected by stereotypes and the expectations of what men and women *should* be like? How would it be if we could find what our potential is as women and girls, and got to be in charge, take the lead and change the narrative?" It's much easier to imagine it, by seeing it on stage. That's where I think stories and theatre comes in. It helps people to live it if they can see it. You're creating the wheels to put on the vehicles and they can go driving off into the sunset with them.

**How has feminism influenced your work?**

It absolutely is the skeleton, the bones, the blood and everything of our work. For a start, we do site-specific, mid-scale and mainstream touring, large-scale theatre tours; we do some television and radio; we work with fusion events, with musicians and animators, we bring all sorts of stuff together. We work a lot with verbatim and community theatre as well as, obviously, commissioning straight-up plays. The only really common thread to such a variety of output is feminism. We're looking for every output that any woman might be doing that's interesting, vibrant, and makes other women feel better about being a woman.

**Has the content of your work changed over time?**

Yes, tons. It starts with my own background being in theatre. I also do a lot of compering, circus, Glastonbury, and big festivals like that. I'm quite involved in that world so, there's a lot of cabaret in our early work as well. There's a lot of comedy, a lot of women's voices, a lot of music, but then that really shifted into quite big stories, big gothic productions. We did an all-female *Dracula*. We got into a period of our lives where we were really interested in taking classic stories and giving them this massive feminist re-envisioning. So, all-female *Dracula*, all-female *Peter Pan*. Then, of course, with COVID-19, because I'm from Cornwall, we did a lot of site-specific work outdoors.

The environment we work in influences our output a lot and with our interest in how literature and performance, people and spaces interact, you fuse really interesting, site-specific work in that way. But then with COVID-19, we've also done tons more digital work, partly because we were in the middle of interviewing the amazing Greenham women, so we've got all of this fantastic archive of women's interviews from non-violent direct action.

Every one of those interviews is like a film in itself. It could be a movie or a series all on its own. During COVID-19, we created an online VR exhibition which we had never done before. We worked with a wonderful tech co-op and made it into this online VR experience. We also did narrative work. We worked with teaching women to make online computing stuff out of their own interviews and things. To exist online in several "interesting" forms as well as it being registered with a university

Rebecca Mordan and Shazz Andrew in *The Full Brontë Literary Cabaret*
Photo: Lee Searle

and, also, on a big website that people just access.

We also do a lot more livestreaming now. We do a lot more putting our content up, not particularly slick, just quite fast responsive work. We were doing that all through lockdown, turning a lot of our storytelling salons that we had been doing live into sort of monthly or weekly little online salons. I was also in the BBC Writersroom, so then we've started to get more work, working with radio, we've just been optioned by World Productions to be looking at a new, recurring legal drama with a very feminist angle. That's really exciting; actually getting paid to start developing stuff for TV.

We are often led by the interests of members of the company. When we were working with Shazz, she was very interested in storytelling, live storytelling, so we got really good at pairing up traditional stories and written narratives. Then, with Vanessa, she was a teacher for years; she is an amazing person with younger people, particularly her knowledge of schools and what they need is fantastic. We're doing a lot more now of the "Scary Little Schools" programme. We've just been commissioned by the Historic Royal Palaces. We've done a play about Sophia Duleep Singh with

Rebecca Mordan & Flo Crowe in *The Tempest,* a co-production with the Minack Theatre

them. That's currently touring and touring, going all over the country.

**Do you feel women have achieved equality in theatre?**

Absolutely, resoundingly not. It's more about the big theatres resolutely keeping us out. There's a lot more talk about how we need women in theatre and how women need to be represented better but when you look at the statistics on how many artistic directors, at a meaningful mainstream level are women, they are still really low. Women's companies in theatre get less funding overall from the Arts Council, so they're clearly less trusted with public money than male artistic directors. Then, the amount of women who have to do secondary work to stay in the industry, is still terrible. We have a lot of women who come to us because they're sick of not being given good parts, or having to take parts in quite sexist, old-fashioned work, because it's the only work that's out there, particularly in regional theatre.

Many of these are still unofficially adhering to a strict policy about what size and age a woman should be to work as actors. The unofficial standard is that no woman who is a size 10 or over is cast in a leading role. We just disallow most women to work on a variety of criteria and when they're actually in work, they're not being promoted or given access to real change-making funding and bigger venues. It is still very frustrating.

The Arts Council doesn't recognise women as a discriminated group. There's a long way to go. I've been involved recently with a reporter from Sky News who knows how much I've spoken about #MeToo and sexual harrassment. He is looking into whether drama schools are any better now in terms of duty of care for female students. He is finding that they absolutely are not. He still hears stories like mine all over the place, in this day and age. I'm not surprised, but he was shocked. It is very upsetting. He is trying very hard to create a big enough story that he can take it to the House of Lords and they can get an independent body to assess drama schools. The drama schools, at the moment, don't even have an independent regulatory body. If there's a complaint, they have a system of investigating each other and that is clearly a conflict of interest. Whereas if there was an independent assessment, that would make some difference and lead to change. That's what universities have to abide by, at least in part.

We're training people in environments that are still sexist. Then, we're sending them out to work in theatres that are still sexist. We can see from the stats just how many women leave the industry and how hard it is to climb in it, and how effective that sexism still is.

**Is it true that for the last 30 years, the stats haven't moved?**

Yes. They show you how firmly men are saying, "Let's not change it. It's working for us" at really key levels, when you get to where the money is. There's little interest in women's stories. Then, that sort of plays out in every other way. When you look at massive successes in mainstream popular culture, people are biting your hand off if you can make a successful police drama. If someone makes *Line of Duty,* let's say, there's usually a rush to make a lot more like it. That didn't happen with *Orange Is the New Black,* which is really interesting. I was one of many women who were brought into the TV industry because they were saying "we need more feminist women and more women in general," and then we would pitch them various ideas, like I've been trying to make something fictional about Greenham Common for years now, and it ticks all the boxes in terms of diverse casting, strong characters etc but it doesn't involve women being prostituted or incarcerated, so they won't take it up. I'm seeing other women at a level a bit beyond me, who have gotten quite far down the line with commissions for series with really active female protagonists. But when it gets to the serious money, these projects are not progressed because the industry is still run by predominantly older, white blokes.

**They won't take the risk?**

In every art form, women dominate in terms of ticket-buying. It doesn't even make fiscal sense. Obviously, on some level, there's an inbuilt resistance to financing female narratives.

**Have you experienced sex-bias while working in theatre?**

Yes. I watch younger men get promoted above and beyond us, or their newer companies getting support from the lead establishments much more quickly. We've been here turning out really high-quality work for 21 years, employing thousands of women, and pouring over a million pounds into the Cornish economy through all of our work. To celebrate 20 years, we commissioned a survey last year to determine how we had impacted the arts. It was carried out by an outside consultant, and the findings were remarkable. In retrospect, I feel that despite the quality and level of output we are known for, our commitment to feminist work may have been viewed as less worthy of funding than those producing more mainstream productions that do little to challenge the status quo.

Right from the beginning, in these very high-end institutions that you really fight to get into, you're going to be told, "Never say no" or "Keep yourself pretty". After drama school, I was shocked, saddened, annoyed and frustrated by the way women around me were being treated and how my early jobs treated me, and by the lack of interesting roles. If I got a good job, it would still be in a sexist vehicle; I would still have to play out these terrible storylines, even if the pay was good and the job was good. It's unrewarding in that way. I didn't feel like it was helping society. I've basically made my own company and tried to create this little bit of a level playing field, in a very small way. We constituted ourselves to always employ more women than men and always employ along the lines of representation and not along the lines of what people should or shouldn't look like, trying to take a really diverse approach to casting, crew and everything. From then on, I have been very lucky to work with the kind of people who want to work like that, and it's a gift that keeps on giving, personally, professionally and creatively.

≈

Photo: Christine Bradshaw

**Rebecca Mordan** After graduating Sheffield University and Bristol Old Vic Theatre School, Rebecca worked as an actor, director, writer and producer and created award-winning feminist production hub Scary Little Girls.

In 2018, she founded the Greenham Women Everywhere project which has interviewed over 200 Greenham Women and helped to put the Greenham Common Women's Peace Camp back into the cultural conversation. In 2021 she was a member of the BBC Writersroom, wrote for the BBC's Archive on Four, Radio 4's The UK Project and her first book was published, *Out of the Darkness: Greenham Voices.*

She is currently under option with World Productions developing an original idea with writer Sarah Rutherford for a recurring feminist legal drama. Rebecca is a regular contributor to tv and radio, including *You and Yours, 5 Live, Women's Hour,* and *Sky News.* She is also a compère in circus and cabaret and is a regular at the Glastonbury Festival Big Top, the Edinburgh Fringe and the Brighton Fringe. She has used these and other performative skills to work with CAAT, CND, Feminism in London, MADD Fest, Object, Stand Up for Women, Not Buying It and London's Reclaim The Night march.

www.scarylittlegirls.co.uk    www.greenhamwomeneverywhere.co.uk

# INTERVIEW WITH AMY NG

**What does feminism mean to you?**

Women are not a means to male flourishing but ends in themselves.

**How has feminism influenced your work?**

Feminism has influenced my work in three key ways:

- Subject Matter: I've written about issues like forced abortions and arranged marriages in China; sexual coercion in educational settings; the long-term effects of rape on female sexuality; and abortion and Catholicism; as well as plays featuring Margaret Thatcher and Jiang Qing (Madam Mao – wife of Mao Zedong) – in my reading of thwarted feminists who became lieutenants of patriarchy.
- Work Environment: I've frequently worked in all-female spaces (women directors, all-female cast and creatives)
- Critical Lens: Feminism has taught me to question received moral codes and intellectual paradigms, encouraging skepticism towards underlying power dynamics and subtexts in societal structures. This perspective drives me to challenge established norms in my narratives.

**Has the content of your work changed over time?**

The content of my work has undergone significant changes over time:

- Experimentation with form: I've taken bolder strides in experimenting with narrative structures, challenging established dramaturgical norms such as the conventional three-act or five-act structures. Rather than forcing stories into forms, I want to find forms that serve the stories. I've grown increasingly impatient with stories where the hero is gender-flipped to become a heroine, but where the narrative structures remain the same. I want stories where the different ways that women move through the world are integral to the warp and weft, the fabric and structure of our art.
- Exploring how the personal is indeed political – how our deepest secret desires, phobias, and dreams shape and are shaped by macro socio-political forces.

• Over time, I have become more and more conscious of the porousness of time past, time present and time future. I think of my work as a form of time travel. Received narratives of history are written by the victors. Bringing to light the failed revolutions, the suppressed protests, the people on the historical margins is a magical act transporting seeds of alternative futures to our present and replanting them. It allows us to construct an alternative feminist canon, alternative genealogies and lineages, to construct a different trajectory for our futures. It is no accident that history has become central to the cultural wars now. Those who benefit from present-day societal structures have a vested interest in reifying the study of history. It is our task to subvert this.

• Translation and adaptation have become significant aspects of my work. I'm on a mission to expand the world theatrical canon beyond Greek tragedies, Shakespeare, Ibsen, and Chekhov to include works from other traditions. For instance, I've adapted plays by Guan Hanqing, a 13th-century Chinese playwright known in the West as 'The Chinese Shakespeare,' and am currently adapting *The Peony Pavilion,* one of the most famous Chinese plays from the 16th century.

**Do you feel that women have achieved equality in theatre?**
No.

Reading of *Rescuing One's Sister in the Wind and the Dust* adapted from a story by Guan Hanqing. Photo: Almeida Theatre

**Have you experienced sex bias while working in theatre?**

Yes, subtly, in the form of condescension and mansplaining. I've also noticed a palpable difference between all-female spaces and mixed-gender spaces. Men tend to dominate the discussions in the latter, though to be fair, part of this is down to internalised misogyny (certainly on my part). I notice that I tend not to speak so much when men are around. It's a work in progress!

**What would improve opportunities for women in theatre today?**

1) Better and affordable childcare!

2) Achieving a critical mass of women in leadership roles.

3) Achieving a critical mass of women playwrights/women directors on main stages.

4) More women theatre critics! By amplifying female voices in critical discourse, we can diversify perspectives and create an environment that values and recognizes the contributions of women.

**Does intersectionalism influence your work?**

Yes, intersectionalism profoundly influences my work. As a woman of colour and a first-generation immigrant from Hong Kong, I continually grapple with the Eurocentric assumptions pervasive in mainstream Western feminism. Simultaneously, I confront the conservative Chinese narrative that perceives feminism as a radical, extremist ideology imported from the West – a Trojan horse aimed at undermining traditional Chinese values. Therefore, I am on a mission to excavate and illuminate subversive proto-feminist narratives from my own cultural tradition to prove that feminism does not start in the West with Mary Wollstonecraft.

For instance, I adapted Guan Hanqing's *Wind and Dust*, a 13th-century proto-feminist comedy which I like to describe as "similar to *Taming of the Shrew* but the women win!" I have also workshopped another Guan Hanqing play, *A Deceived Wench Sports in the Wind and Moon* – probably the world's first play to feature a servant girl as a protagonist of complexity and dignity, as opposed to the usual "cheeky maid" role serving as plot device/comic relief.

Moreover, even celebrated works like *The Peony Pavilion,* revered as the pinnacle of Chinese theatrical achievement, strike me as extremely subversive and proto-feminist. This play celebrates female sexuality and asserts the primacy of female subjectivity over any claims of Confucian filial piety. It is no coincidence that only excerpts are performed nowadays in China, rather than in its gloriously subversive entirety.

**Do you collaborate with other groups?**

I actively engage in various collectives and informal partnerships, such as a group for Hong Kong theatre workers in the UK, a collective of migrant theatre workers, a community for writers of colour, for East and Southeast Asian theatre workers, and for East and Southeast Asian women in theatre.

Too many of us freelance artists have internalised the message that our careers depend on gatekeepers. Consequently, the focus is often on building vertical connections to decision-makers, to the neglect of building horizontal connections with peers. However, in my experience, it's our peers who enable us to produce our best work. We serve as each other's allies, restoring agency to one another by creating networks and partnerships of solidarity.

**Do we still need feminism?**

Yes.

≈

**Amy Ng** is a British-Hong Kong playwright. Her plays include *Under The Umbrella* (Belgrade Theatre Coventry, UK Tour), *Acceptance* (Hampstead Theatre), *Shangri-La* (Finborough Theatre), and *We Like To Move It Move It* (co-writer, Ice and Fire Theatre). Adaptations include *Miss Julie* (Chester Storyhouse and UK tour; Singapore Repertory Theatre and Hong Kong International Arts Festival). Radio plays include *Tiger Girls* (BBC Radio 4) and *Kilburn Passion* (BBC Radio 3). She is under commission to the Almeida Theatre and the Kiln Theatre and was commissioned by the RSC to adapt Guan Hanqing's *Wind and Dust*. Amy is also a historian with a research interest in multinational empires, imperial decline, and nationality conflict, and is the author of *Nationalism and Political Liberty* (Oxford University Press).

Amy was educated at Yale University and at Balliol College, Oxford University, where she was a Rhodes Scholar. She graduated with a D. Phil in Modern History and was an Alexander von Humboldt Research Fellow in Germany. She is currently based in London.

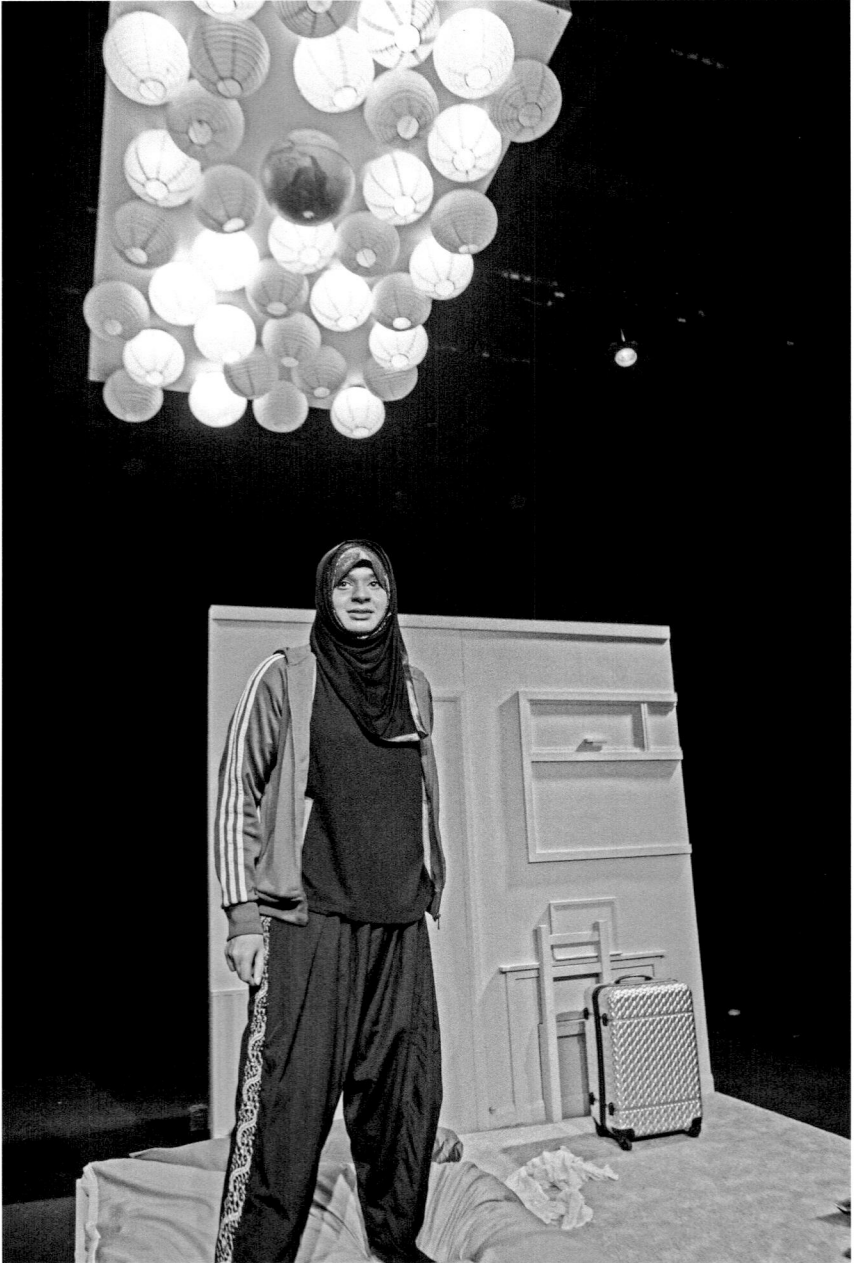

Ambreen Razia in *Diary of a Hounslow Girl,* Ovalhouse Theatre, 2016.
Photo: Richard Davenport

# UNTOLD STORIES
## MAEVE O'NEILL

Theatre, for me, is more than scripts and actors – it's creative teams, directors, designers, stage managers, poets and musicians, collaborating to create a live act, a performance for people to engage with. The 'feminism' in my work comes as much as anything from working with diverse creative teams of talented directors and lighting/sound/set designers such as Sarah Meadows, Wiebke Green, Nicola T Chang, Xana, Martha Godfrey, Zoe Spurr, Mayou Trikerioti, Loren Elstein, Petra Hjortsberg and a long list of creatives who I believe promote inclusivity and equality in their practice. It's about representation and inclusion, not a niche genre but a wide sector of arts activities with audiences and artists at its core.

When I reflect on the productions that I have worked on with female, male and non-binary artists and on the themes that have been explored therein, I begin to understand how my own values, and the political context of that time, are inherent in my professional practice. In 2002, I had joined the Drama Society at Dublin Institute of Technology (DIT) Cathal Brugha Street and discovered *The Vagina Monologues* by Eve Ensler (1996). Written as a series of empowering monologues about the female experience, I performed the monologue *My Vagina Was My Village* which gives a brutal and moving account of rape. Directed by Donnacadh O'Briain we toured to four DIT campuses and raised money for Dublin's Rape Crisis Centre. It proved controversial as posters of 'vagina facts' were removed and the performances included DIT Bolton Street, with a largely male student audience who were enthralled. This gave me an insight into how theatre and performance can inform and have a positive impact.

My professional career as a producer started in 2010 in the UK and since then, I've forged a career in arts administration and project management. For me, the role of a producer is to facilitate the creative process. I do this through project management including writing and managing funding bids with Arts Council England. When I reflect on my portfolio, it features plays that explore themes from a female perspective such as *The Diary of a Hounslow Girl* and *POT* by Ambreen Razia, *Screwed* and *Poisoned Polluted* by Kathryn O'Reilly, *Hidden* by Nicola Werenowska, *WHITE* by Koko Brown and highlights experiences traditionally viewed as 'women's issues' such as abortion: *Vessel* by Laura Wyatt O'Keeffe, and menopause: *Dry Season* by Kat Lyons. I'm drawn to untold stories that we don't frequently see on our main stages.

The context of producing *Vessel,* in which the lead protagonist impregnates herself intentionally to stage a public protest for legalising abortion, was a referendum on legislation to enable abortion, that took place in May 2018 in Northern Ireland. By 2018, legislation in 25 USA states had passed to reduce access to abortion.[1] This resulted in women not having full autonomy over their bodies due to government policies and decisions. Artist and performance maker, Bryony Kimmings said of the play: "*Vessel* is a timely yet timeless play about how we value women and fertility". While I personally am passionately pro-choice, *Vessel* provoked and challenged but didn't patronise or assume anything of its audience. This ability and skill is what I admire in the writers I work with. The referendum in Northern Ireland resulted in the permission to legislate for abortion but there are still 24 countries where abortion is prohibited in any circumstance.[2] When governments create legislation that directly affects women or a particular group in society, it impacts everyone.

At Edinburgh Fringe Festival 2018 I also worked with Koko Brown, writer and performer of *WHITE,* a powerful and entertaining one-person show that shares a story of mixed race heritage and identity. As the sole character says in the opening moments:

I always knew what I was.
I was female, mixed race, aged 8.
'Girl Power' growled through timid teeth!
I was never really a beast.
I was actually quite quiet and shy.
So I wondered why I always had to be Scary Spice.
Now I know why.

Koko's solo performance combined poetry and music with writing that cleverly showed how society categorises people according to their

---

1 National Library of Medicine https://pubmed.ncbi.nlm.nih.gov/33612338/ #:~:text=Medical%20abortion%20laws%20increased%20from,none%20were%20 passed%20in%202018

2 https://focus2030.org/Where-do-abortion-rights-stand-in-the-world-in-2023

gender and race, etc. The piece highlighted the impact of racism and cultural ignorance. A review of *WHITE* in *The Stage* noted that "Brown makes you laugh, but then she makes you hold that laughter up to the light for closer scrutiny."[3] The performance gave an insight into the reality of growing up mixed race in a predominantly white country and unfortunately, we do not see this perspective often enough on our stages. For me *WHITE* highlights systemic racism and unconscious bias, which are issues that intersect directly with feminism and can't be separated. I'm aware of my own privilege and cultural background (white, Irish, raised Catholic) and actively try to learn and improve so that I can support artists who have a story to share. Racism exists in the UK and Ireland, and it exists in our theatres. While the arts industry has begun to address these issues, we still don't see enough representation on stage, backstage or in leadership roles.

When I worked with Ambreen Razia who wrote and originally performed *The Diary of a Hounslow Girl,* terms such as 'Islamic terrorism' featured in UK media and during the Brexit referendum. A coming-of-age story with universal themes, this one-person show tells the story of a British Muslim teenage girl. It struck a chord with audiences, and we did a national tour with Black Theatre Live. In 2017, actress Nyla Levy performed in another national tour with House Theatre and performances at Southbank Centre. It was vital to support the actress and writer from online trolling and bullying, especially when planning and delivering publicity campaigns.

I think it is unfortunate that artists are pushed into being a 'spokesperson' for an entire community, when they are sharing or presenting one story. My frustration with the theatre industry is tokenism. Why are we told that one story from a black person is enough in a theatre's programme? Why are we told that one story from a female perspective is enough in a theatre's season? Reducing a performance to the category of 'feminist theatre' or 'women's theatre' or 'theatre of the global majority' and limiting the number of those performances is damaging to culture. Fortunately, there are many great venues across the UK and Ireland with diverse programmes for their audiences, who work inclusively with artists, but there still isn't enough representation. Since the COVID-19 pandemic, the increasing challenges facing artists and venues highlight

3 Four star review of WHITE at Pleasance Courtyard, 2018 *The Stage* https://www.thestage.co.uk/reviews/2018/white-review-pleasance-courtyard-edinburgh/

the importance of funding. We need cultural leaders and decision makers to actively ensure that the activities they fund and programme are wide ranging in terms of theme, characters and artist representation.

Writer Nicola Werenowska wrote a love story which highlighted her own experience of dyspraxia with *Hidden*, a play that demonstrated to me the lack of understanding, support and infrastructure for people with visible and invisible disabilities and neurodiversity. No artist wants to be pigeonholed but when funding, developing and marketing tours, we need to embrace a target audience as well as reach out to people who would want to see and enjoy the work, but are perhaps harder to engage. Artists sometimes struggle when thinking about who their audience is, specifically, as they frequently reply 'everyone' but it's really useful to approach people from different backgrounds, cultures, ethnicity and genders for input, to see how inclusive your work really is. This requires support from members of those communities who are experienced and knowledgeable in engaging those people, which means we need more paid consultants (eg. a BSL consultant if you want to engage D/deaf audiences). The tried and tested methods of marketing or casting are unlikely to work if they were designed to engage one particular group of people or gender.

There is value in recognising a core audience. Poet Kat Lyons toured their show *Dry Season* (2022-2023 National Tour) which was themed on their experience of peri-menopause, so we embraced the fact that it was likely to attract a core audience of women aged 40yrs+, while also aiming to engage with wider communities and people who would appreciate the performance and story. This decision was reflected in the design, copy and marketing material. It is important to be proud of the work we make. The shame, guilt and secrecy associated with menopause, abortion etc are unhelpful and when you consider these are traditionally presented in the media as 'women's issues', it removes the universality of these themes and doesn't acknowledge the wider impact. Women exist in our workplaces and in our families, so these issues are relevant to all. I would further extend that to LGBTQIA+ communities and race. We need to accept the rich diversity that exists in our communities and embrace it culturally. Theatre and performance can help us realise the commonality of our experiences that cross cultural and religious boundaries. It gives us a shared human experience.

While I don't see myself as a producer of self-consciously feminist or political theatre, the work of producing theatrical performances and events is inherently political. Theatre and performance reflect culture and what exists, as well as what is possible. If we seek to achieve equality, it is not just about women's rights, it is intersectional and requires transparency and accountability.

It is vital to consider the challenges of presenting work with strong themes, set against the backdrop of feminism. There is a danger of presenting 'trauma theatre', especially if artists are sharing autobiographical or semi-autobiographical stories. But we should not assume that female-led theatre or theatre portraying female experiences will be more 'emotional' or 'traumatic'. Working with writer Kathryn O'Reilly on her plays *Screwed* (2016) Theatre503, which highlights 'ladette culture' and alcoholism, and on *Poisoned Polluted* (2019) The Old Red Lion Theatre, which has themes of abuse and addiction, the cast and creative teams for both were female-led and the emphasis was on handling the themes with sensitivity, to engage audiences with challenging and potentially triggering themes. On *Poisoned Polluted*, critic Chloe Billington wrote that, "There are multiple challenges in finding theatrical representations for the repeated cycles of hope and grim despair that characterise

Kathryn O'Reilly and Anna Doolan in *Poisoned Polluted*, Old Red Lion, 2019.
Photo: Robert Workman

unresolved childhood trauma and the attempts to find relief in substance abuse."[4] In this instance the issues were delicately handled, we included Q&As and post-show discussions with experts in addiction and mental health practitioners. Increasingly, we are also seeing care being taken about the impact of rehearsing and performing a show with hard-hitting themes or scenes. This requires more funding and support so that venues, partners and producers can provide artists and audiences with a safe space and expert support (eg. counselling/intimacy coordinators etc) to explore these themes. By side-lining female-led theatre, we risk missing out on gritty, hard-hitting performance and writing.

I would love to see theatres be a little braver in their programming, rather than holding back on the number of female writers they support. On *Screwed*, critic Stephen Bates noted that "O'Reilly's play is both funny and disturbing, showing lives that lie behind the statistics that tell us of increasing alcohol problems among women."[5] Personally, I don't think we've seen enough stories on our stages that represent the many facets and lived experiences of women and intersectionality. Staging these performances and stories is important as it gives people the chance to be entertained, to feel empathy and to learn something new about themselves or other people. I feel privileged to have worked with and continue to work with artists who tackle subjects with bravery and talent. Regardless of gender, the teams I've collaborated with have consistently taken an inclusive approach and prioritised the quality of the work. My work as a producer has included cross-artform performance, theatre, new writing, poetry, spoken word and contemporary dance. There are many great, contemporary writers and artists who have equality and inclusion as an integral part of their work and who inspire me, such as Bryony Kimmings, Joelle Taylor, Kae Tempest, Hollie McNish, Deanna Rodger, The Thelmas (Madelaine Moore & Guleraana Mir), Garry Hynes (Druid Theatre Company), Vicky Featherstone, Adrienne Hart (Neon Dance) and Travis Alabanza, to name but a few.

Changemakers are needed and creatives such as Suzanne Alleyne and Stella Kanu bring attention to the current issues facing the UK arts sector, especially in relation to leadership. We need to listen to and actively support these voices. Suzanna Alleyne has done invaluable research into

---

4 Five Star review of *Poisoned Polluted* by Chloe Billington https://www.theatre-news.com/review/UK/3788/Theatre/Headline

5 Four Star review of *Screwed* by Stephen Bates https://www.theatre-news.com/review/UK/3788/Theatre/Headline

the power structures of the arts industry and the lack of representation specifically for black women. Systemic racism and unconscious bias are significant challenges to overcome. If we're looking for equality, then we have to acknowledge and find the language and actions to process and counteract inequality. It will mean changing the way we recruit and deliver projects. I've learnt a lot through working with people such as Stella Barnes and Naomi Shoba (Brixton House, formerly Ovalhouse) and Lisa Mead (Apples and Snakes). All of this highlights the importance of questions such as 'Who is running our national cultural buildings and institutions? Who is on their board of trustees and who is represented?'. Patriarchal systems are embedded in our economies, structures and politics. At a time when the world seems divided, it's not about highlighting differences but rather, being able to acknowledge and accept our differences to overcome ignorance and hatred.

Can theatre save the world? Maybe not, but it could certainly be a part of the solution.

≈

**Maeve O'Neill** (she/her) is an independent arts producer and founder of Rua Arts. Originally from Dublin, based in the UK since 2003. Maeve is executive producer for Neon Dance and company producer for children's poet Simon Mole. Maeve manages productions, national tours and projects for artists, theatre companies and arts organisations. Maeve facilitates sessions on producing and funding for organisations including RADA, Roundhouse, Apples and Snakes and The Albany. She originally trained at The Gaiety School of Acting, Dublin and completed a BA in Modern Drama Studies at Brunel University. Credits include *Poetry Picnic* (National Tour 2021-22 Simon Mole); *Dry Season* (National Tour, 2022-23 Kat Lyons); *Chicken Burger n Chips* (Brockley Jack 2020 Corey Bovell); *Poisoned Polluted* (Old Red Lion 2019 Kathryn O'Reilly); *POT* (National Tour 2018 Ambreen Razia); *WHITE* (Pleasance Edinburgh Festival Fringe 2018 Koko Brown); *Vessel* (Underbelly Edinburgh Festival Fringe 2018 Laura Wyatt O'Keeffe); *Hidden* (Regional Tour 2017 Nicola Werenowska); *Screwed* (Theatre503 2016 Kathryn O'Reilly); *The Diary of a Hounslow Girl* (UK National Tours 2016-2017 Ambreen Razia); *The Table* (Edinburgh Fringe Festival 2011 Blind Summit Theatre). https://www.ruaarts.earth

*L to R:* Melissa MacNaught, Kirsten Hutchison, Sally Cairns.
Photo: Josie Morrison Young

# GIRLS' NIGHT OUT:

## The Case For Fun in Feminist Theatre

## RACHEL O'REGAN

*"You know, for feminist theatre, that was actually really entertaining."*

Without a doubt, we hear some variation of that sentence after each of our shows. I suppose the implication is that feminist theatre is expected to bore the audience to tears with its self-seriousness. Reviews often praise our work for its avoidance of preachiness or pretentiousness, as if we were a bright pink island in a sea of dreary feminist drama.

Of course, that's not true. As of the time of writing this chapter, F-Bomb is only three years old, and we would be remiss not to acknowledge our contemporaries who inspire us. In Scotland alone, there are numerous feminist theatre companies producing work that is urgent, exciting, radical and joyous. These include the trailblazing intersectional theatre company Stellar Quines, as well as emerging companies like Pretty Knickers, Untie My Tongue and Koi Collective. I'm certain they, too, have heard some version of that sentence more times than they can count.

Even if people were to say, "You know, for theatre, it was actually entertaining," it would probably bother us less. You're not supposed to admit it, but theatre can be quite dull and pretentious at times. I've often left a theatre perplexed about what I had just witnessed and what I was meant to learn from it (though you're not supposed to say that either). Perhaps I'm simply not clever enough to grasp it, or maybe that esoteric style of theatre isn't always engaging…

When I began my playwriting master's programme at Edinburgh Napier University, our class was asked which play had inspired us to pursue theatre. Many can relate to the unique challenge of having to prove oneself in a peer-professor setting. We went around in a circle, citing the Greeks, Antonin Artaud and the "in yer face" movement. I had come to theatre relatively late in life, in my mid-twenties, feeling like a certified relic among the nepo-babies and under-25 schemes. I was completely unprepared for these references. I gave a compliant yet bland response and counted down the seconds until the next writer started discussing Brecht.

Reflecting on it now, I wish I had been brave enough to speak the truth. I wanted to create theatre because I had seen *Mamma Mia!* and it blew my tiny mind. And *The Phantom of the Opera*. And *Wicked* and *The Play That Goes Wrong* and *Fleabag* and *Our Ladies of Perpetual Succour* and *Chewing Gum Dreams*. These were the popular, laugh-out-loud, spectacular productions that you would take someone to who had never seen a theatre show in their life.

I wanted to make theatre with a strong message and urgency towards the issues of today, but entertaining the audience was always just as important a priority. That's why I got along so well with the F-Bomb girls. F-Bomb Theatre was formed by a group of female acting students at the same university I attended. Tired of being saddled with the roles of long-suffering girlfriends and mothers in domestic dramas, they were looking for a playwright who could write a comedy script for women. The rest is herstory.

I was determined to have fun with our play *Afterparty*, a comedy-drama about a scrappy group of benefits-class teen girls awaiting their future after graduating high school. At the time of developing the script, my mum had recently passed away, COVID lockdown was in full force, and the news was a 24/7 doom spiral. Perhaps there's something unsophisticated about a play

Kirsten Hutchison, Linzi Devers, Sally Cairns. Photo: Hannah McEachern

that opens with a direct address in which one of the characters threatens the audience to stop looking at her or she'd batter them "like a sausage". But it made us laugh, and we thought it would make the audience laugh too, and isn't there something urgent in that?

I was workshopping the play with the brilliant Scottish theatre director Niloo-Far Khan when she let me in on a secret: *entertainment is a political act.* Well, it's not really a secret – a lot of people have been saying so for years. Notably, John McGrath. His manifesto, *A Good Night Out: Popular Theatre: Audience, Class and Form*, argues against the bourgeois, intellectualised theatre which is canonised by critics and historians (read: middle class, traditionally educated white men). He makes a case for working class entertainment, where the theatre can be funny, direct, emotional and accessible. What a concept!

"A good night out" is not just relevant to working-class audiences, but to everyone who feels unwelcome and othered in theatre spaces. I find it baffling how theatres will wring their hands about the lack of new and diverse audiences, but the ticket prices remain extortionate, the etiquette is stifling, and the performances are indulgently traumatic without a content warning to be found. I have seen more than enough scenes of women being raped and tortured onstage, and I always think: who is that for? It's certainly not for women, of which one in three will experience violence in her lifetime.

For our company, it comes down to this: surely, we have the right to a good night out? Women and people of marginalised genders are bombarded with enough on a daily basis. When they sit down to watch one of our shows, we don't want it to feel like an onslaught. Our Fringe First-winning play, *The Beatles Were A Boyband*, confronted women's safety, misogyny and femicide… and it was entertaining. Alongside the pain and the rage, the script quoted *Twilight* and *Love Island*, and included pop songs by One Direction and Taylor Swift. (I can talk at length about the justification of such unserious, unapologetically feminine references in a play about male violence, but that may be an essay for another day.)

A side-effect of this approach, we discovered, is that it made the play accessible to men, too. There is an argument that if your feminism is appealing to men, that means it's not working. Respectfully, I disagree. We need men as allies and if an entertaining play helps change their minds, this sounds like a winning scenario for everyone. Of course, it should be discomforting, and I don't want us to slide back into the pattern of playing nice so as to not offend men. But the beauty of theatre is that you have a captive audience and time to make an argument. If you start that dialogue with your audience on a weighty level, and don't allow for respite, the danger is that they will shut down emotionally. Such is human nature – especially when coming into an environment with little education or sympathy towards the cause. Make your audience laugh and relax a little first, and they'll be much more likely to feel something later.

I'd be lying if I didn't say this feels like a trap sometimes. Women are conditioned to swallow down their anger, and if they must show it, do so in a way that is palatable – to not be the angry feminist, the one who can't take a joke, let alone write one. And then if you make the choice to present your feminism in a more entertaining format, there will be criticisms that you haven't gone far enough. As women, as feminists, as theatre makers, you can never do enough, or satisfy everyone, and every choice is met with a thousand contradictions that will make your head spin.

For F-Bomb, right now, our approach is feminism through the vehicle of theatrical entertainment. It's what has worked so far to welcome

Sally Cairns and Rachel O'Regan. Photo: Josie Morrison Young

audiences of all demographics and backgrounds, particularly people who are *not* traditional theatre-goers. It's wonderful to walk into the bar after one of our shows and witness animated conversations between men and women, fathers and daughters, partners and peers, and friends and coworkers.

*"I never thought about it like that. This really opened my eyes."*

*"I was worried the play might be too triggering to watch, but I just felt seen."*

And of course, *"For feminist theatre, that was actually really entertaining."*

It's hoped that, somewhere down the line, this little unsophisticated subgenre of feminist theatre can start to break apart these stigmas. And we can *all* finally just have a good night out.

≈

**Rachel O'Regan** is an award-winning feminist playwright based in Edinburgh, Scotland. Rachel's first full-length play *Hungerland* won the Bread and Roses Playwriting Award in 2019. Her next play, *Afterparty*, was produced by new women's theatre company F-Bomb Theatre and sold out its entire run at Edinburgh Fringe 2021. Her most recent play, *The Beatles Were A Boyband*, was produced by F-Bomb Theatre and debuted at Edinburgh Festival Fringe 2022. Exploring women's safety in a culture of male violence, it won a Scotsman Fringe First Award and the Sit-Up Award for social impact. Rachel has also been a finalist in the Women of the Future Awards and had development from BBC Writersroom as part of Scottish Voices.

F-Bomb Theatre is an award-winning feminist theatre company based in Scotland. Aside from their productions, they have launched community-focused initiatives designed to support women and people of marginalised genders in an industry that has historically been male-dominated. These have included their International Women's Day Showcases, which provide emerging female writers with dramaturgical support and a platform to share their work. They also originated the FemiFringe movement, a vibrant community that celebrates the work led by women and individuals of marginalised genders at the Edinburgh Festival Fringe. The F-Bomb Theatre FemiFringe Guide lists the shows at the Fringe that are created by women, trans, or non-binary people. In August 2023, they distributed 2,000 free print copies of the FemiFringe Guide.

**playing 'the maids'**

Amidst austerity, who is smiling now? Who moves whom? An international ensemble explores the dynamics of servitude...

Flyer for *playing 'The Maids'*

# INTERVIEW WITH KAITE O'REILLY

**What does feminist mean to you?**

I like how Sara Ahmet defines feminism as "the dynamism of making connections... Feminism is bringing people into the room."[1] It can happen through that moment of connection through shared experience – the realisation of prejudice, power relations, misogyny or ableism – or as the young Rebecca West mused over a century ago:

> "I myself have never been able to find out precisely what feminism is:
> I only know that people call me a feminist whenever I express
> sentiments that differentiate me from a doormat."[2]

**How has feminism influenced your work?**

I'm interested in social justice, in what we described (problematically) at the end of last century as 'giving voice to the voiceless'. This sense of fairness and equity, of telling the stories of the excluded and denied, impacts on my politics and identity not just as a woman, but as an Irish-disabled woman. The humanism of feminism and the insistence on fairness, equality, and inclusivity has been my lodestar. So much of my development as an artist has been through creative experimentation with phenomenally talented and generous women, who challenged me, corrected me, fought with me, loved me, guided, and at times made work with me, stretching my practice, making me think about power dynamics and hierarchies. There are many, but some of these women include Jane Arden, Caryl Churchill, Anna Furse, Jenny Sealey, Jean St Clair, Nat Lim, Julie (Mack) McNamara, Christina Katic and my mother Betty O'Reilly. Feminist men who were impactful include John E McGrath, Sam Boardman-Jacobs, and Phillip Zarrilli. I was also fortunate to train extensively with Augusto Boal and his Theatre of the Oppressed from the mid to late 80s and this allied itself to my emerging disability politics and established female-centric identity: the realisation that whether working class, female, queer, disabled, immigrant, or other elements where we have been 'othered' in some way – we are not

---

1    Sarah Ahmet *Living a Feminist Life*, Duke University Press
2    Rebecca West, *The Young Rebecca: Writings 1911-17*

inferior, but oppressed – not insignificant, but excluded. This has impacted on the work I have made throughout my career, initially in applied drama using Boal's techniques in post-conflict reconciliation contexts and then as a playwright, trying to tell stories overlooked or deemed uninteresting to the majority culture and the decision makers/gatekeepers – invariably (but not always) white, non-disabled, straight men.

**Has the content or form of your work changed over time? How?**

Considerably. I was an interpreter (actor) or facilitator early in my career, then I became (and remain) a collaborator and co-creator with devised work. The process and billing is different when I work as a playwright, as then I am the lead artistic voice.

Initially, I was categorised as an Irish feminist playwright (my first piece was one of the winners of the Royal Court Young Playwrights Festival a thousand years ago, and was about the Cumann na mBan, an Irish Republican women's paramilitary organisation founded in 1914 and involved in the Easter Rising of 1916).

I then became known as a disability artist owing to my work within disability arts, inclusivity, and the aesthetics of access. I have become more engaged in themes and contexts exploring the intersectionality of our lived experience – how we can be part of disparate groups regarding geography, gender, sexual preference, disability, cultural heritage, etc, and yet have shared experience and connection. This has been particularly the case in my multi-lingual, international, intercultural work *The 'd' Monologues,* written solely for disabled and Deaf collaborators such as *And Suddenly I Disappear* (Singapore/UK, 2018; South Korea, 2019) and *Something Wonderful* (China, 2022/3).

**Do you feel women have achieved equality in theatre?**

Absolutely not. It's worse this year statistically re: the number of female playwrights/lead artists being produced than in previous years, though I'm encouraged by the recent appointment of female artistic directors (Indhu Rubasingham at NT, Kate Wasserberg at Theatr Clwyd, Tamara Harvey as co-artistic director at RSC, etc)

**Have you experienced sex bias while working in theatre?**

Oh yes. And ableism and discrimination because I'm Irish. It's not a comfortable or easy path when you're a woman. We need to be strong, to be forthright, to be firebrands, to not care about what others think of us or whether we're coming across as 'trouble' when we challenge the bias (whether conscious or otherwise) which we consistently experience. We need to call it out, to support others marginalised or undermined, and boldly address the power dynamics in a room or working situation. My mother always said: 'you have a tongue in your head – use it,' so I delight in being 'mouthy', I celebrate the title 'difficult woman' and the other slights created to silence or demean me and other women. They don't shut me up. Rather, I see them for what they are – weapons which become ineffectual when I persist, ignore, or address their presence in the room. But, like racism and ableism, this prejudice is systemic and ingrained in every aspect of our culture. It's going to take a lot to get rid of it.

**What would improve the opportunities for women in theatre today?**

We need to find ways of encouraging women to consider and apply for these opportunities. At present we're falling at the first hurdle. Women are less likely to apply for jobs they are qualified for than men. I was struck by a study by *Harvard Business Review* which said women only applied for jobs when they were 100% qualified, whereas men would apply when they were just 60% qualified. This is a major issue we urgently need to address. To actively seek out, invite and support women in getting into the industry, and to understand what we can do to unpick this reluctance in going for the few opportunities available. Is it lack of confidence? Imposter syndrome? In an article for *Mslexia* magazine, Susie Orbach believed it's due to fear of rejection. Whatever it is, it has been imprinted, ingrained within our minds and psyches and it needs to be erased.

We also need those who make the decisions and shape the culture of any institution/company/cultural building or initiative to be less corporate-minded and more engaged with notions of multiplicity, diversity, inclusivity, with a flexibility in approach and willingness to expect and foster different ways of doing things…

To consider the welfare of ALL in the industry – to get everyone who works with a company whether full-time or on a short contract to fill out a rider that identifies what conditions would be best for them to engage and make the best work they can… The working day may be different for those with caring responsibilities, or who are managing their energy. We can change the structures, processes, and theatre itself by having a less prescriptive approach. Banish the 'but this is the way it's always been done', as it clearly isn't working.

**Do you collaborate with other groups?**

Since 2014 I've been exploring intercultural collaborations with different groups. *playing 'The Maids'* was a performative exploration of the dynamics of power and female servitude in Genet's *The Maids,* co-created with Gaitkrash (Ireland), The Llanarth Group (Wales) and Theatre P'Yut (South Korea). A co-authored book with a chapter by each of the collaborators from their perspective – dramaturg, director, sound artist, devising performer, etc – will be published by Bloomsbury later this year, titled *Intercultural Processes, Practices and Perspectives – Co-creating playing 'The Maids'.*

I began a long-term project called *The 'd' Monologues* in 2010 ('d' denoting Deaf, disability, diversity, deliciousness, etc) – where I created fictional solos specifically and solely for disabled, Deaf and neuro-divergent artists, informed by interviews and exchanges I had with disabled and Deaf individuals around the world. The first, *In Water I'm Weightless*, was part of the Cultural Olympiad celebrating the 2012 London Olympics/Paralympics and was a collaboration with National Theatre Wales. An international Unlimited Commission led to *And Suddenly I Disappear: The Singapore/UK 'd' Monologues*, an international dialogue about difference and exclusion, collaborating with The Llanarth Group (Wales) and Access Path Productions (Singapore). The work was with an all Deaf, disabled, and neurodivergent international cast using English, Tamil, Mandarin, Malay, Singaporean Sign Language and British Sign Language, premiering in Singapore and then London's Southbank Centre before touring the UK.

I'm always interested in the power dynamics of a collaboration and the intricacies and challenges of making multilingual, intercultural work.

**Do we still need feminist theatre? Why?**

Yes. *The Stage* stated that three quarters of plays produced in 2022 were by men. We have bias in work environments, gender privilege, unequal pay for the same job. Post-pandemic women are shouldering more caring duties. Female-led companies often work in more inclusive ways, or with more flexibility.

But let's dig into what feminist theatre might be… I'm going to adapt Catherine Castellani's quotation[3] and assert there is no formula or definition for feminist theatre, as there's no definitive formula for what it is to be human. For me, feminism has always been about social justice,

3      Castellani, Catherine "What IS a Feminist Play Anyway? What IS vs. What Should Be". Women in Theater Journal Online, Spring 2017.

equity, curiosity, and respecting all – it is radical in that it embraces the possibility of transformation and change. I think we go to theatre because we are endlessly fascinated in what it is to be human and are open to our preconceptions being challenged and possibly changed. Good theatre provokes thought and for me feminist theatre is something exploratory, curious, a practice seeking parity and understanding, with the possibility of changing perception and action – stimulating us to think about and do things differently.

In a recent conversation about this with writer and academic Professor Gill Plain she said:

> 'We need feminist theatre like we need feminism in general: it's about seeing things differently, telling different stories – or telling the same stories from different points of view. Casting women in conventionally male roles, all-female companies, new writing that foregrounds women: all this stuff makes a difference. I'm sure there are statistics… the history of the stuff matters – reminds people what being radical used to mean – and new modes of feminist theatre matter, because we still live in a fucked up patriarchal world, and feminism – at its best – says NO, think differently. It doesn't have to be this way.'

Yes. Yes. Yes.

## Do you think having a theatre dedicated to women's work would have an impact?

There have already been theatre companies dedicated to women's work (Sphinx, Monstrous Regiment, BloodGroup, Women in Theatre, Cunning Stunts, etc) and their presence and contribution have been or continue to be important and frustratingly undervalued. I'm intrigued to see what the impact of Women in Theatre Lab, launched by Her Stories Productions in November 2023, may be.

Yes, a theatre dedicated to women's work is important and needed. we need to address gender disparity, but this is still putting a plaster on a wound. We can't remain on the periphery. To really change things and have an impact "women's work" needs to be commissioned and produced by every company and building-based theatre across the UK – so it becomes ubiquitous, usual, just part of the cultural output. I feel the same around disabled-led work – let it not be a tick box ('we've *done* disability with our interpreted show featuring some disabled and Deaf creatives last year') but a constant and invigorating part of our culture.

### Are prizes important? Why? Why not?

I have certainly benefitted from prizes – winning different awards throughout my career has impacted on my visibility and what was recently described to me as my 'contemporary relevance'. I would not like to be starting out in today's overcrowded, jostling creative industry, so perhaps it's helpful to have platforms that might raise the lucky few above the teeming masses? But again, we get to the gritty issue of few women applying for awards or competitions.

I've found it helpful to consider this from another form – literature. *Mslexia* magazine and the Society of Authors have on several occasions covered the subject of why women writers submit less, and the discussion last summer over whether the Women's Prize for Fiction was pandering to tokenism and creating victim-mentality was stimulating. In her *Observer* feature on retiring the prize, Martha Gill felt, "It is disheartening to feel that you've achieved something on the basis of your identity rather than on merit…. The white men are there because they deserved to be, they are saying – the rest of you are being terribly helpful to us in ticking this box." [4]

In comparison, The Women's Prize for Playwriting, launched in 2019 by Ellie Keel in partnership with Paines Plough, has been called a game-changer through truly advocating for women's voices in theatre. And it is needed – perhaps rather like the original women's fiction prize (then the Orange Prize) was needed in the 1990s owing to not one female novelist being shortlisted for a spread of prizes. Interestingly, women dominated the gender-neutral performing categories in 2023's WhatsonStage Awards – illuminatingly the only award chosen by the public.

### Is arts funding equitable?

I think decisions are made owing to all sorts of in-house selection criteria we the applicants are not privy to. When successful applicants are announced, at times it has been possible to guess what demographics the statistics needed to hit that year…

I've been intrigued by an emerging practice in some funding streams of anonymous initial expressions of interest – obviously, once full applications are required, anonymity is impossible – but I'm keen to see if there is any difference in gender from this practice.

---

4    Martha Gill. https://www.theguardian.com/commentisfree/2023/jun/18/female-novelists-dont-need-their-own-prizes-lets-abolish-them

## How can we improve things for women in theatre?

Campaigning. Complaining. Calling out and refusing to accept the bias and gender disparity in productions, pay and opportunities. To keep the issue alive and in front of people. To have forums and meetings where we can come together and discuss what needs to change, and how we may go about it. To be collective – there's power in numbers – and organise summits with the gatekeepers, commissioners, and decision makers to ask what tangible steps are being taken to improve the situation. By expending energy and keeping the subject current, things will improve – but it's exhausting. I try to remember that the history of social justice is not linear, going from one success to the next, mending our unjust systems as we go – rather, it is cyclical, full of retreats, defeats and set-backs and we need to have resilience and stamina.

Injustice is the result of conscious human decisions – but it's temporary, able to be changed by the will of ordinary people doing extraordinary things.

I try to keep optimistic and hopeful for change – it's a daily practice.

≈

**Kaite O'Reilly** is a multi-award-winning playwright and dramaturg, who writes for radio, screen and live performance. Prizes include the Peggy Ramsay Award, Manchester Theatre Award, Theatre-Wales Award and the Ted Hughes Award for new works in *Poetry for Persians* (National Theatre Wales). She is a two-time finalist in the International James Tait Black Prize for Innovation in Drama (2012, 2019) and The Susan Smith-Blackburn Prize. She was honoured in the 2017/18 International Eliot Hayes Award for Outstanding Achievement in Dramaturgy for developing 'Alternative Dramaturgies informed by a Deaf and Disability Perspective'. A leading figure in disability arts and culture internationally, her *Atypical Plays for Atypical Actors* and *The 'd' Monologues* are published by Oberon/Bloomsbury. Her first feature film, *The Almond and the Seahorse,* featuring Rebel Wilson and Charlotte Gainsbourg, will be released in the UK in 2024. www.kaiteoreilly.com

Nell Murphy in *Hanjo* written by Seami & Yukio Mishima adapted by Diane Esguerra for Sphinx. Photo: Dee Conway

# SPHINX
## SUE PARRISH & SUSAN MCGOUN

The Women's Theatre Group (WTG), relaunched in 1990 as Sphinx Theatre Company, is the longest established women's theatre company in the UK. In the context of the Women's Liberation Movement, WTG was founded as a separatist feminist theatre group for the first Women's Festival at the Almost Free Theatre in 1973. Monstrous Regiment and the Women's Company, were also formed for the landmark festival. Funded by the Arts Council in 1975, the WTG toured education and community venues across the UK with company-devised shows, and in 1978, began to commission women playwrights.

**Susan McGoun:**

When I joined the WTG in 1978, there were two things that moved the company on and assisted in its development as a theatrical force. The first was the commissioning of women writers rather than the collectively devised work coming from within the company. This new play was *Hot Spot* by Melissa Murray and Eileen Fairweather and directed by Sue Dunderdale. We still toured to schools and youth clubs but the second change, the increase in our Arts Council annual grant from £15,000 to £30,000, allowed us to plan ahead and commission new work from Timberlake Wertenbaker, Donna Franceschild and Bryony Lavery among others. We could also employ a part-time administrator and work with women directors and designers. The expansion led to playing bigger venues and small theatres. We also got better digs and better pay!

We were still a touring company and made a statement as an all-woman collective by driving the van, doing the 'get in', putting up the set, sorting out the lighting, doing the show and then reversing the process. It was hard work, but we were often shown great kindness by individuals who gave up their beds and produced food late at night. There was a camaraderie on the road, and we sometimes met up with other touring groups as we made our way up and down the M1, stopping at Leicester East and Watford Gap services. It was a relief when I left the company to not think about getting in the van and driving up to Sheffield – again!

We had a loyal audience and venues that booked us year after year – colleges, universities and women's groups – but we also made an impact with audiences that were not necessarily connected to the demands of the Women's Liberation Movement that first informed the work.

Between 1980-82 we were invited to work abroad to perform at the Souterine and Melkweg in Amsterdam and the Groningen International Women's Festival. One play, *My Mkinga*, about drug dumping in the third world, was translated into Dutch and toured in Holland. *My Mkinga* was one of nine productions I performed in, including *Soap Opera*, a musical set in a launderette, by Donna Franceschild; *Breaking Through*, about nuclear power, and *New Anatomies*, about cross-dressing, colonialism, Isabelle Eberhart and Victorian music hall impersonators, both by Timberlake Wertenbaker.

The last play I performed in, *Dear Girl*, which we later recorded for BBC Radio 4 (under the title *Friend to Friend*) was based on the diaries and letters of four working class women between 1897-1917. It showed the active Women's Movement throughout the 20th century, not just in the 1970s. These women explored personal and sexual freedom as well as campaigning for the vote. The play showed the impact of the women's movement on their everyday lives.

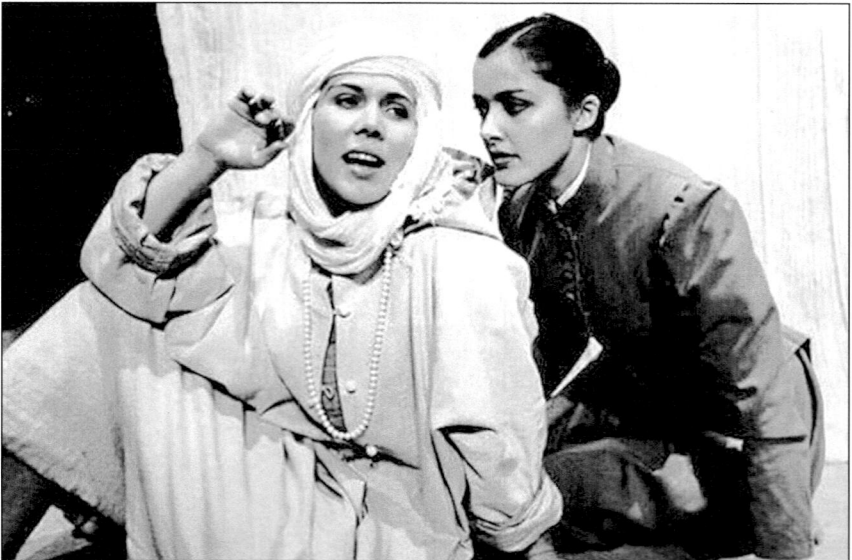

Hazel Maycock and Adele Saleem in *New Anatomies* by Timberlake Wertenbaker

As a collective we all had a say in policy decisions and the direction of the company. Our commitment as a new writing company meant we were able to create stimulating roles for actresses, show the creativity of women writers, and enable women directors and designers to exhibit their skills and talents. This is a unique aspect of our legacy – but we needed the money!

The legacy of the WTG is not only in their plays, which are studied worldwide, but also their roster of now established playwrights and directors who cut their teeth with early productions: Timberlake Wertenbaker, Bryony Lavery, Paulette Randall, Winsome Pinnock, Deborah Levy, Gwenda Hughes and Julie Wilkinson among others, and the wider political impact of touring original feminist theatre across the UK and internationally.

**Sue Parrish:**

I served my theatre apprenticeship after university at the Half Moon Theatre, then a famous political fringe theatre, and home to many productions of Brecht, and Dario Fo, as well as English new writing. Simon Callow was Arturo Ui, and Frances de La Tour, Patti Love, Christopher Malcolm and Denis Lawson starred in the UK premiere of Dario Fo's *Can't Pay, Won't Pay*.

Many alternative and feminist companies played the Half Moon and it was where I first encountered and worked with the playwright Pam Gems. We presented Carole Harrison as *Sandra*, a neglected and abused young woman who murdered her newborn baby in a brilliant, heartrending, hugely successful performance. This was a dive into a then unknown, brutal world written by Pam with devastating authenticity. Carole toured fringe venues and festivals performing *Sandra* for some years. I followed this with a studio tour of Pam's play *Dusa, Fish, Stas and Vi*.

As a freelance director, I benefitted from the contacts I'd made at the Half Moon. There was a cross-fertilisation amongst all the alternative companies. I'm very proud that I directed the first gay play presented at the Soho Poly theatre: *Men*, by Stephen Holt, set in a New York welfare hotel, starred Philip Osment and was designed by Paul Dart, from Gay Sweatshop. Having toured to full houses on the fringe, we enlisted Gay Sweatshop's well-known playwright Noel Greig to advocate for us with the reluctant Soho Poly management, and then had to lay on extra performances as the queues filed round the block! Success!!

After a couple of years with no real progress, a group of female colleagues formed a new organisation: the Conference of Women Theatre Directors and Administrators which held an event at the ICA in 1979 at which the famous writer of *Sexual Politics,* Kate Millet, came from America to speak. (I just phoned her, and she came!) There was a huge 400-strong queue down the Mall, and we continued with a second event, this time at the Young Vic, which also sold out. The most prominent women writers – Beryl Bainbridge, Angela Carter, Caryl Churchill, Fay Weldon and Michelene Wandor came to speak. These numbers demonstrated the widespread hunger for dialogue, networking, and solidarity.

It was clear that we needed statistical evidence to confront endemic inequality so we commissioned a UK-wide survey: 'The Status of Women in British Theatre'. The focus of this survey was female directors and playwrights across 120 UK national, regional, touring and alternative theatres. In 1983, only 7% of produced playwrights were women, and only 12% were women directors. 42 out of 620 plays produced were written by women (22 of these were written by Agatha Christie), which if excluded, brought the 7% figure of female playwrights down to 3.5%. Roles available to women actors were approximately 33% of the total.

Copies of the survey were sent to the Arts Council, major theatres and to the press, to be met with a resounding silence! However, statistical research has developed as a vital tool in each company I have worked with. We came to the realisation that women's roles would not be expanded beyond the stereotypical wife/mother/girlfriend/sister to the central male protagonist in the hands of male writers. Women must write their own stories.

Out of these conference meetings, came the most transformative group in my life – the Women's Playhouse Trust (WPT). This combusted in the basement of Pam Gems' house. She had enjoyed success in the West End with *Dusa, Fish, Stas and Vi*, and with *Queen Christina, Camille*, and most notably *Piaf,* all for the RSC from 1976 to 1978. The Women's Playhouse Trust developed into a company led by Rosemary Squire, Jules Wright (a resident director at the Royal Court Theatre), and me. Rosemary, now a Dame, went on to co-found the Ambassador Theatre Group and then Trafalgar Theatres, but at that point, she was working front-of-house at the Albery Theatre.

WPT demanded a place for women in the mainstream and this prompted the 'coming out' of many leading women actors, until then 'in the closet' about their career opportunities and longevity. We are now used to seeing TV and newspaper reports of leading actresses bemoaning their fate. In 1980, it was the 'elephant in the room'. We convinced Dame Peggy Ashcroft, Glenda Jackson, Jane Lapotaire, Diana Quick, Harriet Walter, Janet Suzman, Juliet Stevenson, and Fiona Shaw, among others, to join us in the search for a West End theatre.

Funded intermittently for education purposes by the Greater London Council, and by investors for productions, the WPT produced the first revival of Aphra Behn's *The Lucky Chance*, starring Harriet Walter and Alan Rickman at the Royal Court, directed by Jules Wright, followed by *Spell #7*, by Ntozake Shange, the first play at the Donmar Warehouse written by a Black playwright, which I directed. This was followed by *My Heart's a Suitcase* by Clare McIntyre and directed by Nancy Meckler. We ran rehearsed readings, women writers' workshops (always over-subscribed), and hosted public discussion events. One of the most memorable talks was with Marilyn French, the American writer and academic, revealing the poverty of Shakespeare's female characters, to the disbelief and anguish of many leading actresses in the audience.

Another unforgettable talk was with Hélène Cixous, the French writer and playwright of the Théâtre Du Soleil, revealing her inspirational relationship with the legendary director Ariane Mnouchkine.

Alan Rickman and Harriet Walter in *The Lucky Chance* by Aphra Behn.
Photo: Donald Cooper

The West End theatre was never realised, but the impact on UK theatre, due to the dynamic and committed advocacy of the star actors, was considerable. The RSC responded by running a women's season, for example, with classics and new plays bringing in women directors, and followed *The Lucky Chance* with a revival of Aphra Behn's *The Rover*.

In 1990, I was appointed to the WTG, shortly before it was relaunched as Sphinx, and at a time of a backlash against feminism and waning audiences. My ambition was to advance women playwrights and to advocate for women as artists. My strategy was to focus on a more epic genre of theatre, and to separate overt political debates from plays. I wanted to develop powerful female protagonists, and I felt that naturalistic dramas tended to reinforce the secondary social roles available to women, reinforcing stereotypes. However, shocks awaited me. When I explained my vision for developing women as artists at my first meeting with our new Arts Council of Great Britain's officer, she responded: "Oh but Sue, women can't be artists, women are mothers." It became clear that this was the prevailing attitude throughout the Arts Council, that women are indeed the Second Sex.

My opening production for Sphinx in 1991 was an all-female *Hamlet*, set in a framing device written by Claire Luckham and starring the witty and brilliant Ruth Mitchell. It was inspired by Moll Cutpurse, the 'Roaring Girl', immortalised by Middleton and Dekker in 1607, a pickpocket who lived in male clothing, an insurgent woman. We discovered that the power of a female interpretation brought Hamlet's cruel treatment of Ophelia, and jealousy of Gertrude into sharp focus, and portrayed the friendship of Horatio and Hamlet as more empathetic than just 'buddies'.

This production set me and the company on a thirty-year journey, of theatrical innovation and brilliant artistic collaborations. *Every Bit of It* by Jackie Kay brought a star D/deaf actor, Elizabeth Quinn, and singer Suzanne Bonnar, together with Bessie Smith; *Playhouse Creatures* by April De Angelis brought the first English actresses onto the Restoration stage, to become a classic produced worldwide; *Chandralekha* by Amrit Wilson brought a female warrior to the Raj; *Sweet Dreams* by Diane Esguerra cast new light on Sigmund Freud and Dora, which toured theatres, psychology departments and the Charleston Festival, among others. Standout productions include the award-winning *Goliath* by Bryony Lavery, directed by Annie Castledine and performed by Nichola McAuliffe, *Vita and Virginia* by Eileen Atkins, directed by Maria Aitken, and importantly, *The Snow Palace* by Pam Gems, directed by Janet Suzman. This told the story of a Polish writer, Stanislawa Przybyszewska, who had written the novel *The Danton Affair* on which the film *Danton* was based. Although the RSC had produced *The Danton Affair*, during her research, Pam had become fascinated by the story of the writer, Przybyszewska, who had died of hypothermia in her unheated hut, in her thirties. This led to her writing *The Snow Palace* which lay unproduced, and I seized on it over a cup of tea with Pam. Janet Suzman took on the production distinguished by Kathryn Pogson's blazing performance. We toured the show to Poland as part of the British Council's festival and it was revived three times for mainstage tours. Pam's last play for us was *The Little Mermaid*, which was a beautiful aerial production. Among my most treasured collaborations, I include Claire van Kampen, whose virtuoso music inspired many productions, and Clare Dale whose vivid choreography expressed the subconscious levels of the drama.

Many of our plays have been published and have a continuous presence in schools, youth groups, drama schools, amateur and professional productions with the legacy of a series of unique heroines.

In creating a feminist artistic forum, I had initiated The Glass Ceiling conferences in 1991. This was the start of the hugely successful annual Glass Ceiling meetings held from 1991 to 2005 principally at the National Theatre's Cottesloe Theatre. They proved landmark events where distinguished women artists and thinkers shared their creative experiences with colleagues and the public. Speakers included Germaine Greer, Deborah Warner, Fiona Shaw, Katie Mitchell, and Janet Suzman in discussions exploring representation of female aggression, victimhood, collaboration, and endemically, women's lack of confidence. Most memorable was a discussion in 1993 around 'The Personal and the Political' with Helena Kennedy QC, Beatrix Campbell OBE, Russian poet Irina Ratushinskaya and Bangladeshi writer-in-exile, Taslima Nasrin. It was accompanied by police snipers on the roof of the adjacent building to the NT in case of attack on Taslima!

The company was a Regularly Funded Company until 2006 when the touring circuit had all but collapsed, and my ambitions for mainstage productions were stalling. It was at the moment of the Gender Equality Act, and we were invited to be a critical friend to the Arts Council's policy creators. This proved an invaluable source of credibility and small-scale funding to support our feminist dialogues, 'Vamps, Vixens and Feminists'.

Conferences and seminars have remained an important tool to raise the question of cultural discrimination and part of our political feminist strategy. In our 2006 survey, women writers made some progress, rising from 3% to 9% (17% of new writing productions), and women directors doubled from 12% to 23%. However, women's roles were still at 35–38%.

Our 2019 *What Share of the Cake* report, forensically researched and authored by Jennifer Tuckett, Sphinx Literary and Research Director at the time, showed continuing inequality, that women's theatre companies were awarded only 0.64% of total theatre funding. Only 21% of NPO funding (three-year funding) went to companies led by female artistic directors and nationally, theatre repertoires are still dominated by male playwrights. To redress this ongoing imbalance, we began a new project titled *Women Centre Stage* which led to two highly successful festivals of new work by women writers, at the National Theatre in 2015 and at Hampstead Theatre in 2016. The project catapulted the work of 25 women playwrights in each festival to a mainstream platform. In the second phase of this project, co-created with Jennifer Tuckett, with the aim of taking more women's plays to mainstages, we commissioned 30 diverse women playwrights in a unique collaboration with 15 regional theatres across the UK. These were showcased brilliantly with Central School of Speech and Drama in 2021-22. To help theatres, and as a tool for playwrights and directors, we created the Sphinx Test, to develop more gender-balanced plays, inspired by the Bechdel Test.

Our 2021 *Women In Theatre* survey, also researched and written by Jennifer Tuckett, was focused on the impact of the pandemic on women theatre makers. This found that 60% were considering leaving working in theatre. The update in 2023 found that the universal demand throughout the survey was for Arts Council England (ACE)and the UK government to make policy changes to better support women in theatre, and for programmes specifically aimed at supporting women.

Political campaigning has remained an important strand to our work. In 2018, we brought together a group of feminist artists, known as the December Group, to confront ACE to include women as a discrete group of underrepresented artists in their 'Let's Create' ten-year strategy. After many meetings and letter writing campaigns, we succeeded.

So, 40 years on, is there real progress for women in theatre? Certainly there is, and especially for women directors such as Indhu Rubasingham at The Kiln and the National Theatre; Tamara Harvey, at Theatr Clwyd and the RSC and Lynette Linton at the Bush, among others. However, the demands of the *Women in Theatre* survey were not reflected in the 2022 NPO awards where no women's professional theatre companies were included, except community and education companies.

**Women can be artists *and* mothers. We remain Roaring Girls.**

≈

**Sue Parrish** completed her BA Hons Eng Lit at UCL. She is an Associate of the Guildhall of Music and Drama and Sphinx Artistic Director and Producer since 1990. Sue has extensive experience producing and directing Fringe, Repertory and Music Theatre. For Sphinx as Producer: *Goliath* by Bryony Lavery, *The Snow Palace* by Pam Gems, *Vita and Virginia* by Eileen Atkins. As Director: *Playhouse Creatures* by April De Angelis, *Every Bit of It* by Jackie Kay, *Sweet Dreams* by Diane Esguerra and the award-winning *A Berlin Kabaret*. Sue produced the Glass Ceiling feminist conferences at the National Theatre for ten years from 1991 and Women Centre Stage Festivals at the National Theatre (2015), Hampstead Theatre (2019) and Trafalgar Theatre (2020). She was a founding member of the Conference of Women Theatre Directors and Administrators in 1979 and of the Women's Playhouse Trust in 1982 and has remained involved in developing the feminist dialogue in theatre.

**Susan McGoun** trained at Central and the Laban Centre for Dance. Theatre credits include *The Crucible* and *Les Liaisons Dangereuses* (RSC), *Vincent in Brixton* and *Noises Off* (NT), *Dancing at Lughnasa* (Torch) *Tell Me* (Manchester Contact), *The Price for the English* (Theatre of Hamburg), *The Last Yankee* (Duke of York's) as well as work at The Gate, The Lyric Hammersmith, Theatre Clwyd and Bolton Octagon. As a member of WTG she commissioned and premiered new work by Donna Franceschild, Bryony Lavery and Clare MacIntyre and appeared in *New Anatomies* by Timberlake Wertenbaker, at Edinburgh. A long-standing member of the Equity Women's Committee, she is also a board member of Sphinx.

Monique Burg in the premiere of *Theresa,* 1990.

# INTERVIEW WITH JULIA PASCAL

**What does feminist mean to you?**

It means equality. The world has had over 5,000 years of patriarchy. Feminism is about women having at least 50% access to all areas of power. When I look at governments and see that they are mainly manned, something inside me screams. There is a parallel between how a society is ruled and theatre. We use theatre as the public face of our society and if that society is led by men consequently so is our theatre.

I believe that we will never have equality in theatre until half of all jobs are filled by women at all levels. Our National Theatre has been over-represented by men since its birth. It has taken almost five decades to appoint a woman artistic director. The same can be said of The Royal Shakespeare Company. In theatre, gender equality is an endless struggle which feels like one step forward and two steps back. Over half of the population is now boxed into the Arts Council term 'Diversity'. We are not part of 'Diversity', we are the majority and we are mainstream.

**How has feminism influenced your work?**

I have always been interested in women's stories. From childhood I have spurned traditional roles that were supposed to be my sole aspiration.
I saw ballet as a child and the role of the dancer interested me as I danced and understood the freedom art gave me as a girl. This early feminism, where the dance teachers were always women, allowed me a portal into creativity. I studied to be an actor and worked for four years on the professional stage and on-screen. I was aware how few opportunities there were for women and how few roles there were. To gain agency over my career I moved to direction and to writing. In both areas I have always been driven to tell women's stories that have been hidden, forgotten or never acknowledged.

My first play *Far Above Rubies,* which premiered at the Drill Hall in 1984, looked at how Islam and Judaism treated women. Feminism cannot be divorced from religion. I see religion as a legal means of controlling women. If I have a religion at all it is theatre.

I have written many dramas with women as the protagonist. The first in my *Holocaust Trilogy*, published by Oberon Books, was *Theresa*. This is the story of Theresa Steiner, a Viennese, Jewish refugee, who came to England to escape the Nazis and ended up on Guernsey. Through her life I could reveal how Guernsey's government collaborated with the Nazis, implemented their Race Laws, and deported their Jews. I am aware of how little of women's experience in the Shoah is profiled. Therefore, my feminism influenced my telling of this story. I could have written about the male slaves that were murdered on Alderney, again with the tacit approval of the Guernsey authorities, but Theresa Steiner's picture spoke to me when I researched this history. I also interviewed women on Guernsey who knew her and this gave me a feeling for her character and her situation that inspired the writing. Steiner seemed to speak to me and want me to tell her story.

Other plays have been centred on women's experience. These include *The Yiddish Queen Lear, A Dead Woman On Holiday, Crossing Jerusalem, The Dybbuk, St Joan* and most recently *As Happy As God In France* which features the lives of Hannah Arendt, Charlotte Salomon and Eva Daube when they were imprisoned with 8,000 other women refugees in a French internment camp just before the German Occupation.

*St Joan* is a satire on the French National Front. When I lived in France, I experienced anti-Arab racism when people thought that I was from North Africa and, when I said I was a Jew, there was naked antisemitism. I wrote a Black Jewish Londoner who imagines herself time-travelling back to change history and abort the historical imperative of slavery and Shoah. This is a deeply feminist play which challenges white supremacy and racism.

1970s feminism has deeply affected my work. It gave voice to my innate feminism which, as a girl, I had no language to protest. Simone de Beauvoir, Andrea Dworkin, Charlotte Bronte, Judy Chicago, Lilian Baylis, Ninette de Valois are disconnected names, those who come to mind as important triggers, as well as Joan Littlewood, Paula Rego and Leonora Carrington.

### Has the content or form of your work changed over time? How?

I started writing non-naturalistic plays which is my primary writing style. I like cabaret, music, dance, satire and heightened theatricality. In 2002,

I was commissioned to write a play about Israel for The Tricycle. As the film director Jack Gold was directing it, I created a more linear structure than usual for *Crossing Jerusalem* which happens sequentially in 24 hours.

Over the years that I have been writing, the content has been varied. In 2015, I was commissioned to write *Old Newland* by Theatre Delicatessen as one of several short political plays collectively called *Walking The Tightrope* in the old *Guardian* offices in Farringdon Road. It was directed by Cressida Brown. Just as I would rather write a novel than a short story, the concept of the short play was not something that came easily to me. The commission meant that I had to write a meaty work that would last 10-14 minutes. This expanded my repertoire and meant that I felt easy writing in a shorter form. I wrote the central role for an older man; this was based on my father whose voice was easy to access in my memory. He was an Irish Jew and here I wanted to profile a hidden Jewish community and connect Irish and Jewish nationalism. Although the structure and content may be very different in each play, there is a pattern of engaging with huge political issues and this is what I love doing.

*L to R:* Thomas Kampe, Sarah Finch, Ruth Posner, Ian Watts in *Theresa,* Vienna, 2003

However, the majority of my dramas are women-centred. *A Manchester Girlhood,* which I toured this year, is quite different from previous work as it deals with three sisters who are seen from the ages of five to eighty-six. I challenged myself to write a text that would allow women to combat stereotypes of ageing. As writer-director, I cast three actors in their sixties to play the sisters. I wanted to put mature female performers centre stage to subvert how theatre mostly marginalises the older woman.

My content has widened to include other cultures. For example, *Blueprint Medea* is based on a Kurdish soldier who I met in London as an asylum seeker. She allowed me to interview her. This encounter plunged me into Kurdish culture as a background for writing this contemporary *Medea*. It premiered at the Finborough Theatre just before COVID-19 closed all venues.

Another departure in my writing content was the more personal *Woman On the Bridge.* This looks at transmitted trauma down the generations; it reflects my interest in the many female suicides in my own family. This offered me the chance of a completely new structure. The Ulyssean trope of a hero on a journey was transformed into the story of a woman on a journey. She was no Greek god but a 50-something Jew. The end of her wild voyage through Manhattan was to the edge of the Brooklyn Bridge and the drop into the Hudson. Her battle was not with mythical figures but with

Ruth Posner in *Theresa*, Vienna 2003

herself and with a female Puerto Rican cop who was forcing her to choose life instead of death.

Director of Theatre Témoin, Aileen Conant, asked me to write a play, *Nineveh,* for four men based on her research with former soldiers. I enjoy writing male characters as I am aware that women are rarely invited to write about men and war. I was interviewed by a Russian journalist at the premiere at Riverside Studios. The female journalist was surprised when she met with me. She told me 'I thought that this play was written by a man.'

**Do you feel women have achieved equality in theatre?**

Not at all. All is stacked against equality. You have only to look at the data which Sphinx has produced. Together with Sue Parrish, Sphinx's director, and a group of other women practitioners, we met several times with the Arts Council to ask for equality. It led nowhere.

**Have you experienced sex bias while working in theatre?**

Many times. As a young actor in 1971, auditioning for Harold Pinter and Simon Gray, I was told that I did not have the large breasts needed for casting in *Butley*.

I was the first woman director at the National Theatre on the South Bank when I directed *Men Seldom Make Passes*. This was a Platform Performance which ran from 1977-1980 at the NT. I adapted the stories and poems of Dorothy Parker and the show starred Sara Kestelman and David Schofield. It was immensely successful and commented on by Peter Hall in his diaries. My work at this moment attracted a great deal of publicity as it was realised how women directors were absent from the subsidised main stages. At that time the NT's posters proclaimed 'THE NATIONAL THEATRE IS YOU!' It certainly wasn't me or any representation of the women living in this country.

Many women have been frightened to speak out for fear of being blacklisted. But remaining silent has not brought about parity. Around 1985 (and later), I wrote in *The Times, The Guardian, City Limits* and elsewhere about the marginalisation of women in our theatres. Michael Rudman, who gave me my first acting job at the Traverse, wrote to me personally to say, 'I love the way that you write but hate what you say'. As Artistic Director of the RSC, Trevor Nunn sent me a letter in 1985 telling me that, because of what I had written in *City Limits* 'I somehow doubt that you will be experiencing much of what we do at first-hand.' I took that threat to the Equal Opportunities Committee (as it then was) and was told I could certainly take this to court as discrimination but I would need to find thousands of pounds to pay lawyers. I did not have the money to do that and therefore could do nothing. I never was invited to work at the Royal Shakespeare Company by Trevor Nunn. But I do still have that letter.

**What would improve the opportunities for women in theatre today?**

A quota system of 50% employment.

**Does intersectionalism influence your work? How?**

I like to write about women on the margins of society as I come from a refugee background; it's the state of exile within a country which excites many of my texts. I tend to write from direct experience or interviews with others. Yet I also create characters which are not sourced by direct experience but which touch me and make me want to expose their stories. In this way intersectionality of cultures and ages fuse. This is not documentary but fiction, as characters are composed of an amalgam of personalities.

I have also written texts for a company of disabled dancers when I was commissioned by Wolfgang Stange's Amici Dance Theatre Company. I found the contact with the disabled company of artists to be disturbing. It provoked me to be more daring as a playwright. Working with Wolfgang showed me how one disability can represent another. In this production of my script *20/20*, disabled dancers played soldiers who had lost legs in World War One. They were tipped out of their wheelchairs and crawled along the stage, as if gassed. The plasticity of the body, and its limitations, can shock an audience into a new way of looking at disability.

**Do you collaborate with other groups?**

I've worked with many other groups and organisations including Amici Dance Theatre, London Contemporary Dance School, St Pancras Community Centre, KOVE, The Bloomsbury Festival, Middlesex University, King's College, London University, Theatre Delicatessen and Dyspla.

**Do we still need feminist theatre? Why?**

We would not need feminist theatre if we had parity. We need to have women's stories on our stages as the face of our nation. They have been missing from the public arena for too long.

**Do you think having a theatre dedicated to women's work would have an impact?**

I am divided on this. In the present sexist theatre, where women's presence is still marginalised, it could be useful as a form of protest, but it could also let theatres off the hook from their obligation of employing representatives of more than half of our population.

**Are prizes important? Why? Why not?**

Yes, they highlight women's work.

**Is arts funding equitable?**

No. Our meetings with Sir Nick Serota show that any attempt to get equity is a waste of time. He listened to us and made sympathetic noises but did nothing.

**How can we improve things for women in theatre?**

Parity.

≈

**Julia Pascal** PhD is a playwright, theatre director and scholar. Julia trained as an actor and worked professionally as a performer. Her scripts have been published by Oberon Books, Faber and Methuen. Productions of her plays have been staged in the UK, Europe and the USA. In New York, scenes from her *St Joan*, about a Black Jewish Londoner, were part of the Lincoln Centre's Director's Lab. Katrin Hilbe directed it at the Edinburgh Festival, the Dublin Gay Festival and in Liechtenstein. Julia's new vision of *The Dybbuk* was seen at Theatre For the New City. *Crossing Jerusalem*, set in the 2002 intifada, premiered at the Tricycle Theatre then was later staged at the Park Theatre, London. *A Manchester Girlhood* toured in 2023. *As Happy As God In France* is the latest script in development. This reveals the imprisonment of Hannah Arendt and Charlotte Salomon by the French in May 1940.

As director of Pascal Theatre Company Julia produces large-scale arts and heritage projects. Site-specific dance theatre works have been at the Bloomsbury Festival 2021-2023. She received a Dreamtime Fellowship from the National Endowment for Science, Technology & The Arts. Her Writer in Residency at the Wiener Library was supported by a Leverhulme grant. She is a Research Fellow Artist at King's College, London University and a Visiting Artist at the Royal Central School of Speech and Drama.

Aedin Moloney in *Low in the Dark*, 1993. Photo: Simon Annand

# OUT OF THE ATTIC – WTW
## CHERYL ROBSON & ANNA BIRCH

**Cheryl Robson:**

A protean group of women writers, directors and actors came together to write and perform work on the fringe in London from the late 1980s onwards under the banner of the Women's Theatre Workshop (WTW). The company grew out of the Writers' Workshops at the Drill Hall Arts Centre which I co-founded with Janet Beck in 1987. These writing workshops were dynamic women-only labs for discussion and experimentation of new ideas and new writing, as well as for the raising of self-esteem and feminist consciousness.

The Drill Hall Arts Centre was a female-centric venue, led by Julie Parker, which became *the* place to hang out for activists, lesbians, and non-binary theatre practitioners just off Tottenham Court Road, its cabaret atmosphere creating an anti-establishment undercurrent. Looking back, I now see how unique this was, being in a building outside of male control, where female values reigned.

The aim of the workshops was to build confidence, and we discouraged members from apologising for their work, and helped them to find and express their original voice, eschewing self-censorship. As they shared their work in pairs and in the group, the support received and the trust gained helped them to go deeper and express painful experiences of abuse, discrimination and rejection. Most of the writers had experienced male literary managers or gatekeepers sending back disparaging remarks about their work. Some had suffered publicly from the savaging of their work by male critics, who, when made to feel uncomfortable in the face of female experience, had slammed the work, with examples of this being common at the time. This had the effect of undermining the importance of female cultural contribution generally and creating anxiety in the minds of women writers about further public humiliation – the critical reaction to Kane's *Blasted* was one example.

215

Through regular playreadings of new work, and nights when we showcased poetry and prose readings with music, the company acted as a breeding ground for emerging talent and our springboard performance events came to be known under the umbrella term of 'Out of the Attic'. We were reeling from the Thatcher years when a woman in power had, on the one hand inspired young women to achieve more, and on the other, turned the tide against social justice in many ways. I went to see David Mamet's *Oleanna* at the Royal Court Theatre in 1993, reflecting the zeitgeist that male-female power struggles were as complex and divisive as ever.

My journey to working in theatre was unusual. Although I studied Drama and French at the University of Bristol, I then found a job at the BBC initially working as a film technician, where I was the only woman in a department of over 100 men. The sexist comments I received from male colleagues were commonplace. Later, working in film editing, sexual harassment could occur when confined to a cutting room with a male director for long hours. I quickly learned not to share my ideas with male producers as these would be taken, commissioned and never credited. I remember encountering Rolf Harris in the lift in the mornings, the worse for wear and smelling of alcohol.

I was employed at the BBC in a variety of roles over several years including film editing, programme acquisition, news picture research and as a producer/director for current affairs. Once I became a parent, the challenges of continually working weekends and overtime without any choice of flexitime, or part-time working, became too hard, and I decided to change direction. During a conversation with Phyllida Lloyd in a pub around this time, she told me she was leaving the BBC to pursue her directing work in theatre, where she would have greater artistic freedom, and this sowed the seeds of setting up a theatre company in my mind.

I decided to retrain as a drama teacher and undertook a PGCE, then found employment part-time teaching Film and Video for Harrow Film School and the Polytechnic of Central London (now Westminster

University). I had written plays since leaving university, the first titled *Basta Ya!,* was given a staged reading at the Half Moon, another titled *The Taking of Liberty,* about women in the French Revolution, won the Croydon International Playwriting Festival where it was directed in a staged reading by Mark Ravenhill, before getting a production on the fringe, directed by Jenny Darnell. *What's On* reviewed it: "'Discarding all previous male interpretations of the French Revolution, Robson comes up with a completely fresh view that exposes those treasured shibboleths of 'liberté, egalité and fraternité' as hollow irrelevances where women were concerned."

*The Independent* said: "... this always watchable play (reminiscent in many ways of Caryl Churchill's *Vinegar Tom*)... has an engaging optimism. And for once in the theatre, the women really do get all the best lines – which gives the quintet of young actresses roles to relish."

Several other productions and readings of my plays took place at small theatres like the New End Theatre, Soho Poly, and the Young Vic where I had a playreading of my play *Versus* (about nature vs science) directed by Rufus Norris; all were well-received. Wanting to develop my skills, I joined the newly-founded MA in Playwriting at Birmingham University established by David Edgar. While David Edgar had an analytical approach, my tutor, Bryony Lavery, offered a more light-hearted, intuitive, and spontaneous way of accessing the playwriting genie. My next play titled *Simply Hostile* was granted an Arts Council Commission award. David Edgar came to see it when it was produced at the Man in the Moon Theatre in Chelsea, praising the production by director Sarah Frankcom.

The title of the play was apt and reflected the hostile environment women often faced in the workplace at that time – the misogyny of the theatre industry was no different to TV, with nepotism and jobs for the boys being common practice. The play depicts a woman struggling to find her way in

The WOMEN'S THEATRE WORKSHOP presents

**SIMPLY HOSTILE**

by Cheryl Robson
*Directed by* Sarah Frankcom
*Designed by* Louisa Beer
Tues. June 7th -
Sat. July 2nd
8.30pm
Tickets
£7.00 / £5.00
Cast:
Rachel Atkins
Mary Chater
Patrick Cremin
Maria McCateer
Rachel Welsh

392 King's Rd, London SW3. ☎ 071 351 2876 / 5701

Mary Chater and Rachel Atkins in *Simply Hostile* by Cheryl Robson

the world and evaluating what she wants from life. *Time Out* said of it "… ambitiously spans the confusion generated by women trying in their various ways to have it all: the baby, the career, the sexual freedom and the security… where Robson and Frankcom make their greatest impact is the way they skilfully nurse their 60s caricatures to become the compromised, damaged individuals we discover in the 90s."

I worked variously as playwright, artistic director, creative producer, and dramaturg during my time with WTW. The company collaborated with many talented young women theatre directors over the decade including Ruth Ben-Tovim, Anna Birch, Viv Cottrell, Kirstie Davis, Lisa Goldman, Janet Gordon, Chrissy Harmar-Brown, Astrid Hilne, Fiona McHugh, Lucy Pitman-Wallace, Shabnam Shabazi, Jacqui Somerville and more. Unusually for the period, we developed and produced plays not only by British playwrights but also by international women playwrights, introducing British audiences to the work of unknown writers such as Dacia Maraini (Italy) with her play *Veronica Franco,* Marina Carr (Ireland) with her play *Low in the Dark,* Nawal El Saadawi (Egypt) with her play *12 Women in a Cell,* Catherine Johnson (USA) with her play *Joined at the Head,* Lluïsa Cunillé (Spain) with her play *Libration* and a rare double-bill of Dutch plays produced at The Gate – *Dossier: Ronald Akkerman* by Suzanne van Lohuizen and *The Caracal* by Judith Herzberg.

From our tiny two-desk office space at Interchange Studios, a rundown community arts centre in Kentish Town, where Paines Plough, New Playwrights Trust and Gay Sweatshop were also based, we dreamt up new projects and applied for funding from numerous trusts and foundations, working mostly unpaid. It was a vibrant place in the 1990s, home to several charities and small-scale arts organizations, with the option of rehearsal rooms and workshop space available inexpensively for hire. We ran workshops on writing, directing and acting with tutors such as April de Angelis, Nancy Duguid, and Phyllis Nagy. Writers who attended our workshops included poets Mimi Khalvati, Deirdre Shanahan, A-dZiko Simba, and Cherry Smyth. We thought that becoming part of the City Lit evening course programme would be beneficial but the administration and paperwork involved eventually sucked the joy from it.

To try and move writers from the page to the stage we collaborated with local venues to stage the most promising plays. We became experts at begging for scaffolding, props and costumes, and designing sets on a shoestring. We produced new writing at small venues such as Theatro Technis, Oval House Theatre, The Gate, The Bridewell, Riverside Studios, Tara Arts, Watermans, Paul Robeson and Soho Poly Theatre. We staged dozens of playreadings by up-and-coming playwrights, encouraging writing and raising the profile of writers such as Nicola Baldwin, Clare Bayley, Sian Evans, Erica Freund, Eva Lewin, Nina Rapi, Jan Ruppe, and Sarah Woods. Many of these writers went on to have their work produced by theatres such as the Royal Court and the National Theatre as well as diverting to write for television where it was easier to earn a living.

Lack of funding and poor pay were continual issues that I faced during the decade I spent working in theatre and it became increasingly hard as a parent to justify continuing. With two children, it was a case of me paying to work in theatre, as the financial rewards rarely covered the cost of childcare and the logistical challenges of juggling performances and rehearsals with

*Joined at the Head* by Catherine Johnson

school and family proved stressful. As my female friends and colleagues became parents, they too drifted away from theatre into teaching, radio or television production, script editing, arts management, and business. It became apparent that the obstacles we faced as women in theatre were part of a systemic problem which we were powerless to affect as individual artists. When I and others met with Arts Council officers to discuss the idea of quotas in terms of commissioning, funding and employment in key posts, they were sympathetic, but dismissed the idea of 'social engineering'. I was always looking for ways to help address the lack of opportunity for women and outright nepotism in theatre. To this end, I was proud to have initiated the first mentoring programme for women writers and directors in the UK in association with The New Playwrights' Trust and the Directors' Guild in 1995.

The last play we presented was *Tucson* by Lisa Perrotti, directed by Janet Gordon. Co-produced with Lisa Goldman's Red Room Theatre Company at the Finborough Theatre in Earls Court, it won a *Time Out* Critics' Choice and was the recipient of a Guinness Theatre Award.

*

Twenty-five years on, Feminist Theatre is still important as a way to investigate power and oppression, to challenge binary notions of gender and to expose continuing inequality. Some women's plays are now reaching the mainstages, and theatre programmers have accepted that we need more diverse repertoires. However, working with theatre companies today to publish dozens of plays, I can see that plays by women and people of colour still tend to be produced in smaller venues. International work is still rare and the industry is unprepared for the coming of AI, VR and avatars, as in *Abba Voyage*.

Psychologists now recognise that toxic masculinity harms men and stunts their emotional well-being, but we still see cases of male directors bullying, coercing, and sexually harassing women in the workplace. Men in theatre could do more to build productive, diverse teams,

Di Sherlock in *Veronica Franco* by Dacia Maraini

training, commissioning, and mentoring women, non-binary people and people of colour to make work that more accurately reflects the society we live in. Misogyny is essentially a male issue which men need to address.

I now co-own a bookstore and cultural space with my husband Steve, at which we curate and sell diverse and inclusive books, and offer arts and literary events. I pivoted from theatre into publishing and over the last decade it's become a female-dominated industry where men and women collaborate to produce great content. Women writers top the bestseller lists in most Western countries. Women publishers run huge organizations turning over large revenues and making decent profits. The Booker win for Bernardine Evaristo helped push diversity to the fore and current issues are sustainability and the impact of AI. The question is why theatre has not made the same progress.

We recently hosted a playreading of Nell Dunn's feminist classic *Steaming*. During the Q&A after the play, my husband commented that he felt ashamed of the men's sexist behaviour as depicted in the play. Men watching the original production, in which the female characters performed nude, might have found the message less cogent.

Feminism challenges patriarchal notions of class, race and gender and, in association with LGBTQI+ people, feminists help to bring respect and human rights to under-represented communities. Those with privilege, blind to their unconscious bias, have been slow to give women and people of colour a seat at the 'big table', and failed to provide equal opportunities. Consequently, many British theatres are missing out on diverse talent and ideas. In other areas of the arts, a little more progress is being made.

For example, Tate Britain has mounted a major exhibition called 'Women in Revolt' celebrating women artists from 1974-1990. In music, the Rock & Roll Hall of Fame in the US has a 'Revolutionary Women in Music' exhibit to pay tribute to feminist artists and musicians since the 1970s. There has been no equivalent major celebration of the groundbreaking cultural contribution over half a century of feminist theatre makers in the UK. Rather than erasing our women's theatre history, we ask that the National Theatre and other flagship organisations such as the V&A, pay tribute and honour women theatre makers who had the courage, determination and creativity to lead our cultural dialogue and help bring about a more equitable and just society.

**Anna Birch:**

I got involved with WTW by attending an acting workshop. Lesley Ferris was there. I knew of her work from the Gender and Performance course at Middlesex University and her book about cross-dressing in theatre which explored the stereotypes of women characters – the whore, the prostitute and the saint. The content was really well managed in the workshop and it felt like a very safe space. I met interesting women there, who probably led on to further work. The content of Ferris's book has remained with me as a platform for my work and that workshop was very formative. I liked the way that Lesley comes to the world of feminist theatre through the lens of women entering the stage in 1600 and the fact that we weren't represented by women, but represented by boys.

The whole idea that gender is performativity is inscribed from that first workshop experience. I had been at Cambridge, I'd done a lot of theatre there and worked on Edward Bond's plays; I had quite a good foundation. I'd also set up a feminist theatre company – Sensible Footwear. It was a really good time. There was this sense that we could build a peer community; people were supporting each other and empowering each other's work in a safe space. It was women for women. And our work was increasingly getting exposure as well. Mel Kenyon was of course one of those women, April de Angelis, etc. We had a feminist sisterhood there supporting each other to get to bigger venues.

Jean Trend and Aedin Moloney in *Low in the Dark*, 1993. Photo: Simon Annand

Aedin Moloney and Matthew Bowyer in *Low in the Dark*

Cheryl suggested the play *Low in the Dark* to me. It reads really well off the script. It was roll-around funny slapstick, and it throws gender roles against the wall and also mothering, which was fascinating for us, because we had young families at the time. We wanted to do some script development, but the writer was less keen to deconstruct the play. What it did mean was that we got a chance to interrogate the play in the rehearsal room with actors. As a director, I really enjoy that way of working. When we got to rehearsals in Theatro Technis, we were in good shape. It had a great creative team with Sylvia Hallett, who I'd worked with before, a really good composer, Shabnam Shabazi was my assistant, and Simon Annand, photographer.

The casting process was memorable. Jean Trend (Bender) was just great. She spent the whole time in a bath covered in all these coloured babies, strings of them. Then Binder her daughter, Aedin Moloney, was a very speedy, mercurial young actor. The women characters spend a lot of time arguing about men, about who they are as women. There is a sense that you're on a street and people are ranting, then something blows up and then it settles down again. Bender is stuck in the bath in the same way as Beckett's characters are stuck in urns etc. This gives it a sort of existential, esoteric feel. Marina Carr speaks across generations of Irish writers. The design included a costume for Bender, which had fabric breasts in it, which were fantastic. I still have that costume. We had really good fun with that.

Baxter and Bone, the male characters are highly bonded. They're not father and son, they're just bonded men really keeping their side going and building a wall! Carr is very interested in this sort of old-boy network. She's very critical of mothering in the play, doesn't feel that it's a nurturing role. Then there's Curtains who is really a mythological character, under a curtain. It's a metaphor that brings a whole different tempo. Curtains talks a lot about what the role of men and women might be. *Low in the Dark*

223

goes a long way to moving on from the tired old binary so I think it's got a lot to say now. It was a sellout production at Theatro Technis. The space worked really well with the set. It's a comedy so people were laughing and having a really good night. The reviews were mostly good, and Carr is celebrated and the production team, the creatives are all celebrated too.

It was part of Out of the Attic, 1993 and we got a lot of people from the festival. We used an image of Sheela Na Gig, which is a mythical Irish woman giving birth, on the flyers. I can see now why people were shocked and why they thought it might not be the best marketing image but it spoke to what we felt was the energy cutting through that play. I feel proud that it worked so well. I think it showed Carr as a premier Irish writer. She wrote *The Mai* after this play and people say that *The Mai* was an expansion of *Low in the Dark*, but the writing became much darker.

Max Stafford-Clark came to see the play. He was less clear on his opinion and I remember standing outside talking with him under the canopy of grapes. He came with Matthew Lloyd – he was really complimentary about it from every angle. I think Mel Kenyon came from the Royal Court and was a fan. There was an evening we made a foray into the Royal Court introducing Marina Carr to the literary department as I'd trained there, winning the Gerald Chapman Trainee Director Award. That was an interesting evening. There seemed to be a lot of interest in Carr's work and that she should be commissioned, but somebody pulled the plug on it. A couple of years later, *The Mai* came through. That play came into London and had a fabulous lead actress and was a hit.

More recently I've been working outside to investigate and celebrate the life of Mary Wollstonecraft, the 18th-century feminist on Newington Green, where she was living and working in the dissenting Enlightenment community there. This involved a play by Kaethe Fine which we performed on the Green. We also made an app in 2019, with Scary Little Girls, which offers a guided walking tour with actors recorded in several locations around Newington Green. You can access it online.

Then I worked in Glasgow and Montreal applying that method of investigating the herstory of the city, creating large-scale public events. In Glasgow, this was in collaboration with Glasgow Women's Library and the Royal Conservatory Scotland, and it was a hundred women performing an expansion of *A Pageant of Great Women* by Cicely Hamilton. Using film was something that I took on from an Irish colleague of mine, Vivienne Dick, a feminist groundbreaker, who used handheld cameras in

New York in the 70s and made very grainy DIY films. That led me to do a Master's in Film. In Montreal, I was an invited artist in a collaboration between Concordia and IMAGO Theater company and a group of theatre creatives. We created four pieces including walks, and projections onto a building, which turned out to be the first building where feminist theatre action had taken place in the 70s. A sound score was made for Cabot Square in Montreal; a post-colonial piece was made for that. There are these big flour urns as you go into Montreal. We made a piece which explored the role of women who worked there. We got caught in COVID. But the works were documented and they are now online as digital artworks. www.performativeurbanism.com/feminist-performance-creation-the-c.

≈

**Cheryl Robson** (see bio on page 1.) The plays *Veronica Franco* by Dacia Maraini, *12 Women in a Cell* by Nawal El Saadawi and *Libration* by Lluïsa Cunillé are in *Mediterranean Plays by Women* ed. Marion Baraitser. *The Caracal* by Judith Herzberg and *Dossier: Ronald Akkerman* by Suzanne van Lohuizen are in *A Touch of the Dutch; plays by women* ed. Cheryl Robson. All Aurora Metro.

**Anna Birch** is Artistic Director of Fragments & Monuments performance and film company. Her site-specific performance, outdoor screenings, marches, processions, book publishing and walks create participative and celebratory public artworks. Trained as a director at the Royal Court Theatre, London, UK early productions of plays by April de Angelis and Marina Carr were notable. Recent work includes a reworking of *Wollstonecraft Live!* by Kaethe Fine (2018), *MARCH* documentary (2016) Glasgow Women's Library and the Royal Conservatoire of Scotland, Glasgow, following March of Women (2015) featuring *A Pageant of Great Women* by Cicely Hamilton. Publications: *Wollstonecraft Live! and The Story of the Statue* by Kaethe Fine & Anna Birch (Aurora Metro), 'Expanding the notion of monument through Performance' in *The Routledge Companion to Site-Specific* eds. Victoria Hunter & Cathy Turner, Routledge (2024). 'Embodied and En-sited Performance: Reflections on Gender in Cooking Miss Julie/Miss Julie Cooks and March of Women,' with Professor Kathleen Irwin in *Analysing Gender in Performance* eds. Halferty, P and Leeney, C (Palgrave). She was made a Professor of Performance at the Royal Conservatoire of Scotland and a Fellow of the Royal Society of Arts (2015).

*L to R:* Abbie Lowe and Rebekah Smith. Photo: Ruby Belassie

# SCYLLA'S BITE
## REBEKAH SMITH & ABBIE LOWE

**What does feminism mean to you?**

Being feminist means actively seeking gender equity, intersectionality and radical social change in all spaces, for everyone. It is about pursuing this equality in all levels of society, understanding that the patriarchal society we currently have does not benefit the majority. If there are voices going unheard, unrepresented and unrespected, then we are undermining the potential of our society as a whole.

**How has feminism influenced your work?**

Feminism provides a model for making an equitable work environment. Our company started as a conversation between two friends tired of being met with consistent disinterest and disregard. It appeared that in a collaborative creative space filled with mostly men, the artistic expression of our own humanity did not reflect theirs and was thus pushed to the side. No matter how unintentional the exclusion was, it was always present. Desperate to have gender minorities represented and respected in theatre, we created our feminist company. Producing theatre within a feminist space allows us to take more risks. We can embrace the femininity we used to avoid as young women burdened with internalised misogyny. We find validity in our own work rather than seeking outside approval. Consequently our art celebrates girliness: our characters are hyper-feminine in a genuine way; it doesn't diminish their worth but provides joy and depth. Our work is better for it because it has the depth and truth we previously redacted to make our work more palatable and marketable to a male-dominated industry. Now, we have the chance to write for us. We don't have to limit ourselves to fit the standards of today because we're trying to achieve the equity of tomorrow. Feminism has led us to unlearn our prescribed inferiority and find the joy in being women. In previous work we've found ourselves giving our meatiest parts and lines to male characters, leaving our female characters smaller and quieter, because that's what we think audiences expect. The benefit of having a women and non-binary artist company is that you're forced to grow out of that. It's a great way to hold ourselves accountable for enabling women to speak of their own humanity instead of having it dictated to them.

**Has the content or form of your work changed over time? How?**

We're a grassroots company still in the infancy of our work, which allows us to adapt, learn and integrate inclusivity. The shift for positive social change within UK theatre is really exciting for us to grow into, and we look forward to how it will influence our future work.

**Do you feel women have achieved equality in theatre?**

At the beginning of our company's creative process, the focus was to discover where gender equity was lacking and why that was the case. Within certain areas of theatre, such as producing, writing and directing, there has been a lot of research in recent years to highlight this inequality. Organisations such as Sphinx Theatre, Mercury Musical Developments and Gender Equality and Diversity in European Theatre do an excellent job in exposing this. However in other areas, particularly tech, there is a severe deficit of research, indicating that we are only at the very beginning of understanding and solving the inequality.

In certain creative spaces, women are still pigeonholed into pursuing producing, stage management and production management. It is as if the industry wants to convince women that they are better suited for admin and multi-tasking roles simply because it isn't a creative position commonly sought by men. We are still not equally embraced in director, writer and technical roles beyond amateur, fringe or education-level productions.

If you look at acting roles available to women, even now, you'll find a disproportionate amount of roles designated to the 'partner', 'mother', 'hysterical' or 'sexually abused woman'. We're presented with characters that don't feel as four-dimensional as our male counterparts. They're not developed and they don't feel like real people, simply shallow plot devices. Until we weasel out this perception that we cannot be as capable or as whole as men, we won't find equality in theatre.

**Have you experienced sex bias while working in theatre?**

We'll take this one individually.

**Rebekah Smith:**

Originally, when I started university, I wanted to specialise in set design and other backstage roles. From faculty and colleagues alike, I experienced gender bias pretty early on. It was made very clear to me that I was a young woman in that space. First and foremost I was just a girl. Not a colleague, but a pretty, amenable, young woman. I didn't feel welcome. The microaggressions and harassment pushed me out of that backstage space. I changed my specialty to acting because it seemed like the only space I could do the work with any respect. We are continually reminded that there are certain spaces where we cannot be safe and therefore cannot belong. To be told, on the one hand, that we are capable of succeeding and yet, on the other, experience neglect, exploitation and harassment, embeds a fear and distrust that is hard to relearn as we embark on our creative career.

**Abbie Lowe:**

Unless it has been a company or cast of gender minority artists, I have never been in a technical space and not been flirted with. I am seen as a commodity because I am the only woman in that space. So many times people have told me that I don't know what I'm talking about. I've had people touch me when I didn't want it. That, to me, is unfair, unsafe and unwelcoming. I've had a venue technician ask "Whose girlfriend are you?" I said, "I'm the technician," and he replied, "So they bought you along as the go-monkey." And that really just lit something in me. When you're a writer in rooms that are predominantly male, you're constantly second-guessed and spoken over. You're constantly told that your ideas aren't enough – they choose other people's over yours. It's an aggressive space to be in. We created our theatre company to be heard, and to have a safe space to create.

## What would improve the opportunities for women in theatre today?

There needs to be far more training in diversity, welfare and accessibility. It's hard to imagine how we've got to the point where theatre feels so unsafe and discriminatory, especially in backstage and technician roles. There are almost no UK based studies on this, but in 2021, the US Institute for Theatre Technicians concluded that 93% of women working in sound and lighting design experienced gender discrimination. Even reputable drama schools are regularly in the news with harassment and assault claims. We need to be overturning from the top and dedicating resources to the creation of safe practice. It's time to demand safe and welcoming work environments across the industry.

**Does intersectionality influence your work? How?**

If our work is not intersectional then it isn't saying what it needs to say. When we are talking about equality, it cannot be an echo chamber of our own experience, we need to include everyone in the conversation. Our company, as it is now, is just two young white women. We are very limited in our own experience of feminist issues. By producing theatre from this position, we are very aware that we don't represent everyone. As we grow, there is no excuse not to make our workplace and our art intersectional. It's at the forefront of our minds in each project because we don't want to be hypocritical. After all, this theatre company was created because we ourselves didn't feel represented in a space.

Theatre has a history of being a safe space for marginalised communities. It's exciting that intersectionality is at the forefront of current feminist discussion, because theatre is a perfect space to practise that. Intersectionality offers a fantastic toolkit to make accessible work authentically and safely.

**Do you collaborate with other groups?**

Since starting, we've discovered so many other women-led artists, theatre groups and production companies that champion feminist work. Play Full Theatre, Framework Theatre, and Disability Arts, for example, have enabled us to produce better, more accessible and more diverse art. Being part of a community of gender minority artists is such an encouraging, nurturing way to see more feminist work and make bolder feminist work ourselves.

**Do we still need feminist theatre? Why?**

As there always has been, both on stage and behind the curtain, there is still a severe lack of equity for gender minorities. Year after year, research and statistics reveal how underrepresented and unsafe women in theatre feel. If it is proven that large, mainstream stages and funding services are not diverse and accessible enough, how does that trickle down to smaller companies, venues and educational institutions? Feminist theatre raises the bar of what it expects equitable theatre to look like. It sets a model that demands change.

Feminist theatre pushes boundaries and starts conversations that we tend to shy away from and ignore. It is still needed because not everyone is confronted with feminism, not everyone knows that these disparities exist. There are young people who could be coming to see these shows, who haven't even thought about the daily inequalities and struggles, it can really start someone's journey with feminism. Feminist Theatre is also extremely confronting; it can hold a mirror up to people and make them truly think about their actions and how they carry themselves in the future. Theatre and art are so powerful in the conversation, it can spark discussion and change in an entry-level or approachable way. There is always someone out there who needs to see that piece of art and that makes it a necessity.

**Do you think having a theatre dedicated to women's work would have an impact?**

This comes with a lot of complicated feelings. On the one hand, it creates a safe space for women to nurture their art, diversify in skill, grow in confidence and develop work in an environment without gender bias. However, women-led theatre deserves to be represented in mainstream

Photo: Ruby Belassie

theatre. There is a danger that in having a theatre dedicated to women's work, we are simply segregating ourselves. We do not want to give the opportunity to those uninterested in women's art to find a way to disengage. We need to be championed and celebrated everywhere – infiltrating spaces where we are not equally represented. We need to demand to be seen in the spaces where men are, as often as men are.

**Are prizes important?**

Having your work accredited by an organisation will open doors, create opportunities and encourage engagement. Prizes make the theatre scene more equitable for those with lower incomes and less connections. For women, it is often a way our work can be consumed without bias and limitation.

**Is arts funding equitable?**

Sphinx Theatre Company did an excellent study on this in 2019 called *What Share of The Cake* based on Arts Council England's official data. The disproportion of funding going to men's art over women's, particularly in new writing, is staggering. We would recommend seeking it out.

**Are there allowances made for people with caring responsibilities – either children or elderly?**

Theatre has a reputation of being an extremely inflexible workplace. Rehearsal rooms, long work days, and late night hours can be relentless. If you are a person who needs to organise childcare or has other priorities, it can be an impossible industry to access. For theatre to be equitable, we need to start offering workspaces that can adapt for carers, especially as those who care for dependents are disproportionately women.

This is, however, something that many smaller theatre companies are beginning to acknowledge. We are at the start of a very exciting movement where spaces are being more flexible in their rehearsals and audience spaces, particularly with new explorations of 'babes-in-arms' policies.

**How can we improve things for women in theatre?**

Fundamentally, we need to be excited about having women in theatre. We need to believe that a diverse space will change things for the better both on stage and behind it. Women need to be wanted in theatre spaces: sought out and not simply allowed to exist. Let's create spaces where we seek diverse voices and accessible work environments. Until the theatre scene actively wants to change, we will continue to see inequality and bias in creative spaces, studies, statistics and reception.

**Anything else you want to add?**

To really make a difference we need to change competitive practice and champion welcoming work environments. We need to mentor other women, setting each other up to win, and demanding a space that is caring and considerate. Let us encourage one another, support each other, listen, go for coffees, check in and give over the floor.

≈

Photo: Lauren Baxter

**Rebekah Smith** (She/Her)
Rebekah studied Scriptwriting and Perform-ance BA at the University of East Anglia, where she regularly contributed to theatrical productions as committee member and artist. Since graduating, she has been regularly writing, acting and producing theatre in Edinburgh. Rebekah has taken three productions to the Edinburgh Fringe Festival in various capacities; as Assistant Director for Minotaur Theatre's *Bottom's Up* (2019), Writer and Ensemble Member in RatsNest Theatre's *This Is Your Captain Speaking* (2022), and Co-Creator/Performer in Scylla's Bite's debut production *Break Up With Your Boyfriend* (2023). Rebekah was awarded the Malcolm Bradbury Prize in 2021 for her play *Of Milk and Honey.*

**Abbie Lowe** (She/Her)
Also a UEA drama graduate, Abbie has worked primarily as a sound designer and writer. Her co-written play *Nothing Happens in a Petrol Station Car Park* was awarded the Minotaur Theatre creative writing slot in 2021. After working as a Company Technician for Minotaur Theatre and technical operator for Pleasance at the 2019 Edinburgh Festival Fringe, Abbie has gone on to design and operate three fringe shows; Balderdash Theatre's *Drown Your Sorrows* (2021), Orange Skies' *Wild Onion* (2022-23), and Rat's Nest Theatre's *This is Your Captain Speaking* (2022) where she was also a writer and production manager. Abbie co-created and performed *Break Up With Your Boyfriend* in 2023 alongside Rebekah and Scylla's Bite.

Helen George as Anna in *The King and I* at the Dominion Theatre

# INTERVIEW WITH DAME ROSEMARY SQUIRE

**Would you describe yourself as a feminist?**

Definitely. I am a founder of the Women's Playhouse Trust (WPT) and I was heavily involved in the early 80s, when I started in theatre, with a lot of feminist theatre production companies and campaigning organisations. The women who founded WPT were Sue Parrish, Jules Wright, who is sadly no longer with us, Nicole Penn-Symons, who is a solicitor, and me. We were the first directors.

**How did you get started in theatre?**

I grew up in Nottingham and we were very fortunate that we had great regional theatre. My mother loved theatre and took me as a child. For my 13th birthday, we went to Stratford-on-Avon to see the RSC. I often went to the Nottingham Playhouse, which, in the 70s, was a real happening place. Richard Eyre took over as artistic director. It was through Richard Eyre, and his wife Sue Birtwhistle who became a television producer, and founded the Theatre in Education Company "Roundabout", which came to my school. I famously stood on the steps of the Nottingham Playhouse when I was 17 or 18, and announced to a friend, "This is what I want to do. I want to be a theatre manager". I didn't know what that meant. But it was a great feeling; my best friend still remembers it.

**What was your first job and who were your mentors?**

I went to university in the UK and then did a postgraduate in the United States. I was business manager for the National Student Drama Festival. Then, when I came back from the US, I wanted to get a job. I had always had summer jobs and holiday jobs in box office. I had a job all the way through university, and I was quite good on the numbers. I had a few skills when I started to look for work and I got a job virtually immediately. I used to do front-of-house duties at night, and the accounts in the morning. It wasn't great; it was split shifts, but I got to see a lot of work and learned a lot of skills. Because I had been to the US, and

I was relatively young and wasn't scared by the prospect of computers, I was a project manager on the first computerized ticketing installation with Ticketmaster in the UK. At the same time, I was being mentored by inspirational women in the feminist groups I was involved with. In 1984, we produced *The Lucky Chance* directed by Jules Wright at the Royal Court Theatre. It was with Harriet Walter, Alan Rickman, Pam Ferris. It was stunning and we recouped and even made money on top of what we had raised through grants and investment from supporters, so we paid our investors back which was great. Jules Wright was a great mentor, as was Christina Smith, the doyenne of Covent Garden, who gave me the confidence to acquire buildings.

**How did you develop a commercial mindset about theatre producing?**

You can't be a theatre producer without being commercial because you'll very rapidly go out of business if you have no idea about the economics of a venture.

**How did you keep the reins on things?**

It's making sure people understand there are budgets to work to. We always tried to mitigate risk by having partners and co-producing. For example, *The Lucky Chance* was co-produced with the Royal Court then *Beauty and the Beast* by Louise Page was with Liverpool Playhouse and then went into The Old Vic. We also produced a play called *Spell #7* by Ntozake Shange that Sue Parrish directed at Donmar. Again, we had some public funding, some co-production money, and topped it up with an embryonic form of investment. I paid the rent, bought my food and ran my car from the earnings of my day job which was entirely in commercial theatre. So, I guess I met people, saw how it worked in commercial theatre, and then in 1988, I was made redundant when I was on maternity leave, which is not a good thing to do.

Women's Playhouse Trust had done a very good property deal – we had quite a lot of cash by then, and Jules Wright and the team carried on the business of the Women's Playhouse Trust and I moved into commercial theatre as a general manager for a production company. Then, I started to move up the ranks. I became executive director, and I started to co-produce, to get my name on the poster and take some risk. I would have to raise funds for the shows. Together with my husband, Howard Panter, we always produced across the piste. We have not just been about big musicals, we've been about new writing and commissioning. Revivals as well, rock 'n' roll musicals, classic musicals and new musicals. Unlike, say, Cameron Mackintosh, who only does very big musicals, or Michael Codron who produced quality plays, we produce across a broad canvas and always have done.

**How would you describe your job now, because it's managing a portfolio of theatres, isn't it?**

Well, they're part of the group; the second largest group of theatres in the UK is part of Trafalgar Entertainment. We previously built up Ambassador Theatre Group (ATG) over 25 years into the largest in the world, and became the first British company to own a Broadway theatre, in the modern time – probably ever. Sonia Friedman was with us for 17 years. She joined in the late 90s and we left ATG in 2016. Then it was a matter of thinking if we wanted to carry on or retire or do non-executive roles. In the end, we decided to carry on and we've created a different, possibly more robust business.

We now have different divisions in Trafalgar Entertainment. For example, we have an education division, and two performing arts businesses – one of which is singing, acting and dancing, called Stagecoach which is for kids from 4 to 18, that operates at the weekends. Then, we also have Drama Kids which is teaching acting, and that's typically an after-school activity for an hour after school. They're very popular. We're talking about 65,000 kids in a week. It's because schools have stopped teaching music and drama. All those extracurricular activities have gone, which is awful. That's one division and it's international – we've just signed our first master franchise in Canada. We're in Australia and Canada and Germany. We also have a ticketing division which has all of the ticketing for our 18 venues, plus we have an agency business in London which is called London Theatre Direct and which sells two or three million tickets in London – about 10 to 12% of the whole London market. They're very robust.

We also have a content division, which includes our production activity, probably 25 productions a year or many more, if we count all of our family entertainment Christmas shows, there are 22 of them. At the moment, we have *The King and I* with Helen George at the Dominion Theatre. We are about to put on sale our summer production, our fourth summer musical at Barbican Theatre which is *Kiss Me, Kate* – it's going to star Stephanie J. Block and Adrian Dunbar. We've also got Tracy-Ann Oberman in *The Merchant of Venice 1936*, we've co-produced it with the RSC, that's playing The Criterion for a season. We've *The Rocky Horror Show* with probably four different productions globally. Jason Donovan is in it in Australia playing the Civic Theatre in Newcastle.

The other business we have on the content side is our live broadcast company which captures live events and then screens them into cinemas. Including for example, The Royal Opera House, RSC, Metropolitan Opera, on the one hand, then on the other, it captures concerts by artists like Taylor Swift, Beyoncé, and K-Pop bands. We do a lot of our own musicals too such as *The King and I, Anything Goes, Rocky Horror*. We do plays as well – we're just about to capture David Tennant in *Macbeth*.

**So, if there's a pandemic, you've got other streams to fall back on?**

Definitely. The education business was still profitable because we moved it all online during the pandemic. I think it's more of a rounded business. It's a sort of flywheel if you like, with creativity and content at the heart

Tracy-Ann Oberman as Shylock in *The Merchant of Venice*, at The Criterion Theatre.

of it. My job is managing the different senior people and reporting to the shareholders, managing the relationship with the board, heading up all the corporate side as well as being experienced at operating theatres and producing shows, and being there as a resource and support to the teams who are doing all of that.

**Have you self-financed this new business or are you using investors?**

We did, to start with. We were able to bring together a group of friends and family, because of who we were and our track record of having built Ambassador Theatre Group to be the largest in the world. In 2018, we brought in institutional finance from the United States. It's a company called Barings who are owned by the oldest insurance company in the US called MassMutual.

**Are you taking risks on new writers and productions?**

Absolutely. We commission new work regularly. I wouldn't say we would commission a brand-new writer because you need to not expose new writers to what we do, producing for broad-based, larger theatres. But, for example, we've got in rehearsal at the moment a brand-new musical version of a much-loved film from the 90s called *Clueless* which is based on the Jane Austen novel *Emma*. The original screenwriter, Amy Heckerling, is writing the book, and we have KT Tunstall who has written music for it. That's all been commissioned. We are working with an American partner for it. You should go see it, it's going to be a fantastic piece with great parts for women. Two young women playing the leads. Of course, it's a journey about self-knowledge. It's very funny, with very perceptive observations of people and relationships. So, yes indeed, we commission new work.

**Have you encountered sexism and, if so, how did you deal with it?**

The most obvious thing was when I was made redundant without any kind of a proper process or consideration when I was on maternity leave. That's pretty sexist. I have a severely disabled daughter and during my career little or no consideration has been given to that. Whilst my daughter does live semi-independently in supported living, I now have a very elderly mother who lives close by that I care for. Even though my kids are grown up, like many women, I'm now caring for an elderly parent. It's tough.

**Do you make any allowances for people with caring responsibilities in your business?**

We've organized job-sharing and working from home since the 90s because women in the organization needed flexibility. I have had wonderful teams. If women are committed to want to make something happen, they are fantastic, almost without exception. I was recently a part of a recruitment process for the CEO of the Trade Association for London and Regional Theatre, and for the first time, in a high-profile job, we appointed two women who have got school-age children, and they job-share. I think it's the third time they have done that really successfully. They're brilliant at the handing over, the communication is amazing, and you get complementary skillsets. Some people are better on the communication, others on the planning or whatever it is. I found it to be very advantageous.

**You were on the board of the Arts Council as well?**

I was on the National Council for nine years which I think is a bit of a record. Diversity and equality were certainly always on the agenda. I have to say the Arts Council sometimes really puts its foot in it and while I was still in my last year, in one of their plans, equality was just completely overlooked. Sue Parrish and others jumped on that. I was a speaker at a conference that Sphinx organized, and Nick Serota came along because it was such a big omission. You can't think the job is done on the equality front because it's just not there yet. I've always said I will get off my soap box when not the first but the second woman is appointed artistic director at the National Theatre. They've not had the big jobs. This is a huge breakthrough [Indhu Rubasingham's appointment]. Even in television. Look at the BBC. There's never been a woman Director General. There's been a temporary chairman, once, recently, but she is the only woman who has been chairman. There's still a lot of work to do. Equal pay and all of the things we all work for. There are a lot of women that work in the arts now, but still not in the senior roles in the big companies that have considerable resource available to them.

**The pandemic has had quite a lasting effect on theatre. How are ticket sales in the West End doing, and around the country?**

In the last quarter, the West End ticket volume was down. I'm sure you can check with the trade associations, Society of London Theatre and UK

Theatre. I would say our regional theatres have been softer this year than they were last, but last year was a bit unusual in that it was the first proper year back from the pandemic. There was a kind of bounce back. There were also a lot of people who had been moved on from one year to another, to another. As you know, the whole family entertainment over the holiday period at Christmas is huge, it's probably 40% of the revenues for a lot of regional theatres. It has been softer than last year but not by much, which I think is pretty good. Theatre is alive and kicking and London has a lot of plays now, because musicals weren't developed during the pandemic. As we know, it takes years to develop a new musical or any musical production. We also import a lot from Broadway and Broadway is much worse impacted than the West End.

**What about the loss of freelancers? Has that impacted theatre?**

Some of the skilled freelancers are in short supply, particularly for regional touring. It's hard to find stage management or wardrobe staff, and all the technical skills, backstage. I think people got put off the notion of a freelance career during the pandemic because they didn't have any money and families started saying, "What's she doing this for?" I chair Mountview, the Performing Arts Academy, and recruiting people into our technical courses is a challenge. I think it's across all the drama schools because it means a freelance life. Some are going straight into things like Amazon or Netflix and they pay for training on the job, so you can't compete in theatre. It's very difficult. We've got a huge piece of work to do to try and recruit more. Typically, the people who do tour are very young because touring is a young person's game. Once you've got a home and you're settled, maybe you've got kids, you can't really manage it. It's really difficult, particularly for women.

**With twice as many theatre tickets being bought by women, why do programmers not commission more plays by women, and for them?**

In our *The King and I,* we cast as Anna, Helen George, who plays Trixie in *Call the Midwife*. I have to say I take my hat off to the producers of *Call the Midwife*. It's the only long-running tv series that has been about working-class women's experiences. It's a fantastic piece of work that is watched by so many women. They remember having tea at home at a kitchen table like the nurses and midwives. They remember children being born at home and the midwife visiting and how important it was. Whilst *The*

*King and I* is written by men, we have tried to cast it with someone that our slightly older female audience will be interested in. We try to make it as interesting and as accessible for women as possible, which, to be honest, it's just commercial common sense. We also try to attract them by casting the men as well, because a lot of women like, for example, the actor Adrian Dunbar. He's a big star from television and somebody a lot of women want to see on stage. We do work a lot with women directors too like on *The Merchant of Venice 1936* and on *Clueless* – it's a woman director, woman writer, woman composer. And that's targeting probably 40-year-olds I would say, who loved the film *Clueless*.

**Is feminist theatre still relevant today?**

Yes. Definitely. The job isn't done yet. I can't get off my soap box.

**What needs to happen to make the theatre industry a more equitable place for women to work?**

Well, you've got to stop the things that happened to you and me. I got made redundant when I was on maternity leave. They were restructuring and there was one job, but they gave it to a 60-year-old white male instead of me – a 31-year-old mother with two small children. It was ridiculous. It wasn't about who was better at the job at all. It was all "she's got a husband" or "she's got a partner, so, she doesn't need this job". There was a kind of assumption around that. We have to accommodate our caring responsibilities, at both ends of life, both ends of our careers. Literally, every day, I am running to have half an hour with my mother over a cappuccino because it brightens up her morning. But then, you know, I am always racing to get to meetings. I won't do meetings now before 11 o'clock. I can't manage it. I get up early, work beforehand, have the time out to go and see her, and then race to meetings. It's hard. If I wasn't the boss, I probably wouldn't be able to do it. We've got to accommodate everybody's needs, and particularly women's.

**Do you think a theatre dedicated to women's work would be helpful?**

Why not? It's what I tried to do with the Women's Playhouse Trust. But on a big scale. Let's not get stuck in a studio. Let's have a decent budget, a decent space.

≈

**Dame Rosemary Squire** was a founder of the Women's Playhouse Trust in the 80s, a landmark theatre production company that produced large-scale work by and with women. In 1992, Rosemary co-founded and ran for its first 25 years, the world's largest and most successful live theatre business – the Ambassador Theatre Group. Her latest venture is Trafalgar Entertainment, a premium international live entertainment business. In 2014, she made history as the first woman to be named EY UK Entrepreneur of the Year. She was a National Member of the Arts Council England Board for nine years, Joint Chairman of The Hall for Cornwall in Truro and is currently Chairman of Mountview Academy of Theatre Arts. As President of the Society of London Theatre, Rosemary became the second only female president in the organisation's history. In 2007 Rosemary was awarded an OBE for Services to Theatre and in 2018 received a Damehood for Services to Theatre and Philanthropy. She has been awarded Honorary Doctorates from Southampton University and De Montfort University in recognition of her achievements as a theatre entrepreneur.

Lucy Stevens as Virginia Woolf. Photo: Laura Doddington

# WOMEN IN THEIR OWN WORDS
## LUCY STEVENS

In 2018, to commemorate and celebrate 100 years of women in the UK being allowed to vote, I wrote, performed and toured *Ethel Smyth: Grasp the Nettle*. A play with music, it told the life story of Dame Ethel Smyth: composer, writer and suffragette.

Smyth lived a full 86 years. She was famous in her lifetime and a contemporary of Edward Elgar and Vaughan Williams. Today, her name ought to be just as well-known. She was the first female composer to have an opera performed at Covent Garden (1902) and at The Met in New York (1903). She composed six operas and many chamber and orchestral works as well as publishing eleven volumes of prose and countless articles.

Since dying in 1944, until very recently, she had been silenced, neglected and forgotten. When searching music libraries for her scores, Smyth's music was rarely on the shelves, hidden in the basements in the original, fading editions or only to be found in the original handwritten manuscript at the British Library. When asked by a male professor in a music library what she was looking for, our pianist answered 'Ethel Smyth' and the response came 'why bother?'.

Ethel Smyth provided the answer to his question in *Female Pipings in Eden*, written in 1933:

> "I have always felt it must be, for women, a question of something yet unvoiced … And as time goes on, even the Faculty, an all-male body, once they have got past the stage of saying 'pooh', may come to perceive that something not quite negligible is being uttered though in a language different to their own; while non-creative women, listening to the song of their sisters, be it literature, painting or music, will say: 'O what is this that knows the way I came?' - a comforting thought, for remember half the world consists of women!"[1]

---

1 *Female Pipings in Eden* by Ethel Smyth, Peter Davies Ltd, 1934 at page 55.

Half the world consists of women … what a rich world that would be, if half of all the artistic output were made by women.

When I studied Acting and Community Theatre Arts at Rose Bruford College of Speech and Drama, it was because I wanted to contribute to the conversation in British theatre. Not, as I saw it, just playing the young female roles that rarely drove the narrative, only looking on admiringly to the male leads who did.

At Rose Bruford, we learnt to devise community touring plays relevant to their audiences. We studied the politics of Brecht's plays and the revolutionary theatre espoused by Augusto Boal. But the theatre world I entered as a young 'jobbing' actor told me that my audition song, *On Suicide* by Brecht and Eisler, was 'too bleak, I can't imagine where you [a young woman] would possibly sing it?'.

My publicity photo wasn't 'smiley enough'. My agent told me that I should remove the directing credits from my CV because I might scare directors because they could feel 'threatened' by me. In the 1990s, the directors he was talking about were invariably male. There was no demand for me to sing my 'bleak' song and my look was 'too strong' to play female leads (God forbit they should be strong!).

Gloriously, I did play a number of witches and animals: the Wolf, In *Peter and the Wolf*, for a year's tour of schools and theatres, the Wicked Witch of the West in *The Wizard of Oz* at the Liverpool Playhouse and the White Witch in *The Lion the Witch and the Wardrobe* at the Arts Theatre in the West End. During that time, I rarely saw mature women actors 'jobbing' in theatre work. In theatre ensembles of about ten actors, two or three would be women, playing the love interest or wives and mothers. None, or perhaps one, would be Black or Asian.

Women's lives and their stories were not being told. As a young woman, I didn't see a path for me as an actor once I had turned 30. If you can't see it, you can't be it. Because of that, I trained at the Royal Welsh College of Music and Drama as a classical singer and turned my gaze to Opera where epic stories are told. But as I searched for my 'Fach' (the German system of classifying opera singers), I realised that it was not only as a contralto that the roles were limited. As an art form, Opera was decades behind theatre in writing, commissioning and performing relevant work that explores women's stories away from the male gaze. In the established opera repertoire the few strong women meet a tragic death, warning that this is

Lucy Stevens as Gertrude Lawrence. Photo: Jon Collins

what happens to feisty women who dare to challenge male supremacy. If the role of art in society is to allow us to reflect on the human condition, as a woman at the end of the twentieth century, I could not see my reflection.

I read the published letters and diaries of the British contralto Kathleen Ferrier who died in 1953. In her recordings, her voice is imbued with serene gravitas, but in her diaries and letters she was funny, gregarious and brutally honest. I immediately wanted an audience to meet her. I began editing her letters, diaries and music into my first play with music: *Kathleen Ferrier Whattalife!*

For me, a new journey had begun. Writing plays for a single female performer, with a pianist on stage providing live music and the text taken solely from women's published autobiographical books, essays, letters and diaries – early 20th-century women telling the stories of their own lives.

These were stories that had only been told before by men, in biographies or plays in which the women or their achievements had been marginalised or even ridiculed. Women's stories were rarely heard in any artistic field, not only in theatres, but also in the visual arts and in classical music. We were therefore unable to place women in our cultural artistic timeline. Virginia Woolf observed in her essay *Women and Fiction*:

'... in those almost unlit corridors of history where the figures of generations of women are so dimly, so fitfully perceived. For very little is known about women. The history of England is the history of the male line, not the female. Of our fathers we know always some fact, some distinction... But of our mothers, our grandmothers, our great-grandmothers, what remains?'[2]

Whilst writing these plays, I'm conscious of the threads of my own experiences drawing directly from that of women's lives, how their lives connect with women's lives today. By revealing the everyday personal details, found in diaries or letters, with glimpses of their battles, frailties and insecurities, we allow the audience to witness their brilliance as well as their moments of powerlessness and vulnerability, enabling them to empathise in solidarity as women. These plays do not try to define the woman's output as 'excellent' or 'worthy'. What the women achieved in their lives is relevant, but my main interest is in them and their lives as *women*.

Collaborating with pianist Elizabeth Marcus, music is an integral element in the pieces and weaves through the text, heightening an emotion, enriching a scene, or creating space for the audience to reflect. With the pianist on stage underscoring a scene, the performer shifts fluidly between spoken and sung words, both of which are integral to the storytelling.

Solely drawing from the individual woman's own words, provides an authenticity to the text. It places the character in her time, weighted with her phrasing, nuance and humour, whilst allowing her to be her own storyteller. This is a discipline that I have adhered to with all my writing. An intimacy develops between the character and the audience drawing them in as her confidantes, privy to private thoughts and desires, and enabling them to suspend their disbelief – the actor 'is' the woman.

My most recent play, *Gertrude Lawrence: A Lovely Way To Spend An Evening*, celebrates the style and determined courage of the 1930s star. It follows her journey from Clapham, performing in revues, to London's swanky night clubs and the bright lights of Broadway. We don't celebrate her feminism, as we do Virginia Woolf, but we celebrate a feisty, strong, independent woman who forged her stage and screen career into her fifties and transcended the class ceiling. In 1949 she bought the stage rights to *Anna and the King of Siam* and commissioned Rodgers and

---

2 *Women and Writing - Virginia Woolf*, Harcourt, 1979, 'Women and Fiction' at page 4

Hammerstein to write *The King and I* as a star vehicle for herself.

In 1931, in the same year as Gertrude Lawrence was performing in *Private Lives* with Noel Coward, Virginia Woolf and her good friend, the composer Ethel Smyth, were invited to speak on 'Music and Literature' at the London Society for Women's Service (later renamed The Fawcett Society). Woolf's speech concerned a woman writer's need to be 'herself', with a free, uncensored imagination. This necessitated killing the 'Angel': '... an experience that was bound to befall all women writers at that time. Killing the Angel in the House was part of the occupation of a woman writer'[3].

Reading this speech was my introduction to Virginia Woolf's polemic writing. It was this, alongside her desire to tell the un-written history of women's lives, that inspired me to write *Virginia Woolf: Killing the Angel*. In *The Common Reader* that same year she wrote, 'For living art presents and records real life, and the only life we can truly know is our own.'[4]

*'Why bother?'* The professor didn't hear Ethel Smyth's response because she wrote it 85 years before he asked the question – that's why I bother.

≈

Photo: Laura Doddington

**Lucy Stevens** is an actor, classical singer and theatre maker. She studied acting at Rose Bruford College of Speech & Drama and voice at Royal Welsh College of Music & Drama and has performed in productions at: The Old Vic, West Yorkshire Playhouse, Arts Theatre, Liverpool Playhouse, Longborough Festival Opera, Opera Holland Park, Sadler's Wells and The Royal Opera House. Recently Lucy has created new small-scale theatre productions in which song and the spoken word weave seamlessly through text drawn from autobiographical writings. *Gertrude Lawrence: A lovely way to spend an evening, Virginia Woolf: Killing the Angel, Ethel Smyth: Grasp the Nettle* and *Kathleen Ferrier Whattalife!* tour throughout the UK and internationally and have featured on BBC 2, BBC Radio 3 and BBC Radio 4. In 2020, Lucy recorded *Dame Ethel Smyth - Songs and Ballads* with Elizabeth Marcus and the Berkeley Ensemble conducted by Odaline de la Martinez for Somm Recordings and in 2022 *Virginia Woolf: Killing the Angel* was published by Aurora Metro. www.lucystevens.com

3 *Death of the Moth*, Hogarth Press, 1943, 'Professions for Women' at page 151.

4 *Women and Writing - Virginia Woolf*, Harcourt, 1979, 'Aurora Leigh' at page 140.

Gerda Stevenson as Phaedra in *Phaedra* by Racine, translated by Edwin Morgan.
Photo: Douglas Robertson

# STELLAR QUINES & AFTER
## GERDA STEVENSON

One aspect of being female is that, unless you're very careful, you can become invisible. I founded Stellar Quines Theatre Company in 1993, because it seemed to me that Scotland's female theatre practitioners, particularly women of around 35 and over, were prone to this fate. Several experiences had informed my outlook on my profession.

In 1986, I had the good fortune to work, as an actor, with Monstrous Regiment, often referred to as the Grandmother of British Women's Theatre. Having worked in Britain as an actor for over a decade, I was surprised on the first day of rehearsals to find only one man (an actor) in our midst. The rest of the cast, the playwright (Susan Yankowitz), director (Penny Cherns), lighting designer, set designer, stage management team, publicity – all were female. This struck me as extraordinary. What struck me as even more extraordinary was my own surprise. Monstrous Regiment was a women's theatre company, so what had I expected? The situation initially felt slightly uncomfortable because of its unfamiliarity. I had often been the only woman, or one of a very small female minority, in many theatre companies, and had never experienced that gender-ratio reversed.

Another impressive, and, to me, innovative building block in Monstrous Regiment's structure, was their policy of paying subsistence to those employees who incurred childcare costs. Under the union agreement at that time, Equity paid subsistence to members who had additional travel and accommodation costs, but not for childcare. Monstrous Regiment, a London-based company, paid subsistence as a contribution to childcare, even if the employee did not have additional travel and accommodation costs.

A couple of years later, when I became a working mother back home in Scotland, living in the same city as the theatre company employing me, I decided to take a leaf out of Monstrous Regiment's book: although the contract didn't include subsistence, I nevertheless requested it, as a contribution towards the cost of childcare. This was refused. I insisted, and the relatively small additional weekly sum was eventually agreed, but not without a letter from the administrator (a mother herself), warning me I'd be very lucky to work again.

In fact, this wasn't the end of my working life in theatre, and as a young mother, I received support and encouragement from many people. From the outset, I took my seven-week-old baby with me, the childminder caring for him in a room next to the rehearsal space, which meant that I could breastfeed him during the breaks. This worked well, supported by the director, Gerry Mulgrew, and gave me a confidence boost just when I needed it, carrying the daunting responsibility of being a young mother playing the central role in a new play. Once the show went into performance, I'd take my son with me into the dressing room until beginners' call. While the musicians were tuning up and the actors getting ready, I'd give him a last breastfeed to keep him going. Then I'd pop downstairs and place him in his carrycot on top of the beer crates behind the bar, watched over by the lovely bar woman, who was happy to oblige. Luckily, my babe always slept!

Some months later, rehearsing for another production (playing Desdemona in Shakespeare's *Othello* at the Royal Lyceum in Edinburgh), I was still breastfeeding, and on a day when the childminder wasn't available, I rehearsed with my baby son strapped to my back. This temporary solution was accepted by the supportive cast and director, Ian Wooldridge.

When my son was two years old, and my husband working away from home, I joined Communicado Theatre Company in *Jock Tamson's Bairns* by Liz Lochhead, at the Tramway in Glasgow. This was a large-scale production with a big cast of musicians, dancers and actors. During performances, while I was on stage, my son sat backstage – a massive barn of a place – happy with his Duplo bricks and books, in the company of various cast members, the dresser and his dog. Those were the days when Health & Safety was hardly on the radar, and you could get away with such arrangements.

Around this period, I also worked with Freefall, a new women's theatre company, established by Paola Dionisotti, Anna Furse and Juliet

Stevenson. Freefall focused on creating acting and directing opportunities for women. The play, *On the Verge,* by Eric Overmeyer, was written for a cast of three women but, unlike Monstrous Regiment, Freefall didn't extend their focus to all other roles within the company – the playwright and lighting designer (Gerry Jenkinson) were male. I found myself comparing different models of feminist theatre.

In 1992, I was cast in *Blue Black Permanent,* written and directed by Margaret Tait, the first feature film to be made by a Scottish woman. Tait was a remarkably single-minded artist. She had spent her life funding her own film projects, and, at the age of 74, *Blue Black Permanent,* produced by the British Film Institute, was a breakthrough for her. We connected immediately, partly through our interest in literature, both being writers. Tait had been a quiet presence on the Scottish cinema and literary scenes, making her own films, as well as writing and publishing her own books, since the 1950s – the heyday of the Scottish Literary Renaissance, led by her friend Hugh MacDiarmid. This movement, as depicted by Alexander Moffat in his famous painting *Poets' Pub* (1980), did not include women in its front ranks, although there was no shortage of stellar Scottish female literary talent at the time – Willa Muir, Nan Shepherd, Naomi Mitchison, Nancy Brysson Morrison, Helen B Cruikshank, to name but a few, though none of these particular women appear in the painting. Moffat's group portrait is an exclusive celebration of men seated in the foreground around the central figure of Hugh MacDiarmid – the women are blurred, semi-naked background figures, relegated to the 'sex interest'. As with so many professions, women remained in the shadows, and often still do.

These experiences stimulated me into thinking about the professional theatre scene in my native Scotland. As far as I knew at that time – the early 90s – our only women's theatre company was MsFits, run by Rona Munro and Fiona Knowles. This was essentially a vehicle for Rona as a playwright and Fiona as a performer. Their excellent, pioneering productions were usually one-woman shows.

I was 37 by this stage, and wasn't being offered quite so many of the 'ingénue' roles – the majority of main parts for women in most plays, historically, fall into this category. It seemed to me that just when women have earned some life experience (becoming a mother, in my case), enabling them to contribute something of real depth to the art form, the opportunities simply evaporate. I felt that Scotland should have its

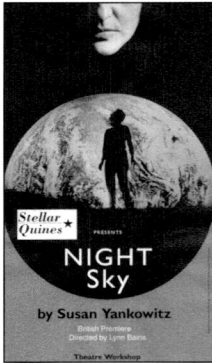

own Monstrous Regiment. I favoured the model that would consciously create opportunities for women in most, if not all areas of production.

I envisaged an international programme. I had in mind an inaugural play – *Night Sky*, by New York playwright Susan Yankowitz. We'd already collaborated when working with Monstrous Regiment, and I admired her writing. I approached Lynn Bains – like Yankowitz, a New Yorker, and Head of Acting at Edinburgh's Queen Margaret College, (later to become Queen Margaret University), to direct *Night Sky*. This multi-layered play is essentially about communication, and was written at the suggestion of Yankowitz's friend, the renowned theatre director Joseph Chaikin, who had become aphasic following a stroke. Before embarking on the central role of 'Anna' in *Night Sky*, I researched aphasia for three months at Queen Margaret College's Speech and Language Therapy Department, my first contact with S.A.L.T., which I found fascinating. (Some years later, this connection proved invaluable, when I gave birth to my daughter who has Down's Syndrome.)

Lynn and I approached the theatre administrator Morag Ballantyne, who was working at the Traverse, and her husband Iain Carmichael, a businessman. The four of us became the core of the new company, which I named Stellar Quines – 'quine' being a fine old Scots word for a girl or a woman, carrying the connotation of feistiness. The word is close to 'queen', yet it resonates with a democratic ring, an aristocracy of the spirit, I like to think – any woman is a 'quine'.

*Night Sky* was produced on a profit-share basis, with no Scottish Arts Council support, and it was agreed that any profit should be ploughed back into the company – I seem to recall the handsome sum of £84! After this inaugural production, actors Muriel Romanes and Irene Macdougall joined the core company. Our second production was Sue Glover's haunting play *The Seal Wife*, which I directed. This time we received a small grant from the Scottish Arts Council. I got in touch with my friends, colleagues and contacts – anyone I could think of who might be interested – including Baroness Helena Kennedy, the Countess of Strathmore, Lady Judy Steel, Edith MacArthur, and Juliet Stevenson, who became Friends of Stellar Quines, generously donating towards the production budget.

We were now receiving recognition, with favourable press comments such as:

*"Bursting with wit, intelligence and energy, Stellar Quines brings a new energy to Scottish Theatre."* – *The Scotsman*, April, 1994

*"A big sense of maturity and skill, an impressive start."* – *Scotland on Sunday*, April, 1994

*"... impeccable... a vintage cast, which brings a rare weight to the proceedings."* – *The List,* November, 1995

We had been working on producing a Stellar Quines repertoire, which would include commissions from Scottish women writers. I'd come across the work of Janet Paisley – alas, now deceased, but still living at the time – a brilliant poet and short story writer, who later became a novelist. Much of her prose is in the form of sizzling dialogue, and I felt that she had a dramatic instinct within her writing. She sent me some monologues, and I suggested she expand one of them into her first full-length play. Stellar Quines commissioned *Refuge* from Janet, a play for six women, set in a women's refuge. This exceptional script – moving, funny, and deeply disturbing – won the coveted British-wide Peggy Ramsay Award, competing with plays submitted by established companies such as the National Theatre, the Bush Theatre and the Royal Court. The almost all-male judging panel included Simon Callow and John Tydeman (former Head of BBC Radio 4 Drama). This award was not made to the playwright,

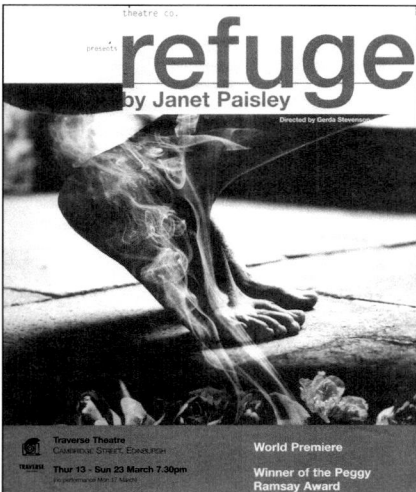

but to the company, as a budget for mounting a production of the winning play. The Peggy Ramsay Foundation awarded Stellar Quines £50,000. Janet Paisley's creativity and imagination was a significant milestone on the journey towards putting Stellar Quines on the map. I directed *Refuge*, which was enthusiastically received by audiences and press. On the week in which *Refuge* opened at Edinburgh's Traverse theatre (March 1997), the *Herald* reported: *"If the Scottish Arts Council is sending out signals about how to run a company, then we should look no further than Stellar Quines."*

*Refuge* has never been published, other than online. It can be read on the Scottish Corpus website: https://www.scottishcorpus.ac.uk/document/?documentid=483

Meanwhile, I had also been making contact with a number of theatre companies and literary agents, in Britain and abroad (including Playbox Theatre at the Malthouse in Melbourne, Australia, run by the indefatigable Aubrey Mellor[1]). I identified a list of plays from beyond Scotland, which I hoped could become part of Stellar Quines' repertoire. These were:

*Honour,* by Joanna Murray-Smith (Australia); *Hotel Sorrento* by Hannie Rayson (Australia); *In Her Sight,* (later entitled *Without A Trace*) by Carol K. Mack (USA); *The Clearing,* by Helen Edmundson (England)*; The Memory of Water,* by Shelagh Stephenson (England).

In tracking down Scottish playwrights, I also discovered, through my interest in the neglected early 19th-century Scottish novelist Mary Brunton, the work of her contemporary, Lanarkshire-born Joanna Baillie. At the National Library in Edinburgh, I read a number of Baillie's considerable repertoire of plays – 27 in all. Sir Walter Scott and Lord Byron rated Baillie's playwriting skills highly. Byron's verdict on her work was: *"If it takes testicles to write drama, then Joanna Baillie certainly has them!"* He also asserted that Baillie was: *"Our only dramatist since Ottway and Southerne,"* adding that *"Women (save Joanna Baillie) cannot write tragedy; they have not seen enough or felt enough of life for it."*

Lynn Bains suggested a moving and thought-provoking American play – *Emma's Child,* by Kristine Thatcher, which took as its theme the issues of childlessness and disability. Under the Stellar Quines Rehearsal Room banner, I directed a rehearsed reading of *Emma's Child* at the Traverse, with Juliet Stevenson and John Bett in the central roles. I was also very keen to give an airing to Carol K. Mack's play *Without A Trace,* a remarkable drama about the blind pianist, Maria Theresia von Paradis, for whom Mozart wrote a piano concerto. She was a patient of Franz Mesmer, the doctor whose unusual practice became known as mesmerism. *Without a Trace* was included in our Rehearsal Room series – a rehearsed reading, under my direction, with live music by Dee Isaacs.

A second tour of *Refuge* was planned, and we continued to seek out Scottish-based writers with a view to further commissions. Dilys Rose,

---

1  See *Southeast Asian Plays* eds. Cheryl Robson & Aubrey Mellor (Aurora Metro)

Donna Franceschild, Zinnie Harris and a second play from Janet Paisley were commissioned. Irene Macdougall directed Dilys's play *Learning the Paso Doble*. Lynn Bains worked with Janet Paisley on the development of *Deep Rising*, with a view to directing the final script – an historical drama, set during the Jacobite uprisings.

Unfortunately, in spite of the endless communications with the playwright's agent, and eventually with the playwright herself, we were unable to secure the rights for Joanna Murray-Smith's *Honour*, which tells the tale of a middle-aged man, who leaves his wife, Honor, and their daughter, for a relationship with a much younger woman. Almost a decade later this play became a hit at the National Theatre's Cottesloe, London (2003), with Eileen Atkins in the title role, and, some time later, with Diana Rigg. The British Theatre Guide's reviewer wrote of the British premiere: "*The National has unearthed an absolute gem with this Australian play written in 1995.*"

Our fourth production was *The Clearing*, by Helen Edmundson (founder of Red Stockings Theatre Company, in 1988), a powerful and profoundly moving play, which combined the personal with the political, set during the early Irish Troubles under Cromwell. As soon as I read it, I felt sure that Scottish audiences would recognise the resonances with our own shameful history of the notorious highland clearances. Muriel Romanes directed this well-received production.

During the first half-dozen years of its existence, Stellar Quines had no core funding. We were supported by donations from our loyal list of Friends, and by the Scottish Arts Council (now renamed Creative Scotland), from their Project Grant fund – one-off awards, which led to a hand-to-mouth existence. The day-to-day running of the company, artistically and administratively, had to be carried out voluntarily. We were paid only when employed as part of the production team, i.e. when we received a modest one-off fee as part of a production budget, once per year at the most. While working for Stellar Quines all year round, building the company from strength to strength, we were simultaneously having to earn elsewhere.

The company had operated for these first six years as a co-operative, with no single artistic director – an idealistic concept, which I favoured, though it proved to be unwieldy. Differences of opinion arose regarding repertoire (one play in particular caused serious divisions), and also the

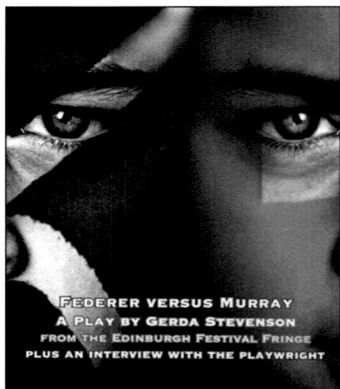

FEDERER VERSUS MURRAY
A PLAY BY GERDA STEVENSON
FROM THE EDINBURGH FESTIVAL FRINGE
PLUS AN INTERVIEW WITH THE PLAYWRIGHT

company model, e.g. whether to employ and commission work from men within the production team, neither of which I supported. I and Irene Macdougall left Stellar Quines, and some of the playwrights withdrew their commissions. The company went on to adopt a more traditional model, with a single artistic director, building on its early success.

I've continued to work in theatre, radio, film, and opera, as director, actor and writer. I eventually directed a production of Carol K. Mack's *Without a Trace* for Sounds of Progress theatre company, Glasgow, an integrated group of disabled and able-bodied performers, with the blind actor Karina Jones playing the central role of the blind pianist, Maria Theresia von Paradis.

I've also written and directed many radio dramas for BBC, was Associate Director with Gerry Mulgrew's Communicado Theatre Company for over a decade, and have directed many plays for Oran Mor, Glasgow, including my own – *Federer Versus Murray*, which toured to New York, under the auspices of the Scottish Government (published there by Salmagundi), and *Skeleton Wumman*, a co-production with the Traverse, Oran Mor and West Yorkshire Playhouse. Most recently I was invited to direct two productions for Orkney's St Magnus International Festival – a film of George Mackay Brown's moving script *The Storm Watchers*, for a cast of seven women, and *Thora*, a powerful play for stage by David McNeish, about the mother of Saint Magnus.

I've recorded an album of my own songs, had a book of short stories and three poetry collections published, two of which have also been translated into Italian and published in Rome. My latest poetry collection, *Tomorrow's Feast*, includes a libretto – a contemporary retelling in verse of Coleridge's epic poem *The Rime of the Ancient Mariner*, which I've set during the current refugee crisis. I particurlarly enjoy research-based writing, reading up on a subject, and interviewing individuals, especially those whose voices are marginalised. My second poetry collection, *Quines: Poems in Tribute to Women of Scotland*, reviewed by Jackie Kay in *The Observer* as *"Fabulous…a groundbreaker of a book,"* looks at

Scottish history and society through the voices of Scottish women from Neolithic times up to the 21st century. The poems are all in monologue form, and, in many ways, the book represents a continuation of my work with Stellar Quines.

My dear friend, the late, great radio producer and theatre director Marilyn Imrie, who was chair of Stellar Quines' board for several years, once told me that if I'd remained with the company I'd have achieved much less in my career. Who knows? In any case, I've never pursued a career trajectory. As a wag once put it, my career has always been more of a verb than a noun. What I do know is that founding and developing Stellar Quines was an exhilarating honour. Three decades and three artistic directors later (Muriel Romanes, Jemima Levick, and currently Caitlin Skinner), I'm glad to say that our feisty quine continues to thrive as a dynamic feminist force in Scottish theatre.

≈

**Gerda Stevenson** is a writer/actor/director/singer-song-writer. She founded Stellar Quines theatre company, was Associate Director of Communicado Theatre Company, has written and directed films, operas, plays for stage, as well as original dramas and adaptations of classic Scottish novels for BBC Radio 4. Acting: Many tv, radio, film and theatre productions, including the title role in Edwin Morgan's *Phaedra* at the Royal Lyceum, Edinburgh. She won a BAFTA Scotland Best Film Actress for her role in Margaret Tait's *Blue Black Permanent*. Nominations include three times for the Critics' Awards for Theatre in Scotland, the Gilder/Coigney International Theatre Award, the MG Alba Awards for an album of her own songs – *Night Touches Day,* and the London Festival Fringe Theatre Writing Award for her play *Federer Versus Murray*. Her publications include three poetry collections, a book of short stories, and collaborations with visual artists. www.gerdastevenson.co.uk

SuAndi. Photo: Julian Kronfli

# DIFFERENCES MATTER
## SUANDI

I am strongly opposed to "blind casting" particularly when the production is based on fact – a lived life. As we struggle to bring the true impact of Black migration to British society (as well as globally), we need to ensure that audiences realise what they are seeing reflects the truth. Despite what I call "The Markle Effect" and the liberal guilt response to #BLM, the extensive casting of Black folk in TV commercials is not reflected in the overall theatre industry – in the commissioning and casting of theatre that is written, produced and performed by Black women.

My life before the arts was without any sense of politics. I was simply a dress, a new one bought weekly for a Saturday night out. Despite the warnings of my mother and my brother's cultural awareness, I was happy to exploit my femininity across a dance floor. The arts were a slap of reality. Here I found a world that had a carefully manicured agenda, polished so highly in order to blindside the individual to the reality that Black artists, artists with disabilities and artists from the gay communities were required to pay lip-service to equality, and accept drip-fed opportunities in changing campaigns under different headings of good intentions. I never once sat on a panel with a fourth seat for women artists. Despite the struggles that feminist artists were facing, they were not as openly marginalised as their Black sisters. They were not sitting at the top table, that is true, but neither were they alongside those of us squashed together as we were at conferences, on what really was 'the guilt panel' made up of those who needed to be tolerated.

I assumed the profession of an artist in 1985. Four years later, the African American feminist movement coined the term intersectionality. Not that I was aware of this at the time. I was too busy facing the lack of understanding and hurdles that other women artists were (and I give them the benefit of the doubt) unconsciously forcing me to push against.

Just as in conferences, we were invited onto panels programmed late in the day, when delegates were beginning to depart early. So, the stages we appeared on were themed for gatherings such as International Women's Week (often without funding support so we were not paid), or Anti-Racist Week, and so on. No one said the actual words, but it was apparent that theatres believed there was no audience for women's work throughout the year, and even less of one for Black and disabled artists. Thankfully, there were voices speaking out in support of opportunities to champion scripts from different life experiences.

I hope I'm not being ageist when I write that I likened The Chuffinelles to my English mother. Created by the late and wonderful Linda Smith, their performances might be considered more cabaret than theatre but with the sharpness of their wit, they told working-class women's stories. Lip Service, with their satirical portrayal of upper-class women and life as written in classical literature, was for me, a way of learning of women at the other end of the social scale. Red Stocking did their own version of "blind casting" but not, of course, on a race level. They were brilliant at casting roles against type, and not based on their looks or physical form.

Although these examples are all white, not marginalised by race, for me, they were allies. Unlike a Greek comedy duo I performed with in Leeds who decided to make me the brunt of their humour for being the straight woman at a mainly lesbian event – proof that women do not always support other women, or respect their heritage and sexuality.

I believe that no artist has a "right" to funding. However, Arts Council England (ACE), financed from public taxes, is dispersed by arts officers whose policies often seem to constrict rather than enhance the arts. ACE headquarters in Great Peter Street (London) had the Access Unit for Disability Arts, Women and whatever the other terminologies were at the time. I'll go for Multicultural, simply because I long ago stopped following the ever-changing labels that have been placed on Black Arts. This meant that in the 90s especially, the opportunities to explore creative ideas and bring them to the stage were often reliant on an arts officer to support the vision within an application, within the access guidelines.

Initially known as Performance Art, Live Art allowed for solo performers, in particular, to take to the stage and tell 'our stories'. Moreover, Live Art was more akin to Black Arts and Culture which does not separate the arts. Here visual art, music, spoken word, all art forms can be utilised in the one piece of work.

Living outside London where there are fewer venues with small theatre spaces, there were rare opportunities to see work that was coming out of the capital such as that by the Theatre of Black Women. The only Black theatre that was available in Manchester was brought over by the Anti-Apartheid Movement, for which we had empathy at the heartbreak of the productions, but they were still stories from a 'strange land'.

Watchers and Seekers was a passport to a fresh start. A confidence booster, a diploma of rights to tell our own stories of womanhood from our perspective as Black women via our own scripts offered openly for all to witness. Staging work remained a difficulty, we needed to break from the limitations of the UK's version of the 'Chitlin circuit' of the Black-managed community centres because we wanted to share our lives and experiences with as broad an audience as possible.

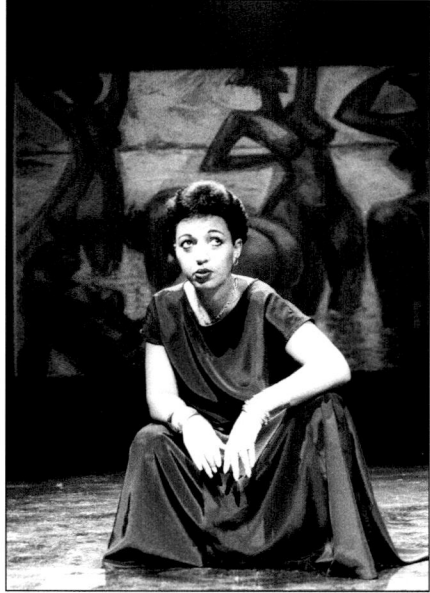

Fortunately, Manchester had The Green Room which brought in shows that "hit the spot" with touring productions from the Market Theatre of Johannesburg, African American artists and UK Arts shows. With increasing Live Art commissions and the diverse programming at the ICA, it became our time, as increasingly we had allies and supporters, and most importantly mentors. I remember Cuban American Coco Fusco performing with Guillermo Gómez-Peña in *The Couple in the Cage* in St Anne's Square, Manchester. Looking back, I see how my response to it was guided by my 'English sensibility'. Was this art? It wasn't even in a theatre? I had seen *Hair* many times so I was used to nudity, but I recoiled witnessing white audiences looking at Black bodies.

American writer and performer, Rhodessa Jones, brought me closer to understanding how performance could not only reflect reality but speak for those who had no voice. Over the years she has conducted her Medea Project in South African prisons, working with incarcerated women and trained correctional personnel and local artists. But it was her portrayal of a homeless woman that really woke me up. When I contributed to the 1995 publication *Let's Get it on: The Politics of Black Performance,* I can still hear Keith Antar Mason berating me for not taking an early opportunity to archive (in print) my work so far. Keith's work with The Hittie Empire was to later inspire two major NBAA productions, namely *In My Father's House* with 147 men and youths and later *In My Father's House 2* which I wrote, produced and directed for 64 men and youth performers.

In my early writing, I was sharing a new poem in BlackScribe and spoke the line 'the black people', or something similar. Tina Tamsho-Thomas asked me who the Black people were. I stumbled for a while giving variations until I finally said, '*We* Black people". I had unwittingly been using the language of those who seek to disempower us.

I have never seen the work of debbie tucker green, except on the television, never had the opportunity to applaud Theatre of Black Women. Is it surprising to share that whenever Black women perform or have their production presented in Manchester, I try my best to be in the audience? Hardly surprising that our eyes strain to see our people there, on stage beyond the footlights, often behind the front row of white faces. Such was the case when the Queens of Sheba performed at HOME in 2019. As my mate and I drove home, I spotted them walking along. I braked and we jumped out of the car and shouted at them. Seeing us, they rushed into our arms to share a hug of unity.

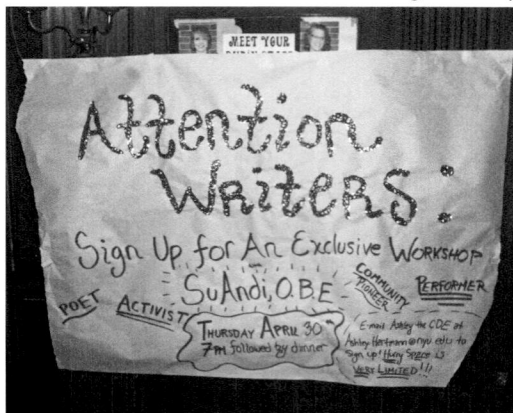

I kept on travelling as my international work increased, giving me the opportunity not just to watch other artists but to spend time with them too: from bell hooks to Ntozake Shange to Maya Angelou. It was seeing Carrie Mae Weems' installation *And 22 Million Very Tired and Very Angry People* during my first New York contract that resulted in my first foray from poetry to Live Art, now known as Performance Art. I was always engaging with other Black women artists but the colonial trickery of 'Divide and Rule' has had a strong grip on the arts so we struggled against each other for the attention of the mainstream. Now I am requesting to backdate my membership to the Sistahood of 'We Are Black Women' speaking across all art forms. I am no longer a student, but a teacher who knows that learning never stops. This means that I continue to question where my work sits in the feminist arena of consciousness.

I now have an OBE. A dear English friend called it an 'Outstanding Black Example', whereas my South Asian friend said it was 'Other People's Efforts' and she is right. (I should add my gong has only served me to tell this story). No achievement is made simply by one individual. Aside from immediate support in the journey from creative idea to the realisation of a production, we walk in the footsteps of those who kicked down so many doors. From the so-called 'Bawdy' music hall singers to the silent screen sirens. They weren't writing their scripts, but they were fighting against how women were portrayed. Taking tiny steps so that over time, women working in theatre were no longer likened to prostitutes.

I do not support the idea of a Women's (only) Theatre because the ONS data shows that there was an increase in the number of sexual offences recorded by the police in the year ending March 2023 (195,315 offences) compared to the previous year (193,559 offences). Of all sexual offences recorded by the police in the year ending March 2023, 35% (68,949) were rape offences. We need to share the joy of our lives, the positives, challenges, successes and difficulties of what it means to be women across our cultural heritages and classes. Even in this 21st century we still live under the threat of some men. However, I do support Black arts centres as 'safe spaces' especially to try out new work. Also accepting that there is a percentage of the population that will never purchase a ticket, nevertheless, we strive for racial equality off and on stage.

The progress of women in the feminist movement has been huge. The progress we have made as Black artists especially over the last few years is amazing. There are so many writers and actors creatively pushing our agenda. We are no longer the chorus line, the back-up singers, the extras walking on and off the set. Nor the annoying best friend of the white shero in films – now we have our own leading men and women.

Many years back after the success of an exhibition with visually impaired women, I started to write what I hoped would become a play. As I drove the women around, I described the scenery. 'Fields' I said. 'What kind of fields are they? Flat or undulating?' Sadly, for Black women, those undulating fields are often of a higher elevation than for their white colleagues, even when we are all walking in the same direction.

ORDINARY WOMAN

I am an ordinary woman
Nothing special
Ordinary. Nothing. Nothing. Ordinary.
There is nothing to show
Nothing to tell
Ordinary. Nothing. Ordinary.

I have cut my hair, grown it
Cut it again. Permed it, straightened it, left it natural
Ordinary. Natural. Naturally ordinary.

I have raised children, alone
Born many, lost a few
Terminated one for my survival, sanity.
Paid the price. Murderer. Nothing. Ordinary.

Will you tell of me?
Remember me in history?
I am not a feminist made no stands
Nor have I been the discarded
Pleasure of a man.
I have loved and left. Loved and lost.
Ordinary. No different. Ordinary.

Yet without me there is no tomorrow
No more generations
Without me the world cannot last
From my loins I have borne life

Ordinary children
Grinded by a man, ordinary just like me.

Do not forget we who have fought battles
Lost and won wars
Worked hard in labour
Settled no scores
You may go down in history
We will simply die.
Ordinary. Nothing.
Ordinary in life. Ordinary in death. Ordinarily special.

≈

**SuAndi** is an internationally renowned British performance poet, writer and arts curator. Based in Manchester, she is particularly acknowledged for raising the profile of Black artists in the North West region as well as nationally. Since 1985 she has been the freelance Cultural Director of the National Black Arts Alliance. She was Cultureword's first Black women writers development worker and one of the founder members of BlackScribe the north west's first Black women poetry group.

Her three published collections are *Style, Nearly Forty* and *There Will Be No Tears;* her one-woman show *The Story of M* is on the curriculum for A-level English Literature and the MA in Black British Literature at Goldsmiths University. An Honorary Writing Fellow at Leicester University, she has received honorary degrees from Lancaster University and Manchester Metropolitan University. In 1999, she was awarded an OBE for her exceptional contribution to Black British art.

SuAndi's career has taken her across Europe and she has performed in North America, Brazil, India and Africa. In 2009, she held a residency at New York University. In 2024 'SussedBlackWoman' for the Mixed Museum will share Manchester's history of racial mixing through a focus on SuAndi's life and creative work. She has also been selected as one of 100 Black Women Who Have Made a Mark. This exciting new project from Serendipity Institute for Black Arts and Heritage will result in a 2024 portraiture exhibition celebrating the stories of Black British women who have made a significant positive change in activism, arts, education, politics, science and technology. She most recently received the Manchester Culture Awards Special Recognition Award. https://tinyurl.com/mrmtpt5f

Clare Summerskill. Photo: Pat Langford

# THEATRE FROM A LESBIAN PERSPECTIVE
## CLARE SUMMERSKILL

Depending on what day of the week it is, I am a writer, actress, stand-up comedian, singer-songwriter, playwright, oral historian and academic! I worked as a professional 'jobbing' actress in the industry for 18 years and, over the last couple of decades, I have toured my one-woman lesbian-themed comedy shows around the UK and occasionally the US, and written and performed in plays produced by my own theatre company, Artemis. I have acted in several national tours of my verbatim theatre productions, where the script is based entirely on extracts from interviews. These plays have addressed matters of social and political concern and have mainly been LGBT-focussed. National tours have included *Gateway to Heaven* (based on interviews with older lesbians and gay men), *Rights of Passage* (based on stories provided by lesbian and gay asylum seekers in the UK) and *Hearing Voices* (based on testimonies given by patients I met whilst on a secure psychiatric ward). Other theatre pieces I have written address issues around LGBT disabled people (*Vis à Visibility*) and experiences and fears older LGBT people have shared about receiving care in later life (*Staying Out Late*, and currently, *At the Rainbow's End*). I have a PhD from Royal Holloway University of London, where I researched connections between verbatim theatre and oral history and I have published books and articles on verbatim theatre processes.

While studying for my first degree in History, at Sussex University (1980-84), I joined the drama society there and discovered my love of theatre. As students, we were allowed to produce and perform plays (usually two each term) in a splendid theatre on campus, then called The Gardner Centre, but now re-named The Attenborough Centre for the Creative Arts. It was one of the most exciting and stimulating times in my life, appearing in plays such as Ben Johnson's *Volpone* and Aristophanes' *The Birds*, taking Joseph Heller's *We Bombed in Newhaven* to the Edinburgh Festival in 1981, and acting in original scripts by my fellow student, and now well-known playwright, April de Angelis.

I directed *Bitter Sweet* by Noel Coward and *The Lesson* by Eugène Ionesco and also began writing sketches and comedy songs for several cabaret groups that I was a part of. These included: *The Sexual Etiquette Show,* which we took to the Edinburgh Festival in 1981; the feminist cabaret group 'Twin Set and Pearls', performed to women's audiences in Brighton; and after drama school, a group called 'The Celibate Three'.

I then formed a lesbian cabaret duo with Alice Arnold (of BBC Radio 4 news-reading and shipping forecast fame) called 'Alice and Clare', while we were both jobbing actors as well. From the mid-80s through to the mid-90s, we performed at gay pride events and LGBT bars and clubs around the country, and we recorded albums of our songs (one of them sponsored by Derek Jarman). But when Alice decided to call it a day, I decided that, rather than going back to simply working as an actress in the industry, I wanted to carry on performing stand-up and comedy songs full-time and write and produce plays for my theatre company, which I have been doing ever since.

After leaving university, I took up a place at The Drama Studio in Ealing, London, on a one-year post-graduate training course, and it was only then that I became fully aware of the extent of sexism and anti-lesbianism from the teachers who claimed to represent the acting profession. My girlfriend was on the same course as I, but she declared herself to be bisexual, whereas I said that I was a lesbian. I soon noticed that her bisexuality was far more accepted by students and tutors alike than my lesbianism and I believe this was because the men still believed that my girlfriend was in some way potentially 'available' to them sexually, and yet I was completely beyond their reach, interest or comprehension.

I began to realise that my time in the drama scene at university had been an oasis of innocent bliss where I was artistically respected by my peers and my sexual orientation had been totally accepted. But in the 'real world' of acting, I discovered that things were quite different. My theatre work was mainly in what were then termed 'Community Theatre' companies, performing plays in non-traditional theatre spaces (schools, community centres, village halls, residential homes for the elderly, etc). These companies included Forest Forge in Hampshire, Interplay in Leeds, Remould in Hull and Age Exchange Reminiscence Theatre in Southeast

London (which is where I first became interested in theatre scripts created from interview content). I also did a few TV jobs and a two-year stint in the West End, appearing in the musical *Buddy* at The Victoria Palace Theatre (1990-92).

Working as an actress, I inevitably experienced many rejections from job applications and that is very much a part of the profession for all actors, gay or straight, but, with hindsight, I'm sure that my being a lesbian undoubtedly worked against me in numerous situations. Of the hundreds of auditions that I attended over the years, probably 95% were for male directors or producers and, of the women, maybe less than 1% of 5% of them may have been lesbians. The acting world – whether in commercial theatre or even in community theatre – is one which is very looks-based. Furthermore, at any job interview, casting directors will often like or dislike you depending on the degree of 'chemistry' between you and them. Inevitably, this chemistry is often sexual chemistry. I had no idea how to flirt with a male director, and no desire at all to access the casting couch, as some of my contemporaries were doing. To compensate for this, as time went by, I just accepted the fact that, in my opinion, I had to show myself in auditions as being more qualified for the roles than most of the other auditionees. It was like a lesbian glass ceiling.

To get good parts, or any parts at all, I often had to demonstrate that I was a strong actress – in serious or comedic roles – that I could sing, and that I could also play several instruments. For example, when I auditioned for *Buddy*, I had to sing, dance a little, act some roles and understudy others, and play piano and piano accordion to a high standard. The cast consisted mainly of male actor-musicians – think members of touring rock bands oozing with testosterone – and I remember how the producers, as soon as they found out I was a lesbian, looked at me as if I had two heads. Although, individually, the male actors in the cast (around fifteen of them) were generally nice blokes, the producers were overtly sexist and misogynistic. This show was their first venture into mainstream theatre, since they usually produced pantos each year and employed, if they could get them, 'names' from TV or the pop industry. I remember feeling that the general atmosphere was probably comparable to working in a garage with car mechanics, but with the Page 3 calendars temporarily hidden away.

After a year of playing minor roles, I expressed an interest in auditioning for one of the very few female lead roles that I knew would be coming up. The day before auditions took place, the musical director, whom I'd approached, seemed to have forgotten that I was on the list and reluctantly allowed me to join the other women auditioning. Since the part I was hoping to get required delivering a show-stopping rock 'n' roll solo piece on the piano during one of the scenes, as well as speaking in a convincing Texan accent (both of which I had nailed), it became clear that very few women were even in the final running. I know in my heart that they were reluctant to give me the part but they couldn't find another woman who could do all that was required.

The next musical I was in was a number one national tour of a show with an extremely thin plot which was basically an excuse to play lots of 60s' songs to middle-aged audiences in middle England! I was treated the same way as I had been in *Buddy* by the producer and also by the actor-musician male cast members. It was horrendous! After that tour, much to my agent's chagrin (because it was deemed a lesser-regarded form of work and also lower paid), I was delighted to return to working for Age Exchange, in plays which were directed and musically directed by women, performing high-quality shows for older people in residential homes and community centres.

A few years ago, the UK actors' union, Equity, ran a campaign which they asked me to support by way of appearing with other out actors on a series of posters and social media posts which stated 'I can act but I won't pretend', raising awareness about actors not being able to be out in their work and, in many cases, even to their agents. Whilst this is, indeed, an extremely important subject, I am compelled to state that, although there are still situations where gay men feel that they will have greater casting opportunities if they 'act straight', they have always had an enormous advantage in theatre, compared to their lesbian counterparts. For more than a century, it has been generally accepted that gay men work in theatre and they have consequently flocked to the profession (Oscar Wilde, Noël Coward, John Gielgud, Ian McKellen, Antony Sher to name but a few), whereas for lesbians in the industry, there has been no such understanding. Working in theatre certainly does not provide a safe and welcoming space for lesbians, except perhaps if they are stage or production managers, when they are more accepted by men, maybe because they are seen as 'one of the boys'. But for lesbian actresses –

especially those who do not conform to stereotypical images of female beauty – the road is a rough one, certainly far more challenging than for gay men in the industry. The fact that lesbians are 'allowed' to work in backstage jobs but are rarely accepted as actresses by predominantly male casting directors and producers is, of course, a classic example of misogyny. Homophobia and anti-lesbian sentiments are natural extensions of sexism, since those who hold prejudices against gay men or lesbians see them as not conforming to traditional societal stereotypes of heterosexual roles. Gay men are regarded as 'feminine' (a term which is seen as an insult when applied to most straight men) and lesbians are seen as rebelling against the submissive feminine role that a fundamentally patriarchal society demands of women.

Non-conforming sexualities are regarded as a threat to the status quo in which a compliant female is the type of woman that many men desire in order to meet their needs. In general, lesbians who present themselves in a more 'masculine' manner are frequently treated with contempt for trying to encroach on male territory by not conforming to socio-normative ideals of female beauty and behaviour. This kind of homophobia is very similar to the sexism that heterosexual women face when attempting to carve out a place in a world that is still dominated by men.

Antonia Kemi Coker and Clare Summerskill in *Rights of Passage* at The Chelsea Theatre, 2016. Photo: Pat Langford

In my kitchen, I have a few posters of my previous shows and on one of them, next to my picture and my name, is a quotation I once received when I was interviewed on Radio 4 *Woman's Hour,* when I was called 'A lesbian Victoria Wood', a compliment which I was flattered to receive. One day I had a plumber at my flat and seeing the poster he read aloud "A lesbian Victoria Wood" and then said to me "Well, that's not very nice, is it?" To him, 'lesbian' was clearly a dirty word and he assumed that the term was meant as an insult. His comment spoke volumes.

When I was in my early twenties, I performed in feminist cabaret shows, flagging up sexist attitudes and gender inequality through sketches and songs. Today, I'm not sure that society is any less sexist than it was back then. My aunt, (the MP, Dr Shirley Summerskill) was involved in drafting The Sex Discrimination Act of 1975 and my grandmother (Dr Edith Summerskill) was a famous feminist politician and so I was familiar with the concept of feminism from an early age. But even in my own family, I've witnessed examples of sexism, (although not by Edith or Shirley, it must be noted!). Boys/men have been put on a pedestal, their bad behaviour excused, while girls/women have not received the same treatment. If women condone or turn a blind eye to men's sexist behaviour, men don't feel the need to question that behaviour or privilege or – more importantly – point out sexist behaviour to other men when they see it. Doing so, I believe would have a far greater impact than any #Me Too Movement or any passing of legal legislation promoting gender equality.

I realise that I have managed to somehow create a theatrical space for my own work where there is a limited possibility of sexism, and maybe that, in itself, is a feminist act. When I'm booked to perform a show or present a talk, since the content is often LGBT-related, the men that I encounter are often gay. This doesn't mean that that they are not sexist, but it does mean that I am not generally working among heterosexual men and women who have to co-exist professionally and in their private lives with someone of the opposite sex. In so many ways I believe that I'm fortunate to be a lesbian but I cannot deny that it has negatively impacted my work and experiences in the theatre industry over the last 40 years. And since homophobia and sexism are intrinsically linked, all women – straight or otherwise – clearly have a very long way to go before we can achieve equality, either in the theatre world or in society at large.

Recently, in London, a handful of productions have had non-binary or lesbian characters as leading roles, notably Virginia Woolf's *Orlando* adapted by Neil Bartlett (at The Garrick Theatre) and *Es and Flo* by Jennifer Lunn (at the Kiln). But in comparison with commercial productions which portray the lives of gay men, theatrical lesbian representation is still extremely rare. However, over the last few years, there has been a significant challenge to previously accepted casting processes. Women have been playing traditional male roles (most notably Glenda Jackson acting the part of King Lear at The Old Vic and Maxine Peake playing Hamlet at The Royal Exchange, Manchester), and some of the largest theatres in the UK have pledged to only cast trans, non-binary or gender non-conforming actors in roles for characters with those identities. The exciting debates around sex and gender that are occurring in society are slowly being reflected in the theatre world and I would hope that this development will bring with it an understanding that the continuing feminist struggle for equality is not only a political necessity but one which creates possibilities for artistic experimentation and advancement, thereby allowing all women in the profession – lesbians and straight – to be valued far more so than they have been to date.

≈

**Clare Summerskill** is a freelance academic, an oral historian, a playwright and a lesbian comedienne and singer-songwriter. Her publications include *Gateway to Heaven: Fifty Years of Lesbian and Gay Oral History* (Tollington Press, 2012), *Creating Verbatim Theatre from Oral Histories* (Routledge, 2019). She co-edited *New Directions in Queer Oral History. Archives of Disruption* (Routledge, 2022) and wrote the introduction for the UK edition of *50 LGBTQI+ who changed the World* with Florent Manelli (Supernova Books, 2023).

Her plays include *Rights of Passage*, based on interviews with lesbian and gay asylum seekers in the UK, and *Hearing Voices*, based on the experiences of patients on a secure psychiatric ward. She regularly tours her one-woman comedy shows to theatres around the UK and the US, bringing lesbian humour to the forefront of alternative comedy.

She co-founded the Oral History Society's LGBTQ Special Interest Group and is a patron of several LGBTQ organisations including Kenric, London Gay Symphony Orchestra, East London Out Project (ELOP), Mind Out, Diversity Choir, and Educate & Celebrate.

Rebecca Hyde in *The Last One* by Zoe Alker, Arcola Theatre. Photo: Steve Gregson

# INTERVIEW WITH IMY WYATT CORNER

**How has feminism influenced your work?**

As a director, the work that I make is necessarily connected with my values. The theatre that I am drawn to tends to be driven by the complexity, comedy, joy, and pain of the contemporary climate. I'm interested in how humans operate, live and love within systems that fail so many people – most often women. I think my work is deeply entrenched in feminist values as they are the starting point from which I come to any project, because they inform the entire way I think.

From the moment a woman's body is on stage in front of an audience it unintentionally carries the weight of history and politics with it. This only increases as the person's identity intersects with other aspects of their being such as race, gender, disability. I work on two different kinds of stories about women: those that are overtly about raising awareness and those that centre brilliant ordinary women navigating the world without referencing their womanhood. For example, I co-directed *BEASTS* by the inimitable Mandi Chivasa at Edinburgh Fringe last year, which was a beautiful piece of magical realism about experiencing street harassment which was intended to prompt conversation around this topic. But I have also directed shows such as *Humane* by the wonderful Polly Creed, which was about a group of apolitical women protesting the export of live animals in Essex in the 1990s. This show was filled with comedy, dancing, friendship and showed women finding their voice. Both shows were equally 'feminist' in vastly different ways.

Often, I pull together all female/non-binary creative teams. This is partially because I enjoy being in these spaces and find that they allow room for listening and creativity. It's also because I'm aware that in more commercial spaces and in larger scale venues there are very few all-female creative teams.

**Do you feel that women have achieved equality in theatre?**

Often when working off-West End, you can be misled into thinking that there is some parity because there are many brilliant women whose work is being programmed in these venues. There is so much vibrant exciting work by women and about women, which is selling out to small studio audiences – *Paradise Now* by Margaret Perry, directed by Jaz Woodcock Stewart at Bush Theatre last year is a great example.

Whereas when you look to programming in the West End or in some regional theatres, the likelihood that a show will be on which has been written or directed by a woman, is very slim. Even slimmer still is the likelihood that there would be several shows centring 'women's stories' staged at the same time in commercial theatres. Some venues take the risk, but crucially, it still feels as though it is a risk to prioritise programming work about women. One of my fears for the industry is that women's stories are cut from programming as venues make more commercially-led decisions due to rising pressures around funding. Venues need to stay afloat and will assume they're far more likely to sell to full houses if they're programming Oscar Wilde than a contemporary female playwright.

Colette Zacca and Francesca Isherwood in *Humane* by Polly Creed, Pleasance Theatre.
Photo: Ali Wright

I'm hopeful that with the appointment of Indhu Rubasingham at the helm at National Theatre there will be some necessary and important pressure on the industry to shift us towards change. There are so many fantastic female directors who are leading the way in the industry now such as Lynette Linton, Lyndsey Turner, Blanche McIntyre and Nancy Medina. While I don't think women have achieved equality in theatre, I am quietly optimistic that the women currently in positions of power can lead the way to affect positive change.

**Have you experienced sex bias while working in theatre?**

Yes. I have experienced sex bias, and more specifically, I have been sexually harassed quite a few times whilst working in this industry. I think that the transience of working as a freelancer, and the unpredictability and scarcity of work, mean that often inappropriate behaviour remains unchecked. It is also vastly different from working within an office environment with an HR department or a line manager. It is often hard to know who to speak to when things are difficult. As jobs are sometimes few and far between, leaving doesn't always feel as though it's a viable option. This is a problem that extends far beyond the theatre industry, but I think the specific precarity of employment means that it remains an unspoken problem.

A couple of years ago, I was a Creative Associate at Jermyn Street Theatre, and we were lucky enough to be given mentorship sessions. I worked with a truly fantastic, experienced director, and one of the first questions I asked her was how to navigate this industry as a young woman. We worked together on creating an armour. I was fortunate to receive this mentorship and to be able to share my experiences with an industry professional. Since then, I talk to my peers in the industry about this subject when I can, as I think it's important that we create our own support network and keep talking to one another.

**Has the content of your work changed over time?**

Something I love about directing is that there is so much scope to continually change and grow. One of the joys of creating a project and staging it is reflecting, and knowing what you want to continue to do and what you want to discard going forward. I enjoy considering what I've put out there, and what type of work I want to make. I hope that my interests continually shift and grow as I gain more experience.

When I first started directing, I was keen to work entirely with new writing and saw myself as a solely text-led director. I still love new writing and find my time developing scripts with playwrights incredibly rewarding. However, as I've worked more, I've realised that I'm also very visually-led and much more interested in the images created on stage than I used to be. With that comes an awareness of what a body in space means. Currently I'm directing a two-hander called *Scarlet Sunday* by James Alston, which is about whether you can separate art and artist. I've been very influenced by art in the staging of the play. We're starting with the two women characters staring at each other across the table and holding this for quite a while, a direct reference to Marina Abramović. At the start of my career, I would have been too nervous to explore the unspoken and would have felt far more beholden to the text.

Going forward, I'm looking to work on more adaptations of classics and to develop ideas with playwrights that I have pitched to them. This is a definite step away from how I've worked up until this point, but I feel ready to bring what I know to something new.

## What would improve the opportunities for women working in theatre today?

- Take "the risk" on work produced, directed and written by women
- Programme stories about women in mid- to large-scale venues
- Ensure that creative teams are 50% female in the commercial sector
- Create spaces which allow women to take risks

Take the risk on women's work and allow women to take risks! Women in theatre can't take the same risks as men in theatre because putting on a female-led story is a risk in and of itself. This means that the programming of more 'cutting edge' work often seems to be very male-dominated. Yet when women do take risks with their work and create plays on a large scale that are a break from tradition, they are often radically brilliant. Over the past few years, we've had plays such as Annie Baker's *Infinite Life,* Lucy Kirkwood's *The Welkin*, Clare Barron's *Dance Nation* and *Fairview* by Jackie Sibblies Drury, which all created a frenzy of discussion around them, inspiring a generation of theatremakers. This is what theatre should be doing! To improve and learn as a theatremaker you must be able to take risks and sometimes fail. As it currently stands, men are far more likely to fail upwards.

As it becomes harder to finance the arts in this country, venues must keep in mind the future of theatre and need to ensure they don't close their doors to progress in favour of perceived financial security.

≈

**Imy Wyatt Corner** is a theatre director from London who trained on the Drama Directing MA at Bristol Old Vic Theatre School. She is currently an Artistic Associate at Arcola Theatre and was a Creative Associate at Jermyn Street Theatre from 2022-3. Last year, she co-directed *BEASTS or why girls shouldn't fear the dark,* which was awarded a Scotsman Fringe First at Edinburgh Fringe.

Other directing includes *The Last One* (Arcola Theatre), *Passing* (Park Theatre), *Duck* (Arcola Theatre, Jermyn Street Theatre), *Scarlet Sunday* (Omnibus Theatre), *Snail* (Vault Festival), *Humane* (Pleasance Theatre), *A Midsummer Night's Dream* (The Grove DIY Skatepark), *Gaslight* (Playground Theatre), *Baby, What Blessings* (Theatre503, Bunker Theatre), *Walk Swiftly & With Purpose* (Theatre503, North Wall Arts Centre) and *Happy Yet?* (International Theatre, Frankfurt).

Associate/Assistant direction includes *Private Lives* (West End), *Relatively Speaking* (Theatre Royal Bath UK Tour), *The Dance of Death* (Theatre Royal Bath UK Tour), *Troilus and Cressida* (Redgrave Theatre), *The Straw Chair* (Finborough Theatre) and *Love All* (Jermyn Street Theatre).

# INDEX

More feminist books and plays

from www.aurorametro.com

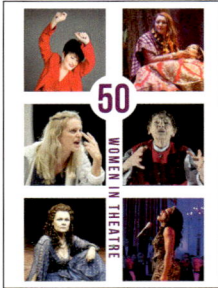

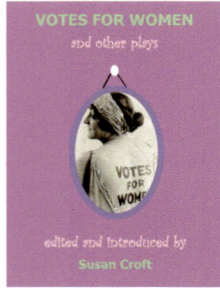

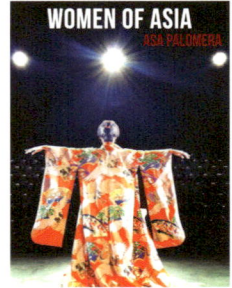

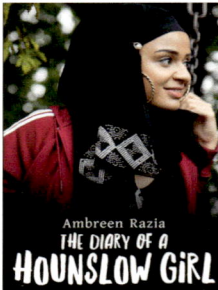

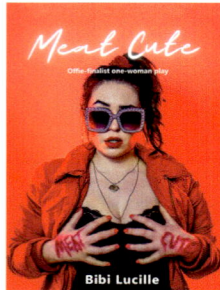

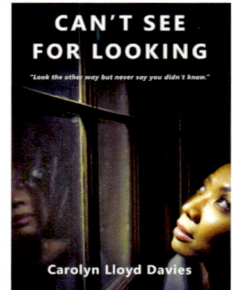

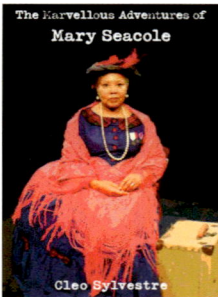

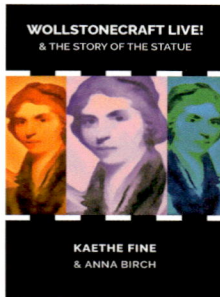

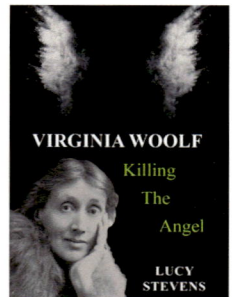

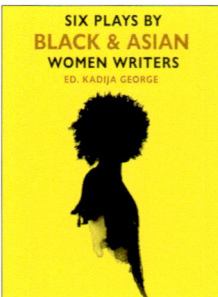

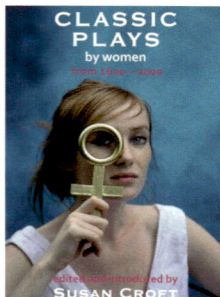

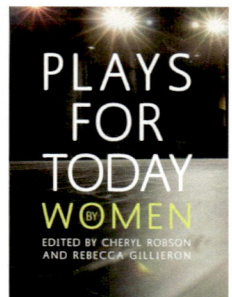